PRAGMATICS AND NATURAL LANGUAGE UNDERSTANDING

Second Edition

Tutorial Essays in Cognitive Science

Advisory Editors

Donald A. Norman
Andrew Ortony

PRAGMATICS AND NATURAL LANGUAGE UNDERSTANDING

Second Edition

Georgia M. Green
University of Illinois

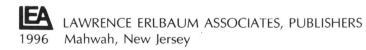
LAWRENCE ERLBAUM ASSOCIATES, PUBLISHERS
1996   Mahwah, New Jersey

Lawrence Erlbaum Associates, Inc., Publishers
10 Industrial Avenue
Mahwah, New Jersey 07430

Library of Congress Cataloging-in-Publication Data

Green, Georgia M.
    Pragmatics and natural language understanding / Georgia M. Green.—
2nd [rev.] ed.
        p.   cm. — (Tutorial essays in cognitive science)
    Includes bibliographical references (p.) and index.
    ISBN 0–8058–2165–1 (alk. paper). — ISBN 0–8058–2166–X (pbk. :
alk. paper).
    1. Pragmatics.· 2. Reference (Linguistics).   3. Semantics
(Philosophy).   4. Discourse analysis.   5. Cognitive science.
I. Title.   II. Series.
P99.4.P72G74   1996
306.4′4—dc20   96–18566
                                                                   CIP

Books published by Lawrence Erlbaum Associates are printed on acid-free paper,
and their bindings are chosen for strength and durability.

Printed in the United States of America
10 9 8 7 6 5 4 3

For my mother, Marjorie Fishbein Clavey

Contents

Notational Conventions Used in This Book

Most of the conventions described below are standard in linguistic writing.

In the text proper:

> *Italics* mark cited expressions.
>
> SINGLE QUOTES [' '] mark meanings of forms.
>
> DOUBLE QUOTES [" "] represent discourse examples. Around brief expressions, they are used as scare quotes.
>
> SMALL CAPS are used for emphasis, and to mark the defining use of technical terms.

In numbered examples:

> *Italics* mark the use of a form being demonstrated.
>
> SLASHES [/] separate expressions that could be substituted as alternatives to illustrate the same point, though no claim is made that the alternatives are semantically or pragmatically equivalent. Thus, (i) abbreviates the two sentences in (ii).

> i. Philip/Her brother thought he would be caught.
> iia. Philip thought he would be caught.
> iib. Her brother thought he would be caught.

> BRACKETS [{}] are used for the same purpose, with longer expressions.
>
> ASTERISK [*] precedes an expression that is ungrammatical; i.e., a correct grammar of the language will not describe it because no context could make it a natural thing for a native speaker to say.
>
> EXCLAMATION POINT [!] marks an expression that is grammatical, but (likely to be) pragmatically bizarre.

Both feminine and masculine personal pronouns are used with generic reference intended. In discussions of relations between speaker and hearer, distinctions in gender are used to help keep the intended reference clear.

Acknowledgments

This book owes much to Sue Ann Kendall, Steve Helmreich, Bill Ladusaw, Wendy Martin, Jerry Morgan, Tsuneko Nakazawa, Andrew Ortony, Craige Roberts, and Ladislav Zgusta for valuable comments on earlier versions, and to Jae Ohk Cho for discussions of honorific phenomena in Korean. Comments and questions from students who used preliminary versions of this book in pragmatics seminars at the University of Illinois in 1986 and 1987 led to clarifications in every chapter. The present form of the work owes a lot to the production staff of Lawrence Erlbaum Associates for their diligence, patience, and equanimity in working around my intolerance for alterations to my choice of relative pronouns, and to Robin Morgan, who dropped everything to prepare the author index.

Acknowledgments to the second edition: A number of individuals and institutions must share the credit for the appearance of this edition. The suggestions and encouragement of Kathleen Dolan, Editorial Associate at Lawrence Erlbaum Associates, were instrumental in making it a reality. Preparation of the second edition of *Pragmatics and Natural Language Understanding* was supported in part by the Beckman Institute for Advanced Science and Technology at the University of Illinois at Urbana–Champaign. Considerable aid and comfort was provided by the technical assistance of Linda May, of the Cognitive Science Group. I owe a special debt to Dylan Morgan, whose critiques were always right on target, to the numerous classes at the University of Illinois, Nagoya University, and Purdue University, whose questions have guided the clarifications and expansions that constitute the revisions, and especially to Atsushi Fukada, whose painstaking care in translating the text into Japanese showed us both how deep the issues are that are only sketched here.

Georgia M. Green

1 What Is Pragmatics and Why Do I Need to Know, Anyway?

INTRODUCTION

Writing is an act of faith, E. B. White said.[1] Speaking is no less so. Pragmatics is the study of the mechanisms that support this faith, a faith so strong that many can use the term *communicate* interchangeably with *speak* or *write*, never noticing that the term *communication* presupposes achievement of the intended effect of verbal action upon the addressee, while *speaking* and *writing* do not. Contrary to popular belief, communication is not accomplished by the exchange of symbolic expressions. Communication is, rather, the successful interpretation by an addressee of a speaker's[2] intent in performing a linguistic act. It is the purpose of this book to give an overview of those mechanisms which allow more to be communicated than is actually said.

Linguistic pragmatics as defined here is at the intersection of a number of fields within and outside of cognitive science: not only linguistics, cognitive

---

[1] Quoting an anonymous writer (Strunk & White, 1979, p. 84).

[2] I use *speaker* as shorthand for *speaker or writer* or the equally cumbersome *language-producer*. The principles described in this book apply generally to all modes of language production addressed to an audience with communicative intent. Quite likely they are trivially extendable to other cases, such as recitation or talking to oneself, but I do not attempt to cover such cases here.

Note that *hearer* and *addressee* are not interchangeable terms (cf. Clark & Carlson, 1982), although it is difficult to define the notion 'addressee' in a noncircular way that distinguishes the addressee of an utterance like (i) from an intended overhearer.

i. I can't believe that this salesclerk has not even acknowledged our existence.

In any case, *addressee* is used for the individual(s) to whom an utterance is addressed, and *hearer* for anyone who happens to hear (or read) the utterance in question.

psychology, cultural anthropology, and philosophy (logic, semantics, action theory), but also sociology (interpersonal dynamics and social convention) and rhetoric contribute to its domain. This volume does not pretend to do justice to the depth of scholarship in all of these fields, but hopes instead to sketch the interrelationships of the phenomena they variously study.

1. WHAT THIS BOOK IS ABOUT

This chapter discusses the foundations of the analysis of language use. Subsequent chapters treat topics encompassed by successively broader interpretations of the domain of pragmatic theory. Chapter 2, therefore, concerns the narrowest interpretation of *pragmatics*: the interpretation of INDEXICAL expressions (words or phrases like *me, here, then* whose REFERENCE cannot be determined without taking into account the context of the utterance of a linguistic expression). Minimally the context required for the interpretation of indexical expressions includes the time, place, speaker, and topic of the utterance. Chapter 2 also discusses the interpretation of anaphoric expressions like *he* and *next day*. Chapter 3 concerns problems of reference generally: how a speaker knows what an expression like *grass* or even *Bill* refers to. Ultimately this leads us to consider also what the conditions for the use of the definite article *the* are, and how one understands the use of common nouns and verbs like *newspaper* and *baste* or *drink*. Chapter 4 addresses two aspects of meaning that interact with the propositional content of utterances: illocutionary force (what a speaker is doing in making an utterance) and presupposition.

Chapters 5 and 6 focus on means which speakers have available to manage how what they say will be interpreted, and strategies for the exploitation of logical relations in arranging the content of one's speech. Chapter 5 begins with a discussion of principles speakers regularly use to convey more than they actually say. The rest of the chapter illustrates how the exploitation of these principles can be invoked in accounts of discourse coherence, illocutionary force, presupposition, and the relation of literal meaning to metaphor. Chapter 6 deals with how a speaker's discourse goals and attitudes may be reflected in the syntax of the utterances that constitute a discourse.

Finally, in chapter 7, we look at conversational interactions, and some of the devices speakers use to regulate control of conversation and maintain or alter social relations among participants via patterns of discourse. The discussion treats topic manipulation, politeness strategies, uses of questions, and other exploitations of linguistic form to affect the course of the interaction.

2. BELIEF AND INTENTION

The broadest interpretation of pragmatics is that it is the study of understanding intentional human action. Thus it involves the interpretation of acts assumed to be undertaken in order to accomplish some purpose. The central notions in pragmatics must then include belief, intention (or goal), plan, and act. Assuming that the means and/or the ends involve communication, pragmatics still encompasses all sorts of means of communication, including nonconventional, nonverbal, nonsymbolic ones, as for example, when a life guard throws a volleyball in the direction of a swimmer struggling in the ocean.[3] The lifeguard believes that the swimmer wants assistance, and that the swimmer will understand that the volleyball thrown in his direction is intended (by the life guard) to be assistance, and that the swimmer will know how to take advantage of the volleyball's property of being lighter than water. That makes at least three beliefs and one intention on the part of the lifeguard, including two beliefs about the swimmer's beliefs, and one about the swimmer's desires.

Reflexive beliefs and intentions (i.e., speaker's and addressee's beliefs and intentions about each other's beliefs and intentions) of this sort are typical of the most ordinary, straightforward uses of language, and such uses cannot be understood without reference to them. For example, belief is what makes the difference (obviously) between a lie and a mistake. When people say something false which they believe to be false, they are lying, but if they say something which is false, but which they happen to believe is true, they are merely mistaken. Belief is also the core of the difference between informing and reminding. If a speaker, S, says to an addressee, A, "The Koreans have a holiday which commemorates the invention of their alphabet," and believes that A does not already know this, S most likely intends to inform A; if S believes that A does already know it, S most likely intends to remind A. Sometimes speakers are content to be vague about this belief, hoping that the remark will be taken as a reminder if A already knows, as information if A doesn't. Other times, speakers may want to make their position clear (for instance, to avoid insulting A by implying that A did not know something which A feels everyone should know that A does know). For example, *As you know, I remind you,* and *Of course* preface utterances that are intended to be taken as reminders; they indicate the speaker's belief that the addressee already knows that the proposition expressed by the sentence is true. Similarly, *Actually* and *In fact* preface utterances that the speaker believes represent information new to the addressee.

Likewise, intent makes the difference between a lie, and a joke or a figure of speech, between a promise and a prediction. Uttering something false like "She phones her mother everytime you say 'Boo!' " is a lie if the speaker intends her addressee to believe that she believes it, a figure of speech if she intends him to understand that it is an exaggeration for effect (hyperbole). Uttering "Johnny will be on time tomorrow" constitutes a promise if the speaker intends to be taken as guaranteeing that it will be true, but it constitutes a prediction if it is only intended to represent her current belief. The nature and interrelationship of

---

[3]Or to borrow an example from Jerry Morgan (1978): when I deposit my quiche in the dog's dish to express my opinion that it isn't fit for human consumption.

beliefs and intentions are explored in the study of philosophy of mind (for an introduction, see Bechtel, 1988).

3. PLANS AND ACTS

Beliefs and intentions are not the whole story, of course. The proverb, "The road to hell is paved with good intentions" means that intentions count for naught unless acted upon. A speaker with an intention and a set of beliefs about her audience acts rationally on that intention by forming a plan to effect it that is consistent with those beliefs. Typically such plans are hierarchical, and involve subgoals and mediating intentions as well as an ultimate goal. Plan formation and reconstruction play an important role in artificial intelligence (AI) work on natural language understanding; the papers in Cohen, Morgan, and Pollack (1990) are representative.

For example, I might have the ultimate goal of having you have a low opinion of a certain mutual acquaintance. Since I cannot effect this by just willing it to happen, I must form a plan which will cause you to have this opinion. I could tell or order you to have a low opinion of him, but given my belief that you are rational, and that you believe that I believe this, I know this is unlikely to be effective. I have to choose a plan (from an infinity of possibilities) which will take advantage of your rationality in causing you to conclude that our acquaintance, call him Eks, is a sleaze. For example, I might choose to tell you that he has instituted a policy in the office he manages which I believe you will find offensive, and having decided that, I must choose exactly how to say this. Shall I just blurt out, "He refuses to hire qualified blacks, Jews, and women!" Or shall I tell an anecdote which gives evidence, with real names and quoted dialogue, which I can expect you will take as indicating that Eks is a despicable character? Or maybe just a single sentence with statistics and one or two names? Once this is decided, the construction of each individual sentence requires many similar decisions (cf. Green, 1982a). And all of this usually takes place without the speaker being aware of even thinking about it. In uttering a single sentence, more decisions have to be made than there are words in the sentence (cf. Green, 1982a), so it is obvious that these decisions must be made very quickly, and below the level of consciousness, or the flow of speech would be considerably more intermittent, and exponentially slower than it is.

The task of the discourse-interpreter is (a) to understand what the speaker has said, that is, to construct a mental model of the situation which the speaker is indicating exists, and (b) to evaluate that model and use it to update his own model of the world. The first task is exemplified by the acts involved in understanding what statement, imperative, question, wish, and so on, a speaker has made. The second involves drawing conclusions which add to one's knowledge of the world and to one's model of the speaker: for example, inferences about what the speaker knows, what the speaker believes that the addressee knows, what the speaker believes that the addressee believes to be false, how the speaker feels about individuals, situations, and events that have been referred to in the conversation. This is also done largely subconsciously, and ordinary competent speakers are rarely able to reconstruct and articulate the logic involved.

Pragmatics, as described in this section, refers to the study of action deliberately undertaken with the intention of causing the intended interpreter to re-assess his model of how things are, including his system of values and his model of the speaker's beliefs, attitudes, and intentions. To narrow our study to linguistic pragmatics, or the pragmatics of language use, we need only stipulate that the principles of pragmatics must account systematically for acts involving linguistic expressions.

4. LINGUISTIC EXPRESSIONS AND THE DETERMINATION OF MEANING

A language (natural or artificial) consists of (a) a set of basic (i.e., unanalyzed) expressions, termed a LEXICON; (b) a set of rules for combining these expressions in well-formed constructions, termed a SYNTAX; and, according to the standard view, (c) a set of rules for deriving the meaning of each construction from the meanings of its parts, called a COMPOSITIONAL SEMANTICS (Montague, 1970, 1973; Dowty, Wall, & Peters, 1981). All of these components are conventional, which means that principles of logic and laws of physics do not force the rules to be exactly as they are.[4] Rather, at least some of the rules are arbitrary to at least some degree, and by custom, speakers act in conformity with them. The issue hardly ever comes to consciousness, but using the language in a way that failed to observe the rules would greatly decrease the likelihood of successful communication. For example, there is no logical reason why English adjectives must go before the nouns they modify (e.g., *united states*) rather than after, as in French (*états unis*). Likewise, the semantic rules that guarantee that *John* is understood as the object of *please* in *John is easy to please* (i.e., that make it equivalent to *It is easy [for people] to please John*), might have been otherwise, allowing *John* to be understood as the subject (making the sentence equivalent to *It is easy for John to please [people]*).

In addition to being conventional, the semantics is compositional and basically TRUTH-CONDITIONAL. It is standard to distinguish between what a sentence means and what a speaker intends to convey by the utterance of that sentence (Grice, 1957), and to restrict the role of semantics to explicating the meaning of a

---

[4]Strictly speaking, the syntax and the semantics are arbitrary and conventional as well, but the syntaxes and semanticses of natural languages are so similar, and so restricted (in the face of all the conceivable possibilities) that the principles constraining them (the so-called rules of universal grammar) must be a consequence, ultimately, if not directly, of the human genetic make-up (cf. Chomsky, 1965, 1968, 1980).

sentence in terms of conditions which must be fulfilled for it to be used to truthfully describe a situation. Aspects of the interpretation of utterances which do not involve truth conditions are commonly considered to be outside the domain of semantics, and that is the approach followed here. Thus, whether an utterance is a promise, a prediction, or a question, and how metaphorical utterances like *India demanded compensation* are understood are considered matters of pragmatics, not semantics (cf. chap. 3–5).

To say that the semantics is COMPOSITIONAL is to say that the meaning of a complex expression will be related in a predictable way to the meanings of the parts from which it is constructed. This is usually expressed by saying that the meaning of the whole is a function of the meanings of the parts, where *function* has its technical, mathematical sense. Consequently, the parts of every structure defined by a particular syntactic rule must be related in the same way, because they are related by a single function.[5] This means that, for example, whatever semantic relation a syntactic subject like *Sandy* bears to its predicate in a sentence like *Sandy cooks potatoes*, the syntactic subject in parallel constructions like *Dana eats turnips* must bear the same semantic relation to its predicate.

To say that the semantics is truth-conditional is to claim that the meaning of sentences (and therefore of their parts, since the semantics is compositional) is explicated in terms of conditions under which they would be true. In other words, the meaning of an expression in a compositional semantics represents a state of affairs that would have to hold if a sentence containing that expression is to be considered true. Although we do not speak of nondeclarative sentences such as questions and commands as being true or false, analyses in modal logic[6] involving such notions as knowledge, necessity, and obligation make truth-conditional analyses of even such sentences possible.

The meanings of the basic expressions are conventional, and arbitrary except for the vagaries of history. That is, there is no particular reason that apples are called *apples*, other than the fact that that is what people are accustomed to calling them. In a seminal paper, Grice (1957) referred to conventional meaning of this sort as NONNATURAL MEANING, and distinguished it from NATURAL MEANING, which he reserved for uses of the word *meaning* which are more akin to 'natural consequence.' Thus, the fact that *apple* "means" 'fruit of a plant of the subgenus *malus*' is much more like the fact that green (in a street light) means$_{nonnatural}$ 'go' than it is like the fact that 'Sandy is allergic to pollens'

---

[5]As a consequence of this principle, noun–noun compounds and expressions like *religious affairs* and *public beaches*, where the adjective is taken as relating to the noun in different ways ('affairs concerning religion', 'beaches for the public'; cf. *religious person, public intoxication*) must be considered either ambiguous, having a plural but finite number of meanings, or vague, having a single meaning, but an indefinite number of potential intended interpretations. This is an interesting and complex matter, and is taken up in more detail in chapter 5.

[6]See, for example, Von Wright (1963), Rescher (1966, 1967), Lemmon (1965); Åqvist (1965, 1971), Harrah (1961), Hintikka (1974), Karttunen (1977), and Lewis (1968).

means*natural* that she will not want flowers in her office. The arbitrary, conventional nature of language is evident in the fact that we call fire *fire* (i.e., [fayr]) because the folks from whom we learned to talk called it [fayr], or something like that, while our German cousins call it *Feuer* (i.e., [foyr]) because somewhere back in history, our respective ancestors began to follow different pronunciation rules. Swahili speakers call it [moto] because that is how they learned it at their mothers' knees. To put it another way, we call fire *fire* because that's what everybody else (in our speech community) calls it. We know that if we call it something else, we cannot expect people to understand that we are talking about fire.

But it is a mistake to assume just because a language has a conventional syntax, semantics, and defined lexicon, that utterances of sentences constructed in accordance with them will be understood as intended.

Up until the 1960s, it was widely assumed among linguists that a theory of meaning framed in terms of conditions under which a sentence would be true (truth conditions) would be able to account for first, the relation between a sentence and the logical proposition it expresses (i.e., to explicate why the sentence *Snow is white* refers to a claim that snow is white (and not to white snow, or Snow White)), and second, the relation between a referring expression and its referent (i.e., to account for how it is that *Snow White* refers to Snow White, or how *the president of the United States* referred in 1986 to Ronald Reagan). It was also taken for granted that the same theory of meaning would account for the illocutionary force of sentences (that aspect of their meaning which distinguishes statements from promises or various sorts of pronouncements; cf. Austin, 1962) and in some cases, for the discourse value of expressions as exemplified by the difference between (1) and (2) or between (3) and (4), or between (5) and (6).

1.   Sandy walked in.
2.   In walked Sandy.
3.   Dana's in prison.
4.   Dana's in the slammer.
5.   Luke killed an imperial guard.
6.   Luke caused an imperial guard to die.

For instance, example (2) contributes a narrative effect (most likely resolving a narrative tension) not evoked by (1). Example (4), in contrast to (3), refers to the place of Dana's incarceration with an expression associated with populations intimately familiar with such places, with the implication that the speaker is familiar with that world, and perhaps that the speaker believes that the addressee is also. The circumlocution in (6), as opposed to (5), implies that Luke's action caused the guard's death in a manner less direct than, say, Luke's mortally wounding him (cf. Horn, 1978; McCawley, 1978a). But it eventually became apparent that these different aspects of what people were used to calling "meaning" were not the same sorts of thing at all. A more current view is that a highly restrictive truth-conditional semantic component must interact with principles of pragmatics which fix or limit what a sentence will convey on an occasion of utterance (Gazdar, 1980). It is often assumed that the pragmatics is independent of the semantics, and takes the "output" of the semantics as "input," the semantics having provided a truth-conditional interpretation of a syntactically well-formed expression.

But even this view is unrealistic if taken literally. There are many cases where a truth-conditional semantics cannot operate independently of pragmatic aspects of meaning (Gazdar, 1979, chap. 7). To take a simple case, consider what a truth-conditional semantics could tell us about the meaning of sentence (7).

7.   He fell down.

A truth-conditional semantics could tell us that it asserts that some sentient male entity came abruptly to be at a point in space lower than its former position at some point in time prior to the asserting of (7). Reference to "the asserting of (7)" is necessary to give truth conditions for the past tense morpheme. This indicates that for a truth-conditional semantics to determine (in the technical sense 'define, specify') the propositional content of a sentence, it must make reference to an agent who is uttering the sentence and to the time of its utterance. (This was recognized early; cf. Bar-Hillel, 1954.)

But even this "liberal" account of the truth conditions of this sentence does not determine (i.e., specify) a proposition, because *he* does not determine a referent. It might refer to the last-mentioned entity which meets the description 'male, sentient,' but very often it does not.[7] Often, language users have to guess at the referent intended by the speaker of a pronoun (or indexical) like *he*, and this is what makes it impossible to claim that a pragmatics in conjunction with a truth-conditional semantics, could determine what a sentence conveys on an occasion of utterance. There is no way of knowing who the italicized *he* in passages like those in (8) is intended to refer to, short of being able to read the speaker's mind.[8]

8a.   When Luke pushed Adam in to give the photograph to Humphrey, *he* fell down in surprise on seeing the golden charm again.

8b.   The dean expelled John because *he* discovered his secret.

---

[7]In an example like (i), *his* could refer just as easily to the mugger, to Robert or to Alex. There are also well-known examples like (ii), where *they* is much more likely to be correctly understood to refer to the farther potential antecedent.

   i. A mugger attacked Robert, and Alex broke his arm.

   ii. The deans refused to let the students picket, because they feared violence.

[8]More exactly: short of being able to know exactly what the speaker expects the addressee to know about the subject under discussion.

The fact that fully competent language users are not always able to tell what the intended referent is would seem to preclude the devising of principles which could compute this mechanically. Since natural language discourse is governed by guesses as well as knowledge, and some of these guesses are themselves based on guesses about what one's interlocutor knows, thinks, or feels, a model which determines (i.e., specifies) a unique interpretation or even a finite range of interpretations from a finitely describable context and a truth-conditional semantics of the usual sort is not a model of natural language processes. To simulate the pragmatic capacity of an ordinary speaker, we would have to build a device that not only would infer which of many possible referents (or illocutionary forces, etc.) a speaker intended, but also would infer a speaker's discourse intentions. For example, a speaker might be intentionally ambiguous (cf. Weiser, 1974), and content to be taken either way. We saw one example of this above, in the discussion of reminders. To take another, A may say (9) to B, hoping the utterance will be taken as a request (cf. chap. 4) if B is willing to talk, but as a mere statement of interest if B is not.

9.   I'd love to know what went on in the hearing today.

Situations like this are probably pretty rare in scientific text, but surely abound in social conversation, in advertising, and in political speech (cf. Myers, 1984). Myers emphasized that part of the politician's art is in saying things in such a way that they will be interpreted in different (favorable) ways by different special interest constituencies. In slightly more complex cases, a speaker may intend to be taken as being intentionally ambiguous, as in one computer company's slogan, "We put people in front of computers."

A more realistic claim about the relation of semantics and pragmatics would be that, given certain contextual conditions or defaults, a pragmatics in conjunction with a truth-conditional semantics could define a ranking of likely candidates for the intended interpretation of an utterance (n.b., not a sentence), but short of claiming clairvoyance, it could never claim to be able to specify the actual (intended or constructed) interpretation of an utterance.

5. VAGUENESS AND INTERPRETATION

It is commonly assumed that language provides a vehicle for thought, that words, or at least connected words (sentences), express thoughts, and do so uniquely. You have a thought, you put it into words which will carry the thought, and any sane and sober person who knows the language will be able effortlessly to behold your thought, to get your idea. But this assumption is mistaken, and for cognitive science, it is a mistake of major proportions.

Reddy (1979) discusses this assumption under the rubric "the conduit metaphor," and presents evidence that it is utterly pervasive in our speech about language and communication. According to the conduit metaphor, linguistic expressions (words, sentences, paragraphs, books, etc.) are compared to vessels or conduits into which thoughts, ideas, or meanings are poured, and from which they can be extracted, exactly as they were sent, accomplishing a transfer of possession. References in the preceding paragraph to *vehicle, put . . . into words, carry, behold, get* are all instances of this conduit metaphor. When we accept the conduit metaphor, we commit ourselves to a view that communication is achieved as easily as serving a glass of milk or sending a package, that any failure to communicate must be due to carelessness or inattention in choosing or construing linguistic expressions, and that properly chosen linguistic expressions do all the work.

Reddy offered an alternative metaphor, which he called the toolmakers' paradigm. Six individuals live in separate environments. None knows what any environment but his own is like, nor even that they are different from each other. The individuals have no common language, but can send each other blueprints of tools they develop to make it easier to cultivate their various terrains. Each one is proud of the tools he invents, and of the blueprints he carefully drafts to instruct the others in making such a tool for themselves. The toolmakers are generally disappointed, disgusted, or angry, not to mention bewildered, when their careful blueprints for their prized tools are returned with what seem to be senseless or even counter-productive modifications, so much so that it is an event for celebration when one is accepted as is.

As a view of linguistic communication, the toolmakers' paradigm assumes first of all that sentences are more like blueprints, from which much may be inferred, but with no assurance of correctness, than they are like programmed instructions or encyclopedias, where everything is explicit. It implies that speakers may have incorrect conceptions of what their addressees know, and of what "everybody" knows, and be utterly unaware of it. It suggests that crafting a message so that it will convey what the speaker wants it to convey to the particular addressee to whom it is addressed is an art, and requires assumptions about what that addressee believes. It also implies that correctly divining what the sender of a message intends the receiver to understand involves real work, and a real risk of failure. Toolmaker metaphors in this description include: *crafting, art, divining, risk.* If this is a more correct model than the conduit metaphor, as I believe it is, then communication probably misfires more often than we realize; the experience of discovering minutes, days, weeks, months or years later that B did not mean 'X' when she said "W," but 'Y,' supports this view.

Reddy argued that the conduit metaphor is not only misleading, but harmfully, perniciously so. For our purposes, however, it is enough to assume that there is more to understanding utterances than parsing them and deriving representations of their propositional meanings in terms of intensional logic or model theory (cf. Dowty et al., 1981). It is necessary also to make inferences about what the utterer believes about what the addressee believes, and about what effect the utterer intends the utterance to have.

A simple demonstration of the necessity of this comes from the work of the psychologists Bransford and Johnson (1973). They asked subjects to read the following paragraph:

> The procedure is actually quite simple. First you arrange things into different groups. Of course, one pile may be sufficient depending on how much there is to do. If you have to go somewhere else due to lack of facilities that is the next step, otherwise you are pretty well set. It is important not to overdo things. That is, it is better to do too few things at once than too many. In the short run this may not seem important but complications can easily arise. A mistake can be expensive as well. At first the whole procedure will seem complicated. Soon, however, it will become just another facet of life. It is difficult to foresee any end to the necessity for this task in the immediate future, but then one can never tell. After the procedure is completed one arranges the materials into different groups again. Then they can be put into their appropriate places. Eventually they will be used once more and the whole cycle will then have to be repeated. However, that is part of life.

Subjects found the paragraph difficult to understand and hard to recall, although there is nothing difficult about any of the words or sentences, or even about the way the sentences are connected to each other to make coherent discourse. When subjects were given the information (by means of a two-word title) that the author intended his text as a description of doing laundry, the text was comprehended and recalled much better. What had been missing was information about what the author expected to be taken as intending to refer to: the paragraph itself is vague in not mentioning washing or clothes.

In fact, most natural language utterances are vague (recall example (7)), and require interpretation of this sort: Who is the speaker referring to? What does she mean by *fell down*? In a race? Off a ladder? Down a hill? Is it good, or bad? For "him" or for her or for me? How does she know? Does she think she is reminding me or informing me? All of these issues can be addressed explicitly in an utterance of this sort, but they rarely are. The problems posed here will be addressed in more detail in chapters 3–5.

Pragmatic "ambiguities" of this sort abound in natural language use. The oral instruction to write your name backwards sounds clear enough, but which of the following is a correct response?

a. writing the last name first: Green Georgia
b. writing the name with the letters within a word in reverse order: aigroeg neerg
c. writing the name as in (b), but last name first: neerg aigroeg
d. writing the name in mirror writing: ИƎƎᴙƆ AIƆᴙOƎƆ
e. writing the name from right to left, last letter first: Georgia Green

<--

f. rotating your body so your back is facing your addressee and writing your name

g.   writing the words "your name backwards"
h.   writing the words "your name" as in (a)
i.   writing the words "your name" as in (b)
j.   writing the words "your name" as in (c)
k.   writing the words "your name" as in (d)
l.   writing the words "your name" as in (e)
m. writing the words "your name" as in (f)

This looks like a finite, though large, number of distinct interpretations. But there are also cases where the number of likely intended interpretations is indefinitely large. For instance, a sentence like *Sandy suggested the fourth amendment* might be intended as a claim that Sandy was the instigator of a fourth amendment to something, or that Sandy suggested that some particular contextually motivated action be undertaken with respect to some fourth amendment (e.g., that it be invoked, opposed, appealed to, mentioned, used as an example, selected as the topic for the next year's conference, and so on). Examples like these support the view of language and communication implied by Reddy's toolmaker metaphor.

6. MUTUAL BELIEF AND PLAN DEDUCTION

We come now to the final notions necessary for a full description of pragmatics—the reflexivity of belief and intention (Grice, 1957; Searle, 1969). When I say to you "He couldn't get mortgage insurance," intending to refer to Captain Frank Furillo, it is not enough for me to just intend it to be taken that way. For communication to be successful, you must recognize my intention, that is, realize that *he* is intended to refer to Captain Furillo. If I intend it to make a reference to Captain Furillo, and you assume it is intended as a reference to Officer Renko, I have not succeeded in communicating, in sharing my opinion with you.

Similarly, on a larger scale, if I ask you to open a window, saying, for example, "Open the window, would you?" I must believe:

(a)   that you know what window I mean you to open
(b)   that you are capable of performing what needs to be done to get that window open
(c)   that the window is not now open
(d)   that the window will not open without the intervention I request
(e)   that you realize I'm addressing you
(f)   that you understand the language I'm speaking, that you are awake, etc.

Still, my believing all this will not by itself guarantee that my request is communicated to you. For that, you must believe that I believe all that. (If I'm addressing you, and believe that you understand that I am, but you believe I'm addressing the child sitting in your lap, I won't have communicated.) Furthermore, you must believe that I believe you believe it. (If you think I believe that you think that the window is already open, you'll conclude I am—perhaps jokingly, or sarcastically—asking you to do something you think is impossible (like touching your chin to your elbow), when in fact it is a perfectly sincere and feasible request.) If you know that the window is operated by a timer set to open it momentarily, and do not know that I do know it, you will find my request extremely puzzling, and conclude either that I am not in my right mind, or am operating on some other wave length, with different beliefs, or that I mean something else by my utterance than a request to open a window (what it might be I'm not sure).

Understanding a speaker's intention in saying what she said the way she said it amounts to inferring[9] the speaker's plan, in all of its hierarchical glory, though there is room for considerable latitude regarding the details. To take a trivially straightforward case, when you understand my saying to you, "Close the window, why don't you" as a request addressed to you, you infer (a) that I want the window closed, (b) that I want you to do it, (c) that I want you to do it because I've asked you (and not, for example, because you think the open window might annoy me), and (d) that I want you to realize that I want you to do it by understanding my utterance as a request as specified in (a–c) (cf. Bach & Harnish, 1979, pp. 3–18), and all without being aware of inferring anything. Schematically,

GOAL STRUCTURE: Get window closed
          by getting X to close window
              by getting X to understand that I want X to close
              the window
                  by requesting that X close the window
                      by saying "Close the window, why don't you."

PLAN RECONSTRUCTION
Speaker has said, "Close the window, why don't you"
  Therefore, Speaker is making a request to close the window.
    Therefore, Speaker wants the addressee to close the window.
      Therefore, Speaker wants the window closed.

Similarly, I might try to get you to decide not to vote for Eks by causing you to have a low opinion of him, by telling you that he has done something which I believe will do this (by showing that his values conflict with yours), by telling you he indulges in discriminatory employment practices, by saying "Eks refuses to hire qualified blacks, Jews, and women." I will preface my remark with *You*

---

[9]In the AI literature, this is referred to as plan deduction (Allen & Perrault, 1980). I reserve the term *deduction* for deductive inferences in a system with a closed, specified set of axioms, which natural language understanding certainly isn't.

know, in order not to come on too strong: I will make it appear that I am reminding you of something I believe you already know, and know that I know you know. And I may well have arrived at this set of intentions without ever consciously considering any of them. Schematically, this plan looks like this:

> Get Y to decide not to vote for Eks
>> by getting Y to have a low opinion of Eks
>>> by causing Y to realize something bad about Eks
>>>> by letting Y know that Eks has done something Y will disapprove of
>>>>> by telling Y that Eks engages in discriminatory employment practices
>>>>> while allowing Y to believe I give Y credit for already knowing this
>>>>>> by saying "You know, Eks refuses to hire qualified blacks, Jews, or women."

Notice that the speaker may not want all of his intentions recognized (for example, his intent to influence the addressee's voting behavior), and that some intentions may not be recognized (e.g., the one just mentioned). Indeed, certain intentions (e.g., rhetorical deceits like using *you know* to diminish the inference of informational superiority implied by the speaker's telling the addressee something (cf. chap. 7)) are such that their being recognized will make the communication less successful than if they go unnoticed.

Plans of intermediate complexity, such as plans to let someone know, by changing the topic, that he has made a faux pas, or plans to achieve actions by asking questions such as *Can you see the time?* are discussed in chapter 5.

Plan reconstruction may start, as in the example of *Close the window, why don't you* with the eventual utterance, or with the goals, if the addressee believes that he and the speaker share a lot of beliefs and are familiar with each other's values and ultimate goals. Either way, knowledge of this sort is constantly necessary as a check on the validity of the inferences made in plan reconstruction: if an inference conflicts with what is believed about the speaker's beliefs, values, and goals, either the inference or the background belief has to be modified.

CHAPTER 1 STUDY QUESTIONS

1. Why are the notions belief, intention, and rational act crucial for pragmatic theory?

2. In what sense are linguistic rules conventional?

3. What does it mean to say that a semantic theory is truth-conditional?

4. What does it mean to say that a semantic theory is compositional?

5. Why is a compositional, truth-conditional semantics insufficient by itself to account for the interpretation of utterances?

6. How does the conduit metaphor provide a misleading view of linguistic communication?

7. What properties of language support the blueprint metaphor of the toolmakers' paradigm?

8. What kinds of speaker-beliefs about the intended audience are relevant in pragmatic investigations? Why?

2 Indexicals and Anaphora; Contextually Identifiable Indeterminacies of Reference

The narrowest interpretation of the term *pragmatics* is that it refers to the study of indexicals, expressions whose reference is a function of the context of their utterance. In this chapter, we examine the adequacy of this interpretation, focusing first on indexical pronouns like *I* and *you*, and adverbs such as *here* and *yesterday*, and then extending the discussion to related phenomena such as tenses, demonstratives like *that*, and anaphoric pronouns (like *he, her*, and *their*), which refer to entities previously mentioned in the discourse. Far from indicating that the domain of pragmatics is narrowly circumscribed by observable contextual phenomena, the interpretation of indexicals and related anaphora is shown to require assumptions of inferences about the speaker's beliefs and/or intended referents, and thus requires a broader interpretation of *pragmatics*.

In his classic 1954 paper "Indexical Expressions,"[1] Bar-Hillel argues that indexicality is an inherent and unavoidable property of natural language, and speculates that more than 90% of the declarative sentences people utter are indexical in that they involve implicit references to the speaker, addressee, time and/or place of utterance in expressions like first and second person pronouns (*I, you*), demonstratives (e.g., *this*), tenses, and adverbs like *here, now, yesterday*. Thus utterances of sentences like those in (1–5) cannot be fully understood (that is, understood enough to judge whether they are true or false) without an indication of who uttered the sentence (1, 2), and when (1, 3, 4, 5), and where it was uttered (4).

---

[1] This must surely be regarded as one of the seminal papers in pragmatics, though many important points made there have had to be rediscovered and made again repeatedly.

1. I am hungry.
2. This is good for coughs.
3. It's raining in Madrid.
4. It's begun to rain.
5. The president of the United States had an audience with the Pope.

Actually, it is an oversimplification, one which it is not clear whether Bar-Hillel appreciated, to suppose that having that information is sufficient to guarantee evaluatability. Strictly speaking, it is irrelevant where the sentence is uttered. What is relevant is what place the speaker intended to be taken as referring to.[2] Sitting in Urbana, Illinois, I can say, "It's raining," referring to the weather in the city where a football game I am watching (or listening to) is being played. Similarly, for uses of tenses: historical presents (e.g., "I try to crawl to safety, but my leg is broken") use a present tense to refer to a past time. Bar-Hillel (1954) may have recognized essentially this problem with *this*:

> 'This' is used to call attention to something in the centre of the field of vision of its producer, but, of course, also to something in his spatial neighborhood, even if not in his centre of vision or not in his field of vision at all, or to some thing or some event or some situation, etc., mentioned by himself or by somebody else in utterances preceding his utterance, and in many more ways. (p. 373)

However, it is probably worth noting that Bar-Hillel does not use the term *intention* or *intended referent* in his description of the phenomenon. Morgan (1978) gives an example[3] which illustrates nicely the problem of identifying the referent of an indexical:

> ... imagine a jar of sugar with a glass lid, on which the word *sugar* is painted in blue; and imagine that someone puts her fingertip just under the letter *u* of the word *sugar* and says, "What's that?" Our answer might be, among other things, *the letter* **u**, *the word* **sugar**, *paint, blue paint, blue, English, a lid, glass, a glass lid, a jar, sugar, a jar of sugar*, and so on, depending on our interpretation of the person's interests—is she learning English, the use of seasoning, physics, or what? (p. 264)

---

[2]This exemplifies the basically pragmatic character of ostensive reference, discussed in more detail in chapter 3.

[3]There is an unwitting example in Bar-Hillel's own paper. He says:

> A clear understanding of the functioning of indexical expressions can be helpful both in avoiding pseudo-problems and in solving genuine philosophical problems (though the borderline between these two cases is somewhat vague). (p. 376)

Does "these two cases" refer to pseudo-problems and general philosophical problems, or to avoiding pseudo-problems and solving genuine philosophical problems?

1. INDEXICAL PRONOUNS

Although the first person singular pronoun is the paradigmatic example of an in-dexical expression, the issue is not so clear with first person pronouns as Bar-Hillel may lead us to believe. Dismissing the case of an actor speaking his lines, where the understander has to know how to distinguish between the actor's references to himself, and the persona's references to himself (a task that can be difficult in certain plays by Pirandello and Thornton Wilder), Bar-Hillel (1954) took utterances of *I* to refer to whoever utters them (p. 363), and displayed the supposed universal absurdity (p. 377) of the assertion of sentences like (6) as corroboration.

6.   I am dead.

But whenever an agent speaks for a counterpart (G. Lakoff, 1968; Lewis, 1968) in another "world," the possibility of a non-absurd utterance of a sentence of this form arises, for example, an actor in *Hamlet* referring offstage to the last scene, or Scrooge or Marley's ghost in Dickens' *A Christmas Carol*. Marley's ghost's line, "In life I was your partner, Jacob Marley" presupposes (6), even if it doesn't assert it, and in his utterance "I wear the chain I forged in life," the first *I* refers to the (speaking) ghost, while the second refers to the then dead Marley.

Thus, the reference of the first person singular pronoun is determined (largely) pragmatically as a function (cf. Nunberg, 1993) of the utterer of the form *I*. This makes the indeterminacy of reference isolatable (in the form *I*) and contextually resolvable, up to counterparts and assumed identities. The second person pronoun poses different problems. It is similar to the first person pronoun in that the form *you* isolates the referent as the individual or individuals whom the speaker is addressing, but there are no linguistic or external clues to who the individual(s) addressed might be. The addressee is whoever the speaker intends to be addressing, and does not have to be physically present where the utterance is made (as in the case of letters, telephone calls, and the like). The addressee does not even have to exist at the time the utterance is produced, as in the case of documents or speeches sent to a recipient light years away or intended for publication or broadcast 50 years after their production. All that is necessary is that the speaker intend and/or expect that at the time of reception, there will be an appropriate addressee.

Even assuming a contemporaneous, physically present addressee, there may be no linguistic clues to indicate which of several candidates is intended. For instance, an utterance of (7a) would appear to be addressed to every individual in hearing distance of the speaker, but it surely would not be intended to include casual overhearers (cf. Clark & Carlson, 1982), and might not include individuals allied with the speaker (e.g., henchmen who were expected or required to be present).

7a.   I'm glad that all of you received my invitation.
7b.   I'm glad that you received my invitation.

All we really know about the referent of *you* in (7a) is that it is plural, and we know that from the phrase *all of you*.[4] Without such a clue (as in (7b)), it is not at all clear whether the intended referent is the whole group or some subset containing one or more members. Finally, different tokens of *you* may have different referents in an utterance like (8), as indicated by the distinct subscripts, and the only clue to who the various referents are may be changes in the direction of eye-gaze or body-position of the speaker.

8.   You$_1$ can vacuum while you$_2$ wash the dishes, and—keep your$_3$ hat on—I'll get the groceries.

Naturally, all the counterpart and assumed persona complications that arise with first person pronouns arise equally here, and with third person pronouns.

First person plural pronouns have all of the indeterminacies of second person pronouns. *We* can refer to the speaker and any number of other individuals, present or not, and not necessarily existing at the time of production. Cases where the addressee (and possibly others as well) is included in the intended reference of *we* (inclusive *we*) must be distinguished from cases where the intended reference is to the speaker and one or more others, not including the addressee (exclusive *we*). Some languages (e.g., Marathi) have different forms for these two sets of cases.

In all of these cases, it is knowledge of (or beliefs about) the speaker, including beliefs about his beliefs and intentions, at all levels, that enables an interpreter (addressee or otherwise) to divine the intended referents of indexical pronouns. This inference is constrained somewhat by the spatio-temporal coordinates of the utterance, but is by no means uniquely entailed by them.

2. TENSES

Bar-Hillel (1954) indicated that tensed verbs also make sentence tokens indexical in that their reference and truth cannot be determined without an indication of the context in which they are uttered (here, crucially, the time of utterance). Although Bar-Hillel's examples include only true present tenses (e.g., *I am hungry* as opposed to *Water is a compound of hydrogen and oxygen*), which define the time of reference as the time of utterance, past and future tenses are equally indexical, referring to times that are a function of the time of utterance. Thus, if I utter (9a) at time t_0, I mean that I am hungry at t_0; if I utter (9b) at t_0, I mean that I was hungry at some point before t_0, and if I say (9c) at t_0, I mean that I will be hungry at some point after t_0.

---

[4]Because *all of* has a partitive use, as in *all of the pudding*, this is not just strictly semantic interpretation, but must be considered an inference from the assumption that it would not be rational to anticipate an addressee contemplating a situation where part of him receives an invitation.

9a.   I am hungry.
9b.   I was hungry.
9c.   I will be hungry.

Notice, however, that although (9a) indicates a unique time, (9b) and (9c) refer very vaguely to some time before or after t_0; one doesn't know if it is on the order of minutes, days, weeks, years, decades, or millenia distant. Furthermore, it is not clear whether the time indicated by (9a) is a moment, or an interval of indefinite duration which includes the moment of utterance. Although on hearing me say (9a), you wouldn't assume my hunger began when I began to speak or ceased when I stopped speaking, one might want to say that it is a moment, and the fact that (9a) is understood to refer to an interval containing moments before and after t_0 is just the same vagueness that is inherent in the past and future time references. This turns out to be a very complicated issue, however (see Dowty, 1979 for further discussion).

Above I said that the time reference of a tensed sentence was a function of the time of utterance of the sentence, but in fact, this is not the whole story. Depending again on the intentions of the speaker, if there is a significant interval between the time of utterance and the time of (assumed) receipt of the utterance, the time reference of a tensed sentence may be partially a function of the anticipated time of receipt. For example, if I write a letter, I most likely will index time references to the time of writing: "It's 3 degrees Fahrenheit here; we are thinking of going to St. Maarten," but the commander of an earth-invasion force from Alpha Centauri might write to earthlings, "There are thousands of Alpha Centaurians among you, disguised as trucks, tripods, and tape recorders," long before the situation described came to pass, knowing or believing that by the time the message was received, it would have come to pass.[5]

---

[5]The following sentence from *Parade* magazine (1-5-86) illustrates the problem of writing for a future audience.

    i. Any day now (if not already), Mrs. Thatcher's administration will have abolished the old trading laws, and the British—suffering from a 13%-plus unemployment rate—will join the ranks of the all-day Sunday shoppers, a move calculated to increase retail employment.

Apparently, at the time of writing, the Sunday trading laws were still in effect, although their abolition seemed imminent to the writer. The sentence involves a blend of *Any day now, Mrs. Thatcher's administration will abolish. . .*, appropriate if the abolition has not occurred before press time, and *Mrs. Thatcher's administration has already abolished. . .*, appropriate if abolition has occurred. But *Any day now Mrs. Thatcher's administration will have abolished the old trading laws* is ordinarily a very odd thing to say, using a future perfect instead of a simple future, since the future perfect is ordinarily used to relate a future event (like abolishing the trading laws) to an event assumed to be farther in the future, as in (ii):

    ii. By the time Prince William is old enough to shop, the Administration will have (already) abolished the old trading laws.

3. ADVERBS

Virtually the same things can be said about time adverbs as were said about tenses:[6] ordinarily *today* refers to the day of its utterance, *now* to the moment of utterance, *yesterday* to the day before its utterance,[7] *last month* to the month prior to its utterance, *next week* to the week after the week of utterance, etc., but all of these could, under the circumstances described in the preceding section, be indexed to the assumed time of reception.

Place adverbs such as *here* likewise determine reference indexically, as at the place of utterance, and present the same problems of vagueness as *now* (does it mean 'this instant,' 'today,' 'this week,' 'this month'?) and *this* (described at the beginning of this chapter). Whether *here* means 'at this spot,' 'in this hotel,' 'in/on this city/state/country/hemisphere/planet/galaxy etc.' is a function not of objective context, but of what the speaker intends it to refer to, and interpreters must guess, again basing their guesses on their knowledge and beliefs about the knowledge, beliefs and intentions of the speaker. What expressions like *this spot* refer to is entirely vague, linguistically, and can only be interpreted with the aid of gestures or knowledge about the speaker's beliefs and intentions (see the section on demonstratives).

In the case of utterances which will be received long after they are sent, the reference of *here* does not seem to be relative to the location of the reception. When I write, "It's going to be cold here" in a letter to be sent across an ocean by surface mail, I will not expect *here* to be taken to refer to the addressee's location. The Alpha Centaurian commander may announce to earthlings his invasion of Earth with the message, "I have been monitoring activities on Earth for some time, and have sent an invasion force there disguised as trucks to control widespread corruption." If he used *here*, it would be taken to mean he was speaking (or writing) from a location on Earth. A message sent from Alpha Centauri saying, "An invasion force from Alpha Centauri will land here in the next 24 hours," could be understood as heralding an invasion of Earth, but interpreters would understand the announcement not as coming directly from the commander, but as coming from the public address system, cassette player, or whatever broadcast the message. On the other hand, it seems that if the Alpha Centaurian commander characterizes the activities he has been monitoring as *your activities*, then *here* can mean 'on Earth' without assuming that the commander or his spokesman is on Earth.

---

[6]Indeed, a number of linguists have proposed that tenses are pronominal forms of time adverbs (e.g., Kiparsky, 1968; McCawley, 1971a; Partee, 1973). For a more recent treatment, see Hinrichs (1986). Articles accompanying Hinrichs' provide a variety of perspectives on the pragmatics and semantics of tense and aspect in discourse.

[7]In some languages (e.g., Hindi), 'tomorrow' and 'yesterday' are expressed by the same word, which must refer to a time one day removed from the day of utterance.

Contrary to what might be expected, *there* does not ordinarily refer to a location indexed with reference to the addressee; *there* refers to a place which does not include what *here* would refer to in the same utterance situation, a place which the speaker expects the addressee to be able to identify. It may refer DEICTICALLY (i.e., involving visual or gestural pointing) to something closer to the addressee than to the speaker (cf. example (10)), or just to something farther from the speaker than some location identifiable by the speaker as being 'here' (example (11)).

10.   Hand me that pen over there, will you?

11a.   There it is.
11b.   There comes the bus.
11c.   Put 'er there. [An invitation to shake hands.]

Alternatively, it may refer ANAPHORICALLY (i.e., by reference to something mentioned or implied in previous discourse), the way third person pronouns do, as in (12).

12a.   Sandy wants to go to the park, but doesn't know how to get there.
12b.   We're supposed to see Dr. Gesundheit today, but Sandy refuses to go there unless she gets a balloon.

Thus, deictic reference involves a relation between an object in the world and a linguistic form with no semantically determined reference (some form X is used to refer to A), while anaphoric reference involves relations between such a form and some other linguistic expression (the form X is used to refer to something indicated or evoked by some other expression).

Anaphora and deixis are two different ways of accomplishing the same thing: directing the addressee's attention to the speaker's intended referent, by pointing to something which rationally can be expected to evoke that referent in the addressee's model of the world. Deictic uses of expressions accompany non-linguistic gestures pointing to an external object. Anaphoric uses of personal pronouns (and also such words as *former, latter, first, second,* etc.) direct attention to a name or a description already used in the discourse, while the BOUND VARIABLE use of personal pronouns (as in *If anyone fumbles, he will incur the wrath of the coach*) points to a logically entailed entity. Definite descriptions (see chap. 3) and discourse anaphors such as *thus, such,* and *but* (discussed in this chapter, section 5) point to a referent implied by something in the discourse context or the physical context of the utterance.

Place indexicals in other languages often carve up the world differently. For example, Japanese has three: one for places close to the speaker, one for places close to the hearer, and one for places distant from both, like archaic English *yonder*.

4. DEMONSTRATIVES

Bar-Hillel (1954) describes *this* as indexical (p. 366), requiring knowledge of the spatiotemporal coordinates of the speaker for interpretation of its reference, though he goes on, as quoted above, to show that that is generally not sufficient. The indexical *this* can thus be intended (a) deictically in (13a), to refer to an indicated photograph of the earth as seen from the moon, (b) anaphorically in (13a), to refer to a just completed discourse presenting evidence that the earth is round, (c) CATAPHORICALLY, to refer to such a discourse to follow shortly (as in (13b)), or (d) META-PHORICALLY, to refer to something evoked by whatever is indicated and deictically referred to (e.g., to evoke the content of a book by indicating an image of its dust jacket), as in (13c), where *this* refers not to a part of a photograph, or to the dust jacket on which it appears, but to the text of the book the dust jacket was designed to protect.

13a. This proves that the earth is round.
13b. OK, this'll prove that Eks is irresponsible: when we were on a committee together, he fell asleep during every meeting that he managed to attend.
13c. [indicating a part of a photograph of a wall papered with dust jackets] Oh, I've read this!

In terms of the pragmatic properties discussed here, cataphoric expressions are not much different from anaphoric, and I will use the latter term to cover both. *That* likewise has a deictic and indexical use, as in (14).

14. Put that in the wastebasket, please.

That in (14) is deictic (strictly speaking, spatiotemporally deictic) when some kind of gesture by the speaker is required for the interpretation of its reference; it is indexical in that it is appropriately used in (14) to refer to an object considered to be outside the speaker's domain. I would not say (14) to someone if I was touching or had in my physical possession whatever *that* was intended to refer to; I would use *this*. Note that a speaker could use (14) to refer to an item that was physically closer to the speaker than to the addressee, as long as the speaker was not in physical possession of it, if the speaker believed that there was a mutual belief that the addressee had or would take responsibility for it, (i.e., that it was, metaphorically speaking, outside the speaker's domain). I could say (14) to one of my children, or even to a guest in my home, but because of the implications of imputing responsibility, I think a prisoner would be more likely to use (15) than (16) in trying to get assistance from his jailer.

15. This needs to be washed.

16.   That needs to be washed.

More uses of *this* and *that*, however, are probably anaphoric, indicating their referent as something identifiable from previous discourse, as in (17).

17.   Columbus reached the New World in 1492, but this/that did not convince anyone that the earth was round.

And, not surprisingly, *that* can be used meta-phorically, just as *this* can; *that* could be substituted for *this* in example (13c) with the same interpretation. For further discussion of *this* and *that*, cf. R. Lakoff (1974) and Prince (1981a).

Table 2.1 summarizes and exemplifies the kinds of indexicals treated in this chapter and elsewhere in this book. The ones discussed so far are enclosed within the box.

TABLE 2.1
Indexical Expressions

Type	Deictic	Anaphoric	Meta-phoric
Pronoun	*I, you, we,* . . .	*he, her,* . . .	*he, her,* . . .
Time expression	tenses, *then, today,* . . .	past tenses, *then*	*then*
Place expression	*here, there,* . . .	*there*	*here, there,* . . .
Demonstrative	*this, that,* . . .	*this, that,* . . .	*this, that,* . . .
Epithet	*the idiot*[a] (pointing)	*the idiot*[a]	—
Definite description	*the referee* (looking)	*the gray sweater*[b]	*the Times*[c]
Pro-predicate	*do it*	*so, as, such, other more, do it,* ellipsis of verb and verb phrase, . . .	—
Pro-adverbial	*thus, again,* . . .	*thus, therefore, however, moreover,* . . .	—
Conjunction	—	*and, but, yet,* . . .	—
Ellipsis	of noun phrase[d]	of noun phrase	—

[a]To refer to someone who is not categorically an idiot
[b]To refer to a gray sweater
[c]To refer to a person, building, corporate body, etc.
[d]See footnote 14.

5. ANAPHORIC REFERENCE

Anaphoric reference, as already indicated, is reference to an entity referred to or evoked in previous discourse. Some writers have thought that the reference of anaphoric elements like third person pronouns was indexical in that it was determined by the utterance situation, but it should be clear from examples like (8) in chapter 1, repeated here as (18), that their reference is indexical only in that it is determined by the speaker's intention.

18a.   When Luke pushed Adam in to give the photograph to Humphrey, *he* fell down in surprise on seeing the golden charm again.

18b.   The dean expelled John because *he* discovered his secret.

Of course, a considerate or calculating speaker will be careful to use such pronouns only when his estimate of the context, including the addressee's assumed beliefs, suggests that there is a reasonable likelihood that the intended referent will be correctly inferred. It is often convenient to speak of the reference of a term like *I* or *here* or *he* as being dependent on context, but ultimately, and most generally, it is what the speaker intends to (be understood to) refer to that determines what a form refers to (strictly: is used to refer to) on an occasion of use; elements of the external context of an utterance (the time, place, speaker, addressee, previous discourse, etc.) only provide clues to what that intention is likely to be.[8]

Third person pronouns are the prototypical anaphoric expressions, but demonstrative pronouns and adjectives (as illustrated in section 4), and expressions of many other grammatical categories, are distributed and interpreted similarly. Prescriptive grammars often imply that an explicit reference that is taken to refer to the same thing as an occurrence of a pronoun must precede the pronoun, but in normal language use this is often not the case, as the possibility of coreference[9] between pronoun and following proper noun in sentences like (13b) and (19) indicates.

---

[8]One could define *context* to include speakers' intentions, so that *I* would just be described as referring to whomever the speaker intended it to refer to—most likely, the speaker herself, but perhaps the addressee, as in Samuel Delany's novel *Babel 17* (a science fiction novel (Ace Books, 1966) which linguists and computer scientists will find either amusing or irritating), and similarly for other indexical expressions.

However, this is not a very useful move, since it obscures the relevance of genuine situational aspects of context in determining how rational it is to use a particular expression to refer to a particular individual in a discourse with a particular addressee about a particular subject. The range of referents likely to be inferred to be intended for a word like *this* (or even a name like *Bob*) is limited by the content of the physical environment of the speaker at the time of utterance, and by the history of discourse among the participants in the speech event. The speaker's intentions are not enough; a three-year-old who wants to call marking pens with permanent ink *pregnant markers* has to learn that it is unreasonable for him to expect others to understand what he intends the phrase to refer to, no matter how intense or sincere his referential intentions might be. See chapter 3, section 4 for further discussion of what is involved here.

[9]As is made clear in the next chapter, the relation between an anaphoric or relative pronoun and a linguistic expression that licenses its interpretation is something less direct than coreference. A pronoun and its so-called antecedent do not always have the same intended referent.

19.　Before he got out of bed, James decided that today would be a good
　　　day to leave for Crisfield.

It is essential to understand that the referent of a form is an entity in some world
which the speaker intends to indicate by using that form. The REFERENT of a
form is what the form refers to—some actual thing in the real world, or at least
some entity, concrete like a table, or abstract like a form of government, in some
possible world.[10] A pronoun does not refer to a noun phrase or other linguistic
expression,[11] although it may refer to the same object in the world that some
other noun phrase (also) refers to.

Linguistic research in the late 1960's (Langacker, 1966; Ross, 1967, 1969)
attempted to discover simple linguistic conditions for the distribution of pronouns
relative to expressions which license their interpretation that would predict that
he and *James* could be coreferential in (19) but not in (20).

20.　He decided that today would be a good day to leave for Crisfield before
　　　James got out of bed.[12]

The most comprehensive discussion of syntactic conditions on so-called pro-
noun-antecedent relations is Lakoff (1976), which circulated in manuscript form
in 1968, but it offers no simple solution. In later research, Kuno (1972, 1975)
sought discourse conditions to account for the possible relations of pronoun and
coreferential noun phrase within and across sentences, arguing that in general,
BACKWARD PRONOMINALIZATION (as in example (19)) was possible only if the
referent of the pronoun was determinable from preceding discourse, and that
even the possibility of ordinary forward pronominalization within a sentence
depended on the discourse role of the pronominal noun phrase. He mentioned,
for example, such variables as whether the noun phrase represented predictable
information or an exhaustive answer to a question. He did not explain what made
reference determinable or information predictable.

Later, Kantor (1977) argued that the ease of comprehending that a pronoun
was intended to refer to the same entity as the closest preceding candidate noun
phrase (one which matched the pronoun in number and gender) depended on the
degree to which the interpreter expected a reference to something other than the
referent of the pronoun. Although Kantor showed how this expectation could be

---

[10]Cf. chapter 3 for discussion of the notion 'possible world.'

[11]Except, of course, in writing about linguistic forms, as in example (i):

i. The first noun phrase in that sentence is singular, and *it* contains four words.

[12]Actually, one occasionally runs across sentences of this form, where the pronoun and full noun
phrase are intended coreferents, but in all of the cases I have seen, the sentence does not contain
the first reference in the discourse to the referent of the pronoun, and the linguistic expression which
does provide it is a full noun phrase in a preceding sentence.

manipulated by both syntactic structure and discourse structure, calculating the interpreter's (or addressee's) expectation has not been comprehensively modelled (but cf. Nunberg 1978a: 90–117 on a parallel problem, and chapter 3 for further discussion).

Contemporary syntactic and semantic work on coreference addresses conditions under which a candidate noun phrase cannot license the interpretation of a given pronoun, and extends that analysis to other anaphoric devices (cf. Reinhart, 1983; Bach & Partee, 1980; and other articles in Kreiman & Ojeda, 1980).

Personal pronouns are the stereotypical anaphoric expressions, but many other expressions pose the same sorts of problems of determining what previously mentioned or implied entities or constructs they are intended to refer to. Reference may be direct, as when an anaphoric expression is used to refer to the same entity that a different expression (usually a FULL or LEXICAL noun phrase) was previously used to refer to, as in most of the preceding examples, or it may be more oblique, as when a pronoun or other anaphoric device is used to refer to an idea expressed in an entire clause (as in example (17)), or to an entire line of thought, expressed in a paragraph-sized or larger stretch of discourse, as in (21).

21.   Of all the preparations, the most stupendous was the portable wooden town to protect and house the invaders upon landing. A huge camp enclosing a place for each captain and his company, it was virtually an artificial Calais to be towed across the Channel. Its dimensions epitomized the fantasy of omnipotence. It was to have a circumference of nine miles and an area of 1,000 acres surrounded by a wooden wall 20 feet high reinforced by towers at intervals of 12 and 22 yards. Houses, barracks, stables, and markets where the companies would come for their provisions were to be laid out along prearranged streets and squares. William the Conqueror had brought a dismountable wooden fort to England in aid of his landing 300 years before, and similar devices had been used many times since, but nothing so daring in concept and size as *this* had ever before been attempted.
(Barbara Tuchman, *A Distant Mirror*, p. 426 (New York: Alfred A. Knopf, 1978))

Demonstrative phrases, epithets, and definite descriptions (i.e., descriptions of the form "the so-and-so," such as *the gray sweater*) can be used anaphorically to refer to a previously indicated entity (as in (22)), subject to the same pragmatic conditions for interpretation as personal pronouns.

22a.   No man or woman of style was fully dressed without a snuffbox; and on *that appendage* the goldsmith, the jeweler, the enameler, and the miniaturist exercised their most delicate craft.
(Will and Ariel Durant, *The Age of Voltaire*, p. 79 (New York: Simon and Schuster, 1965))

22b.   Philip stopped by yesterday. *The bastard/idiot/son-of-a-bitch* can't seem to keep from fooling around with other people's wives.

22c.   Philip stopped by yesterday. *The man* can't seem to keep from fooling around with other people's wives.

22d.   William "Refrigerator" Perry was called a "wasted draft pick" at the start of the 1985 season, but *the rookie defensive lineman* has blocked, rushed, and caught for Bears touchdowns, and once even tried to carry the ballcarrier into the end zone.

Strictly speaking, such phrases are of course ambiguous between coreferential uses and noncoreferential uses, but so are ordinary personal pronouns. The set of possible coreferential expressions for the anaphoric devices illustrated in (22) is limited by constraints which personal pronouns are not subject to, however. Unlike pronouns, if these expressions are in a complement *that-clause*, they cannot be coreferential with an expression in the main clause: although *Sandy* can be coreferential with the pronoun *he* in example (23a), *Eric Dickerson* and *Philip* cannot be coreferential with the italicized expressions in (23b) and (23c).

23a.   Sandy realized that *he* could get into serious trouble.

23b.   Eric Dickerson thought that *the Rams' running-back* would rush for at least 100 yards.

23c.   Philip doubted that *the man/bastard* would be caught.

The particles *so* and *as* are also anaphoric terms, but they refer to properties of entities, rather than to entities themselves, and their interpretation is licensed by predicative phrases (typically adjective phrases as in (24a) or verb phrases as in (24b) (occasionally prepositional phrases as in (24c), less often predicative noun phrases as in (24d)), rather than by referring expressions.

24a.   Sandy was afraid of the dark, as was Dana.

24b.   James got hot lunch at school, and so will his brother.

24c.   Jan is in France, but so is Dale.

24d.   Jo is a lawyer, and so is Mo.

As example (24b) indicates, the referent of *so* is not the verb phrase *got hot lunch at school* but the predicate 'get hot lunch at school.' Or 'get hot lunch'—like other anaphoric devices, PROPREDICATES like *so* and *as* are ambiguous or vague and may require interpretation as to their intended referent. It is only a knowledge of history that allows us to reject as an interpretation of (25) the claim that Eisenhower, Kennedy, and Johnson supported the equal rights amendment in Nixon's 1968 election campaign.

25.   President Nixon supported the Equal Rights amendment in his 1968 election campaign, as did former Presidents Eisenhower, Kennedy,

and Johnson.
(From a 1969 newspaper)

Many other lexical items that are not typically counted among the anaphoric expressions nonetheless contribute to the interpretation of a discourse by referring to something indicated in prior discourse. We cannot understand (26a) without inferring that previous discourse has described an extent of depravity; consequently, without that description, which the adjective *such* refers to, we cannot tell exactly what sort of environment is being claimed to have nourished the salons. Similarly for the set of cities in (26b) (which one or ones are excluded?), the individual in (26c), and in (26d), the number of individuals (obliquely referred to by the adverb *more*) who took precautionary measures short of leaving town.

26a.   Amidst *such* depravity, the salons flourished.
26b.   In *other* cities, support for the war was diminishing.
26c.   *The former* preferred to stay at home, though no reason was given.
26d.   Thousands *more* left Paris altogether.

Some expressions which are not referring expressions (notably conjunctions and adverbs like *thus, therefore, nonetheless*, and *notwithstanding*) nonetheless regularly imply reference to entities evoked or introduced in previous discourse, regardless of whether those entities have been explicitly named or referred to. For example, *thus, so,* and *therefore* as clause introducers (as in (27)) are equivalent to the phrase *for that reason* or *for those reasons*; they introduce the conclusions to a reasoned argument, and therefore refer implicitly to previously stated or implied premises of those arguments.

27a.   Therefore Socrates is mortal.
27b.   Thus, under this plan, the rich will get richer and the poor will get poorer.

The propositions indirectly referred to may be as close as the preceding clause, as in the use in the sentence introducing the examples in (27); or they may extend over pages (or hours) of text (or discourse) and may even be separated from the anaphor by digressions of some length.

The connectives *nonetheless, however,* and *notwithstanding* (when it occurs without its object) are similar, except that they are concessive, equivalent to *in spite of that*. Out of context (that is, with no prior discourse indicating what "that" might be), example (28) is just as puzzling, incomprehensible even, as (27).

28.   Nonetheless, they want you to be their representative.

Adverbs like *moreover* and *too* as in (29) (cf. Green, 1973) function similarly, being equivalent to *in addition to that*.

29a. Moreover, they want you to be their representative.
29b. They want you to be their representative, too.

When conjunctions such as *and, but, or,* and *yet* appear at the beginning of a sentence, they are not grammatical errors (despite what may be taught in grammar books), but serve to conjoin the proposition expressed by the following clause with some proposition or set of propositions expressed or implied in a larger stretch of discourse (usually prior discourse). Thus, in example (30a), *and* is used to conjoin references to the reasoning described in the preceding paragraph with the reason alluded to by *another*, and in (30b), *but* contrasts the proposition in the following clause to the affirmative answer which the previous text indicated that the speaker anticipated. Likewise, in (30c), *yet* contrasts the difference indicated in the following clause to the similarities described in the preceding text.[13]

30a. ... it occurred to him that in fact the arrival of the California police at this exact moment was altogether extraordinary. The Swami had been killed little more than ten minutes before. No one else but himself knew. So how was it that the police were here already?
And hard on the heels of that thought came another. Where was the Swami's murderer? ...
(H. R. F. Keating, *Go West, Inspector Ghote*, p. 84. (New York: Penguin, 1981))

30b. 'Yes,' he jabbed on. 'You are not pure, Nirmala Shahani. There is blood on your hands. Isn't it? Isn't it? That blood.'
He pointed, suddenly and stiff-fingered, at the brownish stain not three yards away from them beside the dark-pink chalk outline that called back to his own mind vividly enough the body that had lain there, its luxuriant black locks outflung.
But Nirmala was slowly shaking her head in negative. (Keating, pp. 184–185)

30c. He sat pretending to be dumbstruck with amazement at the size and magnificence of the houses to either side, at spreading red-tiled roofs that reminded him of a little Catholic enclave he knew in Bombay only multiplied ten or twenty fold, at great white-pillared facades, at wide green gardens under gracefully bending palm trees.
Yet somehow even these palms were different. (Keating, p. 26)

Even though the preceding text in (30c) is only one sentence, the passage quoted in (30c) would have a very different sense if the whole passage were a single

---

[13]Even the lowly semicolon is anaphoric when it serves the grammatical function of connecting two independent clauses in a single sentence. In fact, often simple adjacency of sentences invites the same inference that the semicolon indicates was intended.

sentence, with *yet* a subordinating conjunction introducing the following clause as a proposition that modified or limited the previous sentence, rather than as an independent proposition. A contrast would be implied between the protagonist's pretending and the difference of the palm trees, and it would be unclear what the palm trees were supposed to be different from.

In the case of elliptical constructions like (31), where the gaps are indicated by "∅," the absence of a referring or predicative expression where one is predicted by the syntax or the semantics is an anaphoric device, and must be interpreted as having the same referent or meaning as a linguistic expression somewhere in the discourse.

31a. If Dana volunteers, Jan will ∅.
31b. Kim bought potatoes and Dana ∅ beans.
31c. Sandy picked ∅, Dana washed ∅, and Kim pickled the tomatoes.
31d. ∅ Cooking dinner bores Dale.
31e. Dale likes ∅ cooking dinner.

In (31a) it is claimed that what Jan will do is volunteer; in (31b) Dana is asserted to have bought beans; in (31c) Sandy is claimed to have picked tomatoes and Dana to have washed tomatoes; in (31d) and (31e), it is claimed that it is Dale's cooking dinner that affects Dale. These constructions are anaphoric in that their interpretation depends on their being linked to an expression elsewhere in the discourse;[14] the expressions in (32) could not be sensibly used to begin a discussion, though similar constructions can be independent utterances in a context

------

[14]In constructions like (i) and (ii), linguistic expressions are not required for interpretation of the unexpressed subjects.

  i. Saw your brother yesterday.
  ii. See my hat?

In English, if preceding discourse does not provide a coreferring linguistic expression, the omitted subject of a declarative sentence is always interpreted as the speaker, and the omitted subject of a question as the addressee (Schmerling, 1973). If there is a coreferring linguistic expression, a main clause subject may be omitted with a broader range of referents as long as there is a potentially coreferring linguistic expression somewhere in the preceding linguistic context. In English, sentences like (iii) are normally encountered as answers ((iv)) or metalinguistic corrections ((v)) (cf. Morgan, 1973c), or occasionally in narratives in an obsolescent diary style.

  iii. Broke his bat.
  iv. Jim: What did Danner do then?
      Tim: Broke his bat.
  v. Red: I heard Danner broke his back.
     Ted: No, no. Broke his bat.

In other languages, including Japanese and Spanish, such sentences occur more freely, in both relatively formal uses of language, and in ordinary conversation, and subjects may be omitted in dependent as well as independent clauses. In Japanese, non-subjects may be omitted as well.

where another speaker has provided the expression on which their interpretation depends, as in (33).

32a. Dana beans.
32b. Jan will.
32c. To be president.

33a. Ann: Kim will bring hamburgers, and Sandy potato salad.
      Jan: And Dana beans.
33b. Mo: I don't know who we can get to volunteer.
      Jo: Jan will.
33c. Jed: What does Sandy want?
      Ned: To be president.

The interpretations of the elliptical expressions in the constructions in (31) are unambiguous, but this is not always the case.[15] In many cases, the larger the number of expressions that might provide an interpretation, the greater the ambiguity of an elliptical expression. In example (34a) it could be Grandpa who was to come into town, or it could be Grandma and Grandpa; in (34b) it is not clear whether Mrs. Smith gave Dana a bond, or whether Mr. Smith gave one to Mrs. Smith; in (34c) the null anaphor might refer to getting chocolate ice cream or to wanting to get chocolate ice cream; and in (34d) there are at least 14 possibilities as to who the suggested dog-walkers are, depending on (among other things) the content of the preceding discourse. the speaker, the speaker and addressee jointly, Dale and the speaker, Dale and the addressee, Dale and the speaker and the addressee jointly, some fourth person (call him X), X and the speaker, X and the addressee, X and Dale, etc.

34a. Grandma said that Grandpa wanted ∅ to come into town to watch the Bears game.
34b. Mr. Smith gave Dana a set of encyclopedias and Mrs. Smith ∅ a savings bond.
34c. Maybeth wants to get chocolate ice cream if James does ∅.
34d. Dale suggested ∅ walking the dog.

Some of these constructions may be subject to conditions on the syntactic position of a phrase which licenses their interpretation. Others do not require a linguistic expression at all for the referent to be inferred, although in the absence of one, they require an extralinguistic indication of a referent. For example, the propredicate *do it*, and PRO-PROPOSITIONAL *it* generally, may have an extralinguistic situational referent, while the null propredicate (as in examples (31a) and (32b)) depends on a linguistic expression for interpretation. Evidence for this

---

[15]For comprehensive discussion, see Williams, 1995.

claim comes from the fact that the examples in (35), with *it*, would be comprehensible in a situation where speaker and addressee are watching a silent street performer preparing to juggle a telephone, a stapler, a frisbee, a pearl necklace, and a paperback book, while those in (36), with elliptical verb phrases, would be puzzlingly inappropriate in the same context.

35a. I don't think he can do it.
35b. It'll never work.

36a. I don't think he can.
36b. He won't be able to.

Either of the sentences in (36) would be perfectly OK if one of the conversants (or even the juggler) had provided a linguistic antecedent, e.g., by saying, "I wonder if he'll be able to manage all those things." Hankamer and Sag (1976), using *anaphora* in a broader sense than the one adopted here, have referred to this sort of interpretation as deictic or pragmatically controlled anaphora. They show that intersentential anaphora (as in (22) and even (33)) is generally linguistically constrained in the sense that the referent has to be at least implicit in preceding discourse, rather than being physically present in the utterance situation.

6. SUMMARY

This chapter addressed the pragmatic aspect of language represented by indexical expressions. Some of the semantics literature has implied that the use of indexicals is all there is to pragmatics, and has been interpreted as implying that the use of indexicals involves a small set of terms and a fairly trivial mapping from the spatio-temporal context of an utterance to a (possibly unique) interpretation for each. We have seen that even in 1954, Bar-Hillel realized there was far more to the interpretation of indexicals than a simple algorithm, and that even the interpretation of indexical expressions like *here* and *you* requires an estimate of the speaker's beliefs and intentions at the time of the utterance.

We surveyed a selection of the wide range of indexicals that languages provide for speakers to use to refer to entities that are deictically indicated or that have been referred to or otherwise indicated in preceding discourse. In all cases, their use could be vague or ambiguous, resolvable only to the extent that the speaker's intention could be reconstructed. Thus, the set of indexical expressions is not small, and the interpretation of indexical expressions requires, in all but the most fully specified contexts, a means of estimating speakers' intentions and beliefs about the world, including the whole Gricean regression referred to in section 6 of chapter 1.

The interpretation of indexicals (both deictic and anaphoric) inescapably involves inferences about the speaker's intended referent. Grammatical properties of such expressions (such as part of speech) provide some constraints on possible referents, the linguistic context may make some referents for anaphoric expressions more salient, and the physical situation of the utterance may provide potential referents for deictic expressions, but ultimately, it is guesses about what the speaker intended the addressee to assume or infer that determine what a form or expression will be taken to refer to.

CHAPTER 2 STUDY QUESTIONS

1. What is an indexical expression?

2. What are some examples of indexical expressions?

3. Why are external contextual coordinates (time, place, identity of utterer) insufficient to fix the referents of indexicals?

4. What is the difference between anaphora and deixis?

5. What is a referent?

6. What is the range of anaphoric expressions?

7. What kinds of entities can be the referent of an anaphoric expression?

3 Reference and Indeterminacy of Sense

In the last chapter, in discussing the reference of indexical and anaphoric expressions, it was taken for granted that the reader would understand what was meant by saying that some form referred (or was used to refer) to a certain entity. It was enough to understand the term *reference* as indicating the means by which a speaker utters a linguistic expression in the expectation that it will enable his addressee to infer correctly what entity, property, relation, event, or the like he is talking about. Now it is time to examine that notion more critically, and observe the extent to which the pragmatic indeterminacies inherent in it pervade the ordinary use of language.

The modern consideration of the central problem, how one knows what is meant[1] by a referring expression, dates back to the nineteenth century as a philosophical issue.[2] Let us take REFERRING EXPRESSION to refer to whatever kinds of expressions can be used to refer, with REFER understood as in the preceding paragraph. In the initial discussions among philosophers (e.g., Mill, 1843; Frege, 1952; Russell, 1905), the class of referring expressions analyzed was usually the set of PROPER NAMES (e.g., *Socrates*) and definite descriptions

---

[1]This formulation of the question fails to indicate whether it is the speaker or the linguistic expression that is supposed (i.e., believed) to do the referring. This is a serious omission, but typical of many discussions. Many modern logicians (and linguists) write as if linguistic expressions refer even when considered outside the context of any utterance. Others, myself included, treat referring as something that speakers do, often by using linguistic expressions, but occasionally with gestures, vocal or otherwise (cf. Bar-Hillel, 1954; Linsky, 1966; Green, 1984).

[2]Here as elsewhere, discussion is framed within the boundaries of contemporary questions. Some of the issues touched upon have a history dating back to the Middle Ages, or even to Antiquity, but limitations of space preclude extensive historical discussion here.

(e.g., *the author of Waverly*); later on, common nouns referring to natural kinds (e.g., *water, gold*) were added (cf. Putnam, 1965, 1970, 1973, 1975a, 1975b, and Kripke, 1972). Arguments in section 4 suggest that an adequate analysis of these extends to many other kinds of expressions as well, including artifact names, adjectives, verbs, prepositions, and adverbs.

1. SENSE AND REFERENCE

Frege is generally credited with establishing the necessity of distinguishing between the REFERENCE of an expression, "that to which the sign refers" (Frege, 1952, p. 116), and its SENSE, an interpretation of the sign provided by the grammar of the language, "wherein the mode of presentation is contained" (p. 116). The terms EXTENSION (Carnap, 1947) DENOMINATION, and DENOTATION (Mill, 1843) are used by other writers for Frege's *reference*, and the term INTENSION (Carnap, 1947) or CONNOTATION[3] (Mill, 1843) for *sense*. Thus, to use one of Frege's examples, the noun phrase *the morning star* would have a sense paraphrasable as 'the star that is seen in the morning,' but its referent would be the planet Venus. The noun phrase *the present king of France* has a clear sense even in the 20th century, but no reference.

There is some dispute over whether names like *Aristotle* or *George Washington* have sense as well as reference, with Frege and many followers claiming that they do have a sense, namely that of the description of their referent (e.g., 'the teacher of Alexander the Great, the well-known Greek philosopher born in Stagira . . .'; 'the first president of the United States'), which, it was asserted, they "stood for."[4] Others, (e.g., Kripke and Putnam) maintain that proper names and nouns denoting kinds do not, properly speaking, have senses at all, but indicate their referent directly (and arbitrarily), without the mediation of interpreting the sense of the name. According to this CAUSAL THEORY of names, names don't "mean" anything; they are just labels for individuals, given at some more or less remote point in history and passed on in the course of normal cultural transmission

---

[3]Mill's uses of *denotation* and *connotation* do not correspond to their current ordinary uses. Mill used *connotation* to refer to the "meaning" of a term, the means by which it referred to its denotation (a thing in the real world). This chapter deals with ordinary-language "denotation," or "meaning," as well as reference. Ordinary-language "connotation" will be touched on in chapter 4.

[4]It is undeniable that some names (e.g., Jackson, Green) are morphologically analyzable; *Jackson* is analyzable as *Jack's son*, *Green* is in some sense related to the color name. However, any meaning that the morphemes in a proper name may have in other contexts is irrelevant to the concerns of truth-conditional semantics: defining the conditions under which a sentence may be said to be true of a situation. A sentence like (i) will be true just in case someone identified as "Jackson" did something that can be described as speaking, regardless of whether or not that person happens to be the son of anyone named Jack.

i. Jackson spoke.

("That stuff is called *water*"; "I am going to tell you about a great philosopher. His name was Aristotle. He lived . . .").

That is, according to this theory, *Aristotle* can be used to refer to Aristotle because the actual fourth century B.C. philosopher who Mr. Bagnoli told me was called Aristotle (on the grounds that his teacher Miss Jones had told him that that man was called Aristotle) is the same man as the man your teacher(s) told you was Aristotle. These chains of transmission, ultimately leading back to an assumed initial "dubbing" are called CAUSAL or HISTORICAL CHAINS. Thus the causal chain via which such names designate their referents involves deixis or ostension (pointing to the intended referent) or anaphora, and therefore in-dexicality, ultimately. The causal (historical) connection is that kinds and individuals are called what they are called because somewhere, sometime, someone called them that, and it stuck. Who, or when, or where makes no difference. All that is required is that there be a continuous chain, and this requirement is really no more than the claim that language is a social, cooperative institution. As Kripke (1972) said: "the way the reference of a name is fixed is of little importance; what matters is that there be a chain, and that for each name, speakers understand the same referent" (p. 331).

2. SOME OTHER DISTINCTIONS

Donnellan (1966) showed that definite descriptions like (1) can be used to talk about something in two quite distinct ways, referentially and attributively.

1a. the 1984 Democratic presidential nominee
1b. the man with the martini

On the REFERENTIAL use, the noun phrase is used to refer to a particular person whom the speaker chooses to describe this particular way, though countless other ways, including perhaps a proper name, may be available and equally likely to succeed in enabling the addressee to know who is being referred to. An individual referentially indicated will generally be assumed to be familiar to the addressee, independently of the referential expression now being used. The ATTRIBUTIVE use is equivalent to 'whoever fits this description,' i.e., in the case of the expressions in (1) 'whoever the Democratic Party nominated for president in 1984' and 'whoever that is with the martini.' In the attributive use, what is referred to depends strictly on the description, and it may be that no alternative description is available to the speaker. If (1a) was uttered prior to the spring of 1984, it would have to be intended to refer attributively, because no one knew who the Democratic nominee would be. After the Democratic National Convention, it could have been used referentially by anyone who knew (and believed that her addressee knew, etc.), but it might have been used attributively by someone who forgot, or didn't care, or was so out of touch that he never knew who had been nominated. (Someone who knew that it was Mondale, but couldn't remember Mondale's name, would be using (1a) referentially, however, if he meant to refer to Mondale.)

Because referential uses are independent of the actual identity of the intended referent, a referential use may involve a (mistaken) description that is false of its intended referent, or is in fact true of no one. Even in such a case, it may still serve to pick out that intended referent. If you and I are in a crowd where only one man is holding a stemmed glass, and I refer to him with (1b), you may be able to tell who I am referring to even if the drink he is holding is not a martini, but rather a Shirley Temple or some other drink, and even if you know that it is no martini in his glass, as long as you think that I believe it is a martini. But if an attributive use involves a mistaken description, it will refer to no one, or be taken to refer to a referent not intended by the speaker. Suppose a detective is instructed that his suspect drinks martinis, and tells his operative to go to a certain restaurant and "shadow the man with the martini." If no one in the restaurant has a martini, then even if the suspect is there, there will be no one whom he has been told to shadow. If someone other than the suspect has the only martini, the operative will be shadowing someone not intended by his employer when he used (1b) to describe the suspect. In many cases, a noun phrase may be used either attributively or referentially in a given context and successfully refer to the same entity, though the two uses may be intended and understood in different ways. Whether this difference is semantic or pragmatic (and if semantic, how it should be represented) is still a matter of some controversy. See Russell (1905), Quine (1953, 1956, 1960), Donnellan (1978), McCawley (1971b), Keenan (1972), Montague (1974), Cole (1978b), Kaplan (1978), and Over (1985) for some proposals.

Kripke (1972) distinguished between RIGID DESIGNATORS (referring expressions with a single descriptional sense which would pick out the same referent in all possible worlds in which that referent existed), and NON-RIGID designators (like *the Pope*, or *the president of the United States*), that pick out different individuals in different worlds. Before continuing with the discussion of how reference is accomplished, it is necessary to clarify what is meant here by "different worlds."

There is a large philosophical literature on the logic and semantics of POSSIBLE WORLDS (cf. Kripke, 1959; Lewis, 1968—McCawley, 1993 provides a good overview), including some critical of the notion (e.g., Copi & Gould, 1967; Scott, 1970), though it is by now so standard a notion among logicians that references are not made to its origin. For our purposes, it is enough to understand that a possible world is not a place, but a possible way the world could be, or could have been. There are an infinite number of possible worlds. For example, there are possible worlds exactly like the real world except that the Panama Canal had never been dug, or the United States in 1950 had a population of 50 million, or I had red hair, and so on.

There are many linguistic expressions and constructions which are used to define worlds other than the real world, or at least to indicate that reference is being made to such a world. Among these are conditional clauses, both indefinite as in (A), and counterfactual as in (B), clauses with modal auxiliary verbs as in (B) and (C), complements of certain WORLD-CREATING terms (words whose sentential objects describe possible states of affairs which need not correspond to what the speaker believes is true in the real world) as in (D), clauses introduced by adverbs indicating potentiality as in (E), and no doubt many others.

A1. If it rains tomorrow, that will be 25 days of rain in one month.

A2. If Dylan has finished his homework, he may watch TV.

A3. If that book is where it belongs, it's in the middle of the third shelf from the top.

B. If number 10 hadn't fouled out, the Wildcats might/could have won the game.

C. The Cubs might/could/may/will win the pennant next year.

D1. I dreamed/imagined I discovered three new rooms in my house.

D2. Alice wondered whether pigs knew how to fly.

D3. Suppose you're on a desert island.

E. Perhaps/Maybe there is life on Mars.

Expressions like *the Pope* and *Miss America* are non-rigid designators, because who they refer to depends on what world is being discussed. In example (2a), *the Pope* refers to Pius XII;[5] in (2b), to John-Paul II. Similarly, the two occurrences of *the King* in (2c) refer to two different kings.

2a. Before 1945, the Pope had discussed the situation of European Jews with many world leaders.

2b. The Pope survived an assassination attempt shortly after his election in 1978.

2c. The King is dead. Long live the King!

Proper names are rigid designators, however. The name *John Stuart Mill* refers to the 19th century British philosopher and political economist, no matter what sort of world is indicated,[6] e.g., in all of the examples of (3).

---

[5]Most readily, anyway. It could be taken to refer (referentially) to any individual who was Pope prior or subsequent to 1945 (including whoever is Pope at the time of uttering (2a), if that individual was established as a topic of the discourse in which (2a) occurs, and was (mutually believed to be) old enough to talk before 1945.)

[6]Except, of course, where it is intended and understood to refer to another individual with the same name, in which case it refers exclusively to the latter; its reference still does not change according to what possible world is intended in the context of its utterance.

3a. John Stuart Mill published several important books before Karl Marx was born.
3b. John Stuart Mill must be turning over in his grave.
3c. If John Stuart Mill were alive, this would amuse him.
3d. If John Stuart Mill had been drafted to go to Vietnam, he would never have written *A System of Logic.*

Note however, that although a name like *Joe* will (be used to) refer to different individuals on different occasions of use, that does not make it a non-rigid designator. Rather, since there are many individuals who have been named or dubbed *Joe*, on each occasion of use, *Joe* is a rigid designator whose successful use to refer depends on speaker and addressee taking it to be a name of the same individual.

Rigid/non-rigid and referential/attributive are similar distinctions in some ways, but they are not the same. A non-rigid designator such as *the Pope* or *the tallest man in Ohio* can be referential as in (4), or attributive as in the most likely interpretation of the sentences in (5).

4a. The Pope visited India in 1986.
4b. The tallest man in Ohio came to the ball game.

5a. If you have an audience with the Pope, you must kiss his ring.
5b. Since 1805, the tallest man in Ohio has been allowed to live in the house rent-free.

3. MODERN TREATMENTS

In most modern semantic theories, including various intensional logics (cf. Dowty et al., 1981 for further discussion of this term), the sense of an expression is supposed to determine its reference, and the goal of the intensional logic that makes explicit the mechanism by which this can happen is to determine the possible sorts of functions from possible INDICES (coordinations of worlds, times, speakers, etc.), to their EXTENSIONS or DENOTATIONS (the entities or sets of entities denoted by an expression at an index). These functions are taken to represent the senses of linguistic expressions in such a way that the meaning of a composite expression is a function of the meanings of its parts. This sounds very complicated, and it is, but more by involving long sequences of operations than by being conceptually difficult. Dowty et al. (1981) provides an excellent introduction. The point is that it is a fundamental assumption that linguistic expressions indicate (denote) extensions in the real world, and they do this compositionally, with one subpart of the intension extending or delimiting the extension indicated by another. For example, in Montague semantics (cf. Montague 1970, 1973; and Dowty et al., 1981 for an introduction), a name like

Aristotle is treated as if it denoted the (infinite) set of Aristotle's properties, whatever they may be; a definite description like *the gray sweater* gets an analysis paraphrasable as "the unique thing which is gray and is a sweater" (and essentially equivalent to the one Russell (1905) proposed). Common nouns (and adjectives and intransitive verbs) are taken to have extensions equivalent to sets of individual concepts, while their intensions are properties. Thus the intension of *sweater* is paraphrasable as "the property that makes something a sweater" and the intension of *gray* is paraphrasable as "the property necessarily shared by gray things."

Kripke and Putnam provide a view of the way common nouns refer that avoids reference to properties. According to the causal theory of names, names are just names; they are not abbreviations for descriptions, and they do not "mean" anything, not even 'the man called Aristotle' (or whatever). Giving someone or something a name, or transmitting that name, does not define a meaning for the name, but simply fixes or determines its reference. Both Kripke and Putnam extend this analysis to the names of natural kinds (e.g., water, gold, tigers, horses, beeches, elms, lemons, etc.). Thus, in this analysis, *water* does not "mean" H_2O; it is the name of some stuff which happens to be a liquid at temperatures between 32°F and 212°F, chemically analyzable as containing two parts hydrogen and one part oxygen, and so on. Likewise, *horse* is the name of a certain sort of animal, just as *Aristotle* and *Jimmy Carter* are the names of certain individual men. *Horse* doesn't mean a large, short-haired, vegetarian quadruped with solid hooves and flowing mane and tail, used for drawing or carrying loads, etc., even though horses generally have those properties.

In this view of things, it is important not to confuse the analysis of the name of a kind such as *fish* or *water*, with analysis of the kind itself, or with people's knowledge, beliefs, or understandings about that kind. The first is part of the study of language (specifically, semantics or pragmatics); the second belongs to biology, chemistry, mechanical engineering, or whatever; and the last is part of cognitive psychology (cf. Rosch & Mervis, 1975; Smith & Medin, 1981) or anthropology (Conklin, 1972). It is as nonsensical to do a semantic analysis of the word *horse* as it would be to do one of *Fred* or *Panasonic*, even though inferences, including inferences of relations among sets referred to, may be derivable from the use of the term, for the inferences are about the sets, not about the words. I cannot emphasize this point enough; most of the enormous literature on semantic memory by psychologists (e.g., Meyer, 1970; Collins & Quillian, 1972; Tulving, 1972; Smith, Shoben, & Rips, 1974; Collins & Loftus, 1975) is really not about words but about the kinds which words name.

Saying that common nouns like *water* or *lemon* are literally names for kinds of things implies that they are semantically unanalyzable, although the concepts of kinds of things which they designate may be analyzable to some degree. Just because a concept is analyzable, it does not follow that its name is analyzable. It is, I think, uncontroversial that we categorize the world and classify objects into kinds. That is how we know that Fido and Sam and Skipper and indeed, poodles, and huskies and mongrels generally, are all dogs. However, it does not follow from our ability to do this that in doing so we assume each entity or type of entity to be of only one kind. Our classifications may be, as in the example just given, hierarchical, but they may also (instead or in addition) cut across each other: running is a kind of exercise, a kind of sport, and a kind of locomotion. A particular species of bird may be a kind of shore bird, a kind of sexually dimorphic bird, and a kind of migratory bird. In both cases, the categories which subsume the activity or object mentioned are neither proper subsets of each other, nor mutually exclusive with each other.

It also happens that the same word may be used to refer to quite diverse kinds, even ignoring metaphorical uses, just as different individuals may have the same personal names. Thus, *plant* is the name of a large category of organisms, of a kind of building, and of a kind of activity involving seeds, a growing medium and an intention that the seeds grow. *Bank* is the name of a kind of financial institution, of a part of a river or creek bed, and of a kind of maneuver involving causing a projectile to ricochet off a fixed surface towards a target.

Of course, our classifications are not exhaustive, either; we may encounter an object and not know what sort of thing it is (e.g., a westerner encountering tofu or peastarch noodles for the first time). We might be unable to classify the novel object because we do not know what its characteristics are; this is an empirical question, and is, in principle at least, easily resolved. On the other hand, we may know what its properties are, but still not know if it is a member of a kind we have previous knowledge of, or perhaps, of a novel kind.

Thus, just as any interpreter of a discourse has to make a calculated guess about what is intended by the use of indexical terms, he must guess at what kinds were intended by the utterance of various lexical referring expressions. It is clear enough that this sort of guessing is required to interpret anaphoric terms like *he*, a little less obvious with proper names like *Bob*, but it is equally required with kind names in definite and indefinite noun phrases such as *the ham sandwich* or *an elm*. Despite this, communication through language succeeds to a satisfactory extent, and it succeeds to the extent that it does because language use is a social and cultural phenomenon. It is in the best interests of the members of a linguistic community to act as if there were a social contract, and assume more or less standard references for standard words in the language, even though strictly speaking, it is impossible for there to be standard references for standard words when what a word is used to refer to depends on what the speaker intends it to be taken to be intended to refer to, and it is impossible to know what is in another person's mind, and know what she uses, say, *drug*, to refer to. We return to this issue in section 4.

There is no reason not to extend the analysis of natural kind words to non-natural kinds (artifacts) such as pencil, table, clock, robot, plastic, corduroy, and the like, and to what Putnam (1962) called physical magnitudes: heat, kinetic energy, straight line, and even to what might be called social magnitudes:

democracy, prayer, aggression. Indeed, Putnam suggested that artifact names, and at least some verbs (e.g., *grow*) and adjectives (e.g., *red*) refer as rigid designators, connected to their referent by some causal/historical chain, and Kripke suggested the same for at least the adjectives that correspond to natural kinds of phenomena (e.g., *hot, wet*). In fact, a case can be made (cf. Green, 1984) for treating names for kinds of activities (e.g., running, basting,[7] drinking, cramming), states (intending, jealousy, cleanliness), properties (tall, dark, handsome), and situations (giving, growing) as rigidly designating the kind of activity, state, property, and so forth that they refer to.

Not all referring expressions refer by virtue of being names for their referents. Some (e.g., *orphan, weed*) refer by (implicitly) describing their referents. And there are other sorts of words which are not used to refer at all, and so are logically neither names nor descriptions: *and, all; ouch, damn, hello* (see Green, 1984, 1993, for discussion).

If we adopt the view that in general, descriptive terms are rigidly designating names for kinds, we can say[8] that a use of the expression *the gray sweater* indicates a thing of the sort called *sweater* which has the (color) property of the sort called *gray*. How about *the*? Is it the name of some kind also, maybe the property of being unique? Probably not; at least, nobody appears to have advanced this position. As hinted at in the beginning of this section, Russell (1905) and subsequently many other logicians have treated it as an operator which asserts the existence of a unique individual with the properties indicated by the other components of the noun phrase it introduces. The problems with this analysis are that (a) uniqueness is relative, and (b) so is existence. The first problem is demonstrated by an infinite number of ordinary sentences like those in (6).

6a. If you don't hang your coat up, *the* cat will make a puddle in it.

6b. Water *the* plants before you go out, please.

6c. *The* mailman thinks that those five mailmen are throwing mail in the lake.[9]

One can use (6a) without assuming that there is only one cat in the universe, and (6b) is not an order to water all the plants in the universe. If *the* involved an assertion of uniqueness, (6c) would contain a contradiction, but it does not. The cat, the plants, and the mailman are not assumed by speaker or addressee to be unique (cf. also Kantor et al., 1982, p. 262).

The second problem is illustrated by sentences like (7), where the speaker and the addressee do not have to suppose that there are unicorns, or that a northwest passage was discovered.

---

[7]Whether in sewing or in cooking.

[8]Probably, assuming some more or less elaborated form of predicate calculus, treating the property designated by *gray* as a function applied to the kind represented by *sweater*.

[9]Example like this attributed by Morgan (1975a) to J. D. McCawley.

7a. *The* unicorn is a mythical beast.
7b. *The* unicorn does not exist.[10]
7c. *The* discovery of a northwest passage to the Pacific was the goal of many early explorers.

In fact, as the example in (8) shows, the supposition of existence may be explicitly suspended.

8.   Place *the* remaining stitches, if any, on a stitch holder.

In light of these difficulties (and others; cf. Morgan, 1975a), a more attractive analysis, suggested by Strawson (1950) and again by Morgan (1975a), (cf. also Kamp, 1981 and Heim, 1982) is that *the* is neither a name nor a semantic function or operator, but merely a linguistic sign prefixable to the beginning of noun phrases, which a speaker uses to indicate that she has a definite referent in mind which she expects the addressee to be able to identify from whatever clues are available.[11] This is what makes it possible to understand sentences like (6) correctly in context. Out of context, of course, where the interpreter has no way of knowing what cat, plants, or mailman is intended, such sentences cannot be fully understood, in that the interpreter cannot correctly infer exactly when they would be true. *The* has the pragmatic function of aiding the addressee in inferring the speaker's intended referent, but no semantic function beyond that in fixing or delimiting truth conditions. The role of *the* in enabling an interpreter to infer the intended referent is actually quite small compared to the extent to which it is necessary to rely on the interpreter's ability to utilize assumptions about the topic and context of the discourse. Thus, even in a context where, out of the millions of cats presumed to exist, there are two which are equally familiar to speaker and addressee, sentence (6a) could be successfully used to refer to a

---

[10]It might be thought that examples like (i) also illustrate the absence of an existence claim inherent in the use of the definite article.

i. The cat didn't make that mess; we don't have a cat.

However, it is the phenomenon of contradiction by metalinguistic negation that makes (i) acceptable; *the cat* here echoes a previous utterance where the existence of a cat was taken for granted. See Horn 1985, 1989 for full discussion of this phenomenon and its consequences for semantic theory.

The analysis of definite noun phrases in INTENTIONAL or REFERENTIALLY OPAQUE contexts (cf. Dowty et al. 1981, p. 143ff for discussion of this notion) like (ii) where a possible world is invoked which may be different from what the speaker believes to be the real world presents a major problem for contemporary logic and semantic theory (cf. e.g., Quine 1960, Montague 1970, Kaplan 1977, Stalnaker 1978).

ii. The unicorn Dana is looking for is supposed to have golden hooves.

[11]This might be an individual, as in *the gray sweater*, or a species as in (7a). Cf. Nunberg & Pan 1975 and Carlson 1978 for discussions of the treatment of generic noun phrases.

unique cat, if only one of the two cats has an acknowledged reputation for making puddles in inappropriate places.

4. REFERRING FUNCTIONS:
GETTING FROM KINDS TO REFERENTS

The question is not what the writer meant, but what he conveyed to those who heard or read. (Gatley, *Libel and Slander*, quoted in Frederick Philbrick, *Language and the Law*, p. 29 (New York: Macmillan, 1949))

Discussion in this chapter and the preceding ones has suggested that the mechanism by which referring expressions enable an interpreter to infer an intended referent is not strictly semantic or truth-conditional, but involves the cooperative exploitation of supposed mutual knowledge: the speaker must suppose that the addressee knows some proposition P and assumes that the speaker knows that the addressee not only knows P but will use that information in inferring the intended referent. Since there are many more kinds (an infinite number, actually) than kind names, sometimes a kind name is used as the name of more than one kind, as was mentioned in the preceding section. In fact, this situation arises much more often than it comes to our conscious attention, and exponentially compounds the number of potential inferences that an interpreter might make. But by considering it at more length, we can see in more detail how that inferencing mechanism might work.

We noted above the ambiguity of *bank*. The usual lexicographic analysis of this ambiguity is that *bank* is HOMONYMOUS, that is, that there are separate words, with distinct meanings and origins, which coincidentally have the same pronunciation, [bæŋk]. But not all words which can be used to refer to two or more kinds of referents are treated as homonyms. For example, lexicographers treat the two uses of *chicken* in (9) as two senses of a single POLYSEMOUS word (a word with more than one sense).

9a. The chicken ate the grubs, and also the lettuce seedlings.
9b. I had chicken for dinner yesterday.

The difference between polysemy and homonymy appears to be psychologically real, but it is clear that in the vast middle ground, speakers may differ on whether two senses of some phonologically unique form are senses of the same polysemous word, or two different homonymous words. For some people, the 'novel' sense of *original* may be unrelated to the 'initial' sense, but to others, the relationship may be clear. The relation between *cheap* 'inexpensive' and *cheap* 'tawdry' may be obvious to many people, but come as a revelation to others. Generally, whenever one sense can be taken or reconstructed as a metaphorical extension of another (see chap. 5, sec. 4), the two senses are polysemously related, although it is possible for relationships that are originally clear to become obscure over time, so that senses that were once polysemously related may become grammaticized as senses of homonymous words (cf. Morgan, 1978).

The distinction is syntactically real as well, in that in constructions which presuppose linguistic identity[12] (cf. chap. 2, Section 5), homophones like *pear* and *pair*, and homonyms like *bank* and *bank* exhibit different syntactic behavior from distinct senses of polysemous items. In particular, syntactic constructions such as relative clauses and pronominalization treat different senses of polysemous items (as in (10)) as being the same, homonyms (as in (11)) as different.

10a. Pick up the glass, and pour it into the pitcher.
10b. The newspaper Jan's reading almost went bankrupt in 1983.

11a. Dana's bank is eroding, but it is closed on Saturday.
11b. The lawyer's case(,) which was made of genuine leather(,) suffered from logical flaws.

Thus, in (10a), it is a container that is to be picked up, but its contents that must be deposited in the pitcher, and in (10b), what Jan is reading is a copy of an issue of a newspaper, but it was the corporation that publishes the newspaper that nearly went bankrupt. In contrast, if we can interpret (11a) at all, we do not understand that land is eroding and a financial institution is closed on Saturday. Rather, if we can make any sense of it, we must understand either that a financial institution is (in some sense) eroding, and closed on Saturday, or that some land is eroding, and (in some sense) closed on Saturday. Similarly, we do not understand (11b) to be about both a leather carrying container and a set of legal arguments. To make sense of it, we have to understand it to be about either a container or (less plausibly) a set of arguments.

Many ordinary nouns have the property of being usable to refer to quite a variety of distinct kinds of referents, as illustrated with the noun *newspaper* in (12).

12a. The newspaper raised the price per inch for its classified advertising.
12b. The newspaper fell from my lap.
12c. "Dear Abby" isn't in that newspaper on Saturdays anymore.
12d. The printers' union wants to buy that newspaper.
12e. That newspaper has always supported a Republican candidate for president.

---

[12]The identity is not identity of intended reference, for if it were, the uses of *glass* and *newspaper* could not count as identical with the pronouns whose interpretations they support in (10), nor is it identity of form, for then *bank* and *case* should support the corresponding pronouns in (11), but they do not.

In fact, most ordinary common nouns, and even many proper nouns, have a multiplicity of senses of this sort.

13a. Pour a glass of water into the pitcher.
13b. Put a glass of water on the picture.
13c. Put a glass of water in the picture.
13d. France protested the investigation.
13c. France is hexagonal.

Does this mean that all of these words (and names!) are polysemous? If nouns like *glass, newspaper* are names, and names don't have senses, then there is no difference between polysemy and homonymy. We would have to say that there are as many different words *glass,* as there are kinds which that word is used to name. If names do have senses, we would have to say that there are that many distinct senses. There are two problems with this conclusion.

First of all, there is a difference between polysemy and homonymy. As illustrated above, there are demonstrable differences in the syntactic behavior of homonyms and the senses of polysemous terms.

Second, it is possible to show that virtually every noun is polysemous (indeed, virtually every verb, adjective, and preposition as well), and possibly infinitely so. If every distinct sort of use is a distinct sense that has to be learned, there is no way to account for our ability to understand sorts of uses we have never encountered before. Thus, almost all nouns taken to refer to concrete objects can be used to refer to particular individual objects as in (14a), or to the TYPES of which such individual objects are exemplars (or TOKENS), as in (14b).

14a. Dana bought a convertible.
14b. In the fall, GM will market a convertible for the first time since 1970.

Many nouns have several less universal sorts of senses as well (cf. Nunberg, 1978a, chap. 2). Nominalizations like *manufacture, nomination, opposition, construction, approval, election* and other abstract nouns (*committee, culture, adventure*) are multiply polysemous, as evidenced by their behavior with relative clauses and pronouns; they can refer to, among other things:

- the fact that something has been done, or is a certain way, as in (15a),
- the extent to which something has been done, or is a certain way, as in (15b),
- whether or not something happens, as in (15c),
- the act of doing something, as in (15d),
- the product of some action, as in (15e),
- the way something was done, as in (15f).

15a. $\left\{\begin{array}{l}\text{The construction of the builiding} \\ \text{(which took ten weeks)} \\ \text{His opposition (which was vehement)} \\ \text{His presence} \\ \text{His nomination}\end{array}\right\}$ meant that the bill would never pass.

15b. $\left\{\begin{array}{l}\text{The inadequacy of the report} \\ \text{The opposition to the report} \\ \text{The court's construal of the law} \\ \text{The construction in Kuwait}\end{array}\right\}$ surprised the senators.

15c. $\left\{\begin{array}{l}\text{The nomination of Sen. Leffingwell} \\ \text{The approval of the bill}\end{array}\right\}$ depends on there being a quorum.

15d. $\left\{\begin{array}{l}\text{The nomination of Sen. Leffingwell} \\ \text{The construction of the building}\end{array}\right\}$ took four days.

15e. $\left\{\begin{array}{l}\text{Dana's construction} \\ \text{Dale's cooking}\end{array}\right\}$ won awards from international organizations.

15f. $\left\{\begin{array}{l}\text{The construction of the building} \\ \text{The 1986 elections}\end{array}\right\}$ shocked the investigators.

The same sort of evidence shows that even proper names are extensively polysemous. *Shakespeare* is the name of a man, but in (16a) it refers to his works, while the pronoun which that use licenses refers to the man himself, and in (16b) it refers to books containing those works. *Chicago* is the name of a city, but in (16c) it refers to an athletic team. *Xerox* is the name of a corporation, but in (16d) it refers to shares of stock in that corporation (cf. Borkin, 1972).

16a. Shakespeare can be difficult for 8th graders to read, although he didn't use difficult words.
16b. Shakespeare takes up five feet of Dale's bookshelves.
16c. Chicago beat Dallas, 44–0.
16d. I bought Xerox at 49.

Furthermore, in context, just about any noun can be used to refer to just about any sort of thing. A waitress might identify a customer as what he has ordered (giving new meaning to the observation that you are what you eat), as in (17a); a member of a woodwind ensemble might identify another member by her instrument, as in (17b); a detergent might be identified in a TV commercial by the garment it is being used to remove soil from, as in (17c).

17a. The ham sandwich wants a side order of fries.
17b. The clarinet had to go to the powder room.

17c. Now, the T-shirt is fortified with enzymes, and the apron has phosphates.

The potential uses of this sort are infinite. There is no limit to the kinds of uses (or PSENSES, to use a term Nunberg coined (1978a, p. 6) to avoid confusion with the technical use of *sense* in formal semantics) that a noun like *ham sandwich* or *newspaper* can have; if each kind of use was a distinct meaning, then *ham sandwich* could "mean" 'person who ordered a ham sandwich' or 'person who ate a ham sandwich' or 'person who said he hated ham sandwiches' or 'person who knocked my ham sandwich to the floor,' etc., and proper names would be equally ambiguous.[13]

Thus, the multiplicity of kinds of uses a term may have is extensive and pervasive. Since human memory is finite, all of these "senses" cannot be stored as part of the mental representation of linguistic knowledge. There must be some general principles which people use to interpret such terms in referring expressions. Without a pragmatic theory of how terms are used to refer, there is no hope of accounting for cases like (17). With such a theory, cases like (14–16) can be explained as well, without hypothesizing massive homonymy or polysemy. The rest of this section, therefore, describes the pragmatic theory of reference developed by Nunberg (1978a) to explain how uses of terms, even apparently novel ones like those in (17), are readily understood according to general, independently needed principles.

Nunberg argued that (a) in general there are no basic or standard psenses for referring terms (although there are psenses which speakers in particular subcultures take to be normal in some kinds of contexts), and that (b) successful reference is possible because our linguistic competence includes the ability to derive additional psenses from a given psense using a fairly small number of recursively combinable functions. He showed that deictic indexicals like those in (18) have the same range of reference as descriptive terms designating the same intended referents.[14]

---

[13]Alternatively (cf. Nunberg, 1995), *wants* could "mean" 'has an orderer who wants' and *had to go to the powder room* could "mean" 'has a player who had to go to the powder room.'

[14]Nunberg has pointed out (personal communication) that deictic pronouns in sentences like (18) are selected on the basis of properties of the intended referent, not the indicated object. Thus *He* (not *That*) is used in (i) to refer to a customer, and *That* in (ii) refers to a phenomenon (e.g., a sound) or the event which produced it, as shown by the fact that a sentence like (iii) would not be possible in the same situation.

    i. He wants more coffee. [indicating a ham sandwich]
    ii. That must be my piano teacher. [indicating a ringing doorbell]
    iii. That taught me piano.

Notice also that, used in the same situation as (i), (iv) would seem to imply an inanimate customer or impute to the bread and meat a desire for more coffee.

    iv. That wants more coffee.

Thus the function relating the demonstratum and the intended referent is not strictly an identity function. For more discussion, see Nunberg, 1993, 1995.

18a. *That tastes good. [pointing to a picture of a grilled tomato].*
18b. Hearst bought *that* for $3.5 million. [indicating a copy of a newspaper]

This means that the particular intended psense cannot inhere in the individual terms *ham sandwich* and *newspaper*, any more than it can inhere in a pronoun like *that*. Nunberg proposed that speakers make use of REFERRING FUNCTIONS which relate one psense of an expression to another.[15] These are to be understood as functions in the mathematical sense, from psenses (kinds of uses) to other psenses. Thus, in (10a), the two uses of *glass* are related by the function 'contents of' (or 'container of'), and in (10b), the two uses of *newspaper* are related by the function 'publisher of' (or 'product of'). Nunberg suggested that speakers have the ability to relate objects by means of such functions as 'type of' (e.g., (14b), 'cause of,' 'possessor of,' 'location of,' and the like, plus the trivial combinatorial ability to recursively construct an infinite number of composites of these functions, such as 'location of possessor of' (as in (16c)), or 'cause of type of,' and so on. From this perspective, the problem of reference is to determine which of the vast number of potential referring functions relates what is indicated (some object or some basic concept)[16] to what is intended as the referent of one's remarks. Nunberg described several principles which speakers must use to narrow down the set of referring functions that might be relied upon in a given situation.

First, the demonstratum (whatever is pointed to) must be what it appears to be, and appear to be what it is. You cannot point at candy made to look like a newspaper and expect it to be recognized as candy. The addressee has to know that it is candy, and know that he is expected to know, and so on. This holds even for the identity function (i.e., when the speaker points at an object to refer to that object, rather than something it evokes). Second, the addressee has to be assumed (etc.) to know that there are values of the candidate referring function in the set to which the intended referent belongs. If I point to a ham sandwich and say, "He's a conservative," invoking the referring function 'orderer of,' I have to believe that you believe (etc.) that the set of all ham-sandwich-orderers includes some individual male human beings.

Third, it has to be possible to distinguish the demonstratum from other things like it for which the candidate referring function has different values. When Nunberg was writing, in the 1970s, automobiles manufactured in different years were distinguishable enough to allow a speaker to point to a car and use it to indicate a date, as in (19a), but cars of the same make, model, and year were then, as now, pretty much indistinguishable, so one couldn't point to a 1975 Chevy Nova and expect anyone to use the referring function 'location of manufacture' to derive an intended city from an accompanying utterance like (19b).

---

[15]Nunberg (1995) describes predicate transfer functions which define analogous relations among predicates.

[16]This is an oversimplification in that Nunberg argued that the assumption of basic senses is unjustifiable. See discussion surrounding (21–22) to follow.

19a. I was in Germany then.
19b. We visited some lovely parks there.

Now maybe a better example would refer to hearing an old song on the radio, and saying something like (19c).

19c. Oh, I was in college then.

Fourth, when the demonstratum could be the referent, it must be. I can't expect to be understood to be talking about someone who ordered a ham sandwich when I say either of the sentences in (20), if it's plausible for me to be intending to refer to the sandwich itself.

20a. The ham sandwich fell on the floor.
20b. The ham sandwich needs mustard.

This may be what accounts for the fact that when one reads the following passage, it is difficult not to understand *the little blue flowers called faeries'-eyes scattered across the coverlet* as a reference to embroidered decoration on the coverlet, using the common referring function 'image of' (the one which relates, for example, drawings, photographs, statuettes, manufactured miniatures of dogs, and stuffed toy dogs to real dogs) to interpret *flowers*. The passage, from a modern fairy tale, occurs at the point where a princess discovers that her sister has been kidnapped by faeries.

> The little blue flowers called faeries'-eyes scattered across the coverlet were not more dreadful to her now than the fact of the empty bed itself. (Robin McKinley, *The Door in the Hedge*, p. 12 (New York: Greenwillow, 1981))

It is only a reference, two sentences later, to "a faint mysterious smell from the bruised flowers she had lain on" that suggests that the intended interpretation is natural flowers.

Referring functions were described earlier as if they were functions from a basic psense of a descriptive term to a more secondary psense, though it was indicated in footnote 16 that this is an oversimplification. The oversimplification is this: for many descriptive terms or referring expressions, none of the obvious potential psenses is rationally more basic or standard than the others. To demonstrate with some of Nunberg's examples, does *window* refer "inherently" to a kind of hole in a building, or to the framed apparatus that goes in the hole, or to the (usually) transparent material that is part of that apparatus (the part you're referring to when you say that someone's home run broke a window)? Is *newspaper* the name of a kind of regularly published document, or an organization that publishes that kind of document regularly, or to the kind of paper they print it on? For many nouns it is not clear which is more basic: the mass use as in (21), or the countable use as in (22).

21a. Fire destroyed the garage.
21b. Night is 15 hours long at the winter solstice.

22a. A fire destroyed the garage.
22b. Nights are 15 hours long by mid-December.

Even more generally, which is more basic, the type use of a common count noun, or the token use; the species cat, or individual cats?

Nunberg suggested[17] that in these cases, and therefore in general, neither use is basic. Applied to descriptive referring expressions,[18] referring functions relate potentially intended descriptions, but to each other, not to any privileged, inherently designated referents. To quote Nunberg (1978a):

> A rational speaker, even in a linguistically homogeneous speech-community, may never be able to determine the form of the conventions governing the uses of words; the best he will be able to say is that, say, "*w* is used as if it designated *a* or *b*." (p. 74)

Verb uses display the same broad and pervasive variety we saw with nouns in examples (9–17). The intransitive verb *run*, for example, names a kind of goal-directed locomotive activity (23a), and regular participation in a sport consisting of that activity (23b,c). Sometimes the goal-directed activity isn't even locomotive (23d). *Run* also describes the excursus of a liquid from a source (23e,f), and probably by extension, the flow of electric current (23g) and the functioning of engines or batteries powered by electricity, and machines powered by them (23h,i). The execution of computer programs is also called running (23j), perhaps by a further extension. And by extension from one or more of these uses, the goal-directed swimming of fish is also called running (23k). In a related

---

[17]Not for nothing did Nunberg coin the term *radical pragmatics* to refer to his view of reference. This view contrasts with the traditional view of word meaning as wholly conventional, but it is entirely consistent with the claim that semantics is compositional. Whether or not semantics is compositional is independent of how reference is determined, but determination of reference is unavoidably pragmatic in any case for indexicals like pronouns. Names have the same referential vagueness as pronouns, and it has to be resolved the same way, independently of whether common nouns are typically names and similarly vague. The pragmatic determination of reference depends on semantics being compositional in that knowing what is predicated of what is invoked in conditions on inferring referring functions from apparent demonstrata (cf. pp. 57–58), and thus in assigning referents to referring expressions.

[18]Applied to a demonstrated physical object, the same referring functions relate potentially intended referents to the primary demonstratum. The indeterminacies here are the familiar ones of determining what has been demonstrated (cf. chap. 2) and of inferring the referring function intended by the speaker.

use, any machine with moving parts may be said to run when it is operating (23L). And related to its use to refer to the coursing of a river (23f), *run* can be used for other kinds of trade routes (23m). (Anyone who knows Latin may have noticed the Latin word for 'run' showing up in these descriptions in *current, excursus, coursing*.) This discussion does not even begin to exhaust the senses of *run* that are listed in desk dictionaries, but it should suffice to show the depth of the problem.

23a. Dale ran to the grocery store.
23b. Dale runs with the cross-country team.
23c. Dale runs every day.
23d. He ran for president.
23e. The water is running.
23f. The Mississippi runs from Minnesota to the Gulf of Mexico.
23g. The electricity is running again.
23h. The engine/car/refrigerator is running.
23i. A quartz watch will run for a year before the battery needs to be replaced.
23j. Your program won't run until you correct the typos.
23k. The salmon are running.
23L. A wind-up alarm clock will run for 26 hours.
23m. Highway 136/The railroad runs through San Jose and Havana, Illinois.

There are causative senses ('cause to . . .') of transitive *run* as well. Some refer to locomotive activity (24a–24c), others to directing the operation of a complex organization (24d–24f), perhaps by application of the causative function to the machine operation senses of intransitive *run* in (23h, 24i). Perhaps by analogy to a different sense of intransitive *run* as in (23g) or (23m), transitive *run* is used for extending something from one place to another, as in (24g). Transitive *run* is also used to refer to encountering (24h) and overcoming (24i) obstacles.

24a. They ran a race.
24b. They ran her ragged.
24c. They ran Eks out of town.
24d. They ran the company for 12 years.
24e. They ran the company into the ground.
24f. They ran a clean campaign.
24g. They ran a wire from the upstairs to the basement.
24h. They ran the risk of exposing the whole operation.
24i. The ship ran the blockade and got through to the open sea.

Notice that, within the limits imposed by requirements on parallel syntax, these uses of *run* count as the same for syntactic constructions which require identity of sense, as illustrated by the acceptability of sentences like (25).

25a. This program will run if your computer will.
25b. It's a good thing the salmon are running, because the refrigerator isn't.
25c. The Mississippi has run down to the Gulf for millions of years, the river road for only a hundred or so.
25d. The captain ran the blockade, and in doing so, the risk of losing his entire cargo.

Furthermore, practically every verb is subject to a multiplicity of uses of this sort.[19] *Slap* is used to refer to an act of striking something with a flexible, flat surface; you can slap something with a hand or a rolled-up newspaper, but not a hardback book or a rock. But the motion gestalt involved in back-slapping is not the same as for face-slapping. Slapping handcuffs on someone doesn't involve striking or a flat surface at all, and slapping someone with a sentence or a subpoena only involves motion to the extent that every interpersonal interaction involves motion. *Write* refers to the act of inscribing letters (26a), the act of inscribing cursive letters (as opposed to printing) (26b), to making visual representations of linguistic expressions (26c, 26d), and to producing a document (26e).

26a. Write your name on the top line.
26b. Write it; don't print.
26c. He wrote a word/sentence/formula on the blackboard.
26d. He wrote his name in the air.
26e. He wrote a book/a three-page letter to his mother.

Finally, there is a parallel to the fact that in context any noun can be used to refer to an individual associated with something that noun designates (example (17), and accompanying discussion), in that almost any verb that can normally be used to refer to an action can apparently be used (metaphorically) in the context of athletic competition to describe the outcome of a contest.[20] Teams or individuals

---

[19]As evidence for the pervasiveness and creativity of extended uses, a survey of 22 arbitrarily chosen 200-word passages from works of modern English-language fiction revealed that an average of 13% of the nouns, verbs, and adjectives in them were used in senses that are not covered by the entries in a large desk dictionary. (The range was 3% to 29%.)

[20]For example, (i) headlines a story about the Clemson University baseball team getting nine hits and five runs from the pitching of University of Illinois player Boo Champagne.

i. Clemson uncorks on Champagne

Taking advantage of pitching is also described with metaphorical expressions (*jump on x for, rock x for*) whose pragmatic nature is taken up in chapter 5 section 4. Similarly, example (ii) is the headline from an article describing a 10–6 Illinois victory over Eastern Illinois University in which Illinois player Darrin Fletcher hit a grand slam home run.

ii. Illinois' Fletcher slams EIU

hardly ever just beat, defeat, overcome, or win over their opponents. They walk over them, roll past them, crush them, stomp them, tip them, skin them, bruise them, and so on. If a game involved a dispute over rules that involved display of a rule book, a sports reporter would probably be understood if he reported the outcome of the game by saying that the winners read the losers their rights.

Prepositions are notorious for rampant polysemy, though it rarely leads to confusion. The preposition *in*, for example means something different in *in town, in the road, in the sidewalk, in March, in time, in tune, in red, in trouble*, and the like. (cf. Green, 1985a).

Many adjectives demonstrate extensive multiplicity of use also. *Red*, for example, refers to different hues when applied to hair, bricks, human skin, mucous membranes, or marking pens. *Rich* refers to different properties when applied to economic entities, nutritional substances, and prose.

If most ordinary words have such an extensive multiplicity of ordinary uses, and no single basic use or psense, how do language users ever figure out what is being referred to?

Nunberg describes two conditions (pp. 97–100) which serve to limit the number of normal interpretations the use of a word can have in an utterance, assuming beliefs assumed to be (a) normal in the community (Nunberg, 1978a, pp. 94–97), and (b) relevant in aiding the interpreter in selecting the best referring function for the interpretation of that use. In Nunberg's use, a NORMAL BELIEF is one which is included in the body of beliefs that a speaker takes "to constitute the background against which all utterances in a community are rationally made" (pp. 94–95). A normal belief is one that all speakers act as if they believe, and believe that everyone else believes. This technical use of *normal belief* should not be confused with other notions that may have the same name. A normal belief in the sense intended is only remotely related to an individual's belief about how things normally are, and only remotely related (in a different direction) to a judgement that it is unremarkable to hold such a belief. Thus, *normal* as used here has nothing to do with statistics, and makes no claims about clinical psychological fitness. It has more in common with the indefinitely regressive forms of notions that have been referred to as MUTUAL KNOWLEDGE (Schiffer, 1972), MUTUAL BELIEF (Cohen & Perrault, 1979; Cohen & Levesque, 1990), and MUTUAL MANIFESTNESS (Sperber & Wilson, 1986).

A normal use is then one which speakers judge to be consistent with the system of normal beliefs. Consequently, what it is considered normal to use *tack* or *host* or *rock* or *metal* to refer to varies with the community. These are social facts, facts about societies, and only incidentally and contingently and secondarily facts about words. More precisely, they are facts about what speakers believe other speakers believe about conventions for using words.

The first condition which limits the normal interpretations of a use of a word is that if a word is used to designate an object a in such a way that some predicate ϕ is predicated of it, then if ϕ can be rationally predicted only if members of some set R, the use is normal only if there is some member *b* of R such that *b* is best identified as being the value of some function f applied to *a*, given the system of normal beliefs (Nunberg, 1978a, p. 99). In other words, a use of a word *w* is normal if and only if there is something which is best identified (in the community, on the basis of the system of normal beliefs) as the value of some referring function applied to what that word designates, and it is rational to predicate of that thing whatever is apparently predicated of the designatum of *w*. Thus, the use of a newspaper name as the subject of *endorse* (as in *The Herald endorsed three Democrats last year*) is normal because publishers are readily identifiable as the value of the referring function 'publisher of,' applied to 'newspaper,' and it is rational to speak of a publisher as endorsing political candidates.

This condition says that uses which presuppose beliefs foreign to the system of normal beliefs are not normal uses. For example, it rules out any normal interpretation for a sentence like *That idea slept late*, because there is no plausible entity (b) that intends to awaken before a certain time (a member of the set R which the predicate *sleep late* (ϕ) is rationally predicated of) which is best identified as the value of any function (f) from the set (a) of abstract propositions (normally taken to be) designated by *idea*.[21]

A second condition allows uses of a word *w* to refer to things that are not normally the argument of the predicate predicated of *w* only if there is no good function from what *w* designates to something that can be the argument of that predicate. Thus *chicken* could refer to chicken feathers in a discussion of substances to fill pillows with, as in (27a), because there is a good function from feather-bearing creatures to their feathers, and having loft can be rationally predicated of its output. But in a discussion of edibles, as in (27b), *chicken* could not rationally be expected to be taken to refer to chicken feathers, because there is a function (from creatures to their meat) whose output, applied to *chicken*, better satisfies the predicate 'is tasty.'

27a.   Chicken doesn't have much loft.
27b.   Chicken is tasty.

The second condition thus predicts that in normal contexts, neither (28a) nor (28b) will be ambiguous, although *alligator* can be used normally to refer to either a kind of meat or a kind of leather or hide.

28a.   Alligator is tasty.
28b.   Alligator is waterproof.

---

[21]One could also take *idea* literally, and say that *sleep late* is not a normal use since logically, *sleep late* represents a predicate predicated of something in the set of things that sleep late, and it is not rational to predicate idea-hood of such things.

With conditions like this, it is not crucial which psense is evoked first; all that matters is that a plausible psense can be reconstructed or inferred.

Notice that the notion of normal use provided here does not depend on abstracting away from contexts. Theorists who perceive the dependence of the referential use of expressions on users' beliefs about each other's beliefs as inconvenient sometimes try to circumnavigate it by articulating a theory of meaning that is independent of particular contexts in that it depends instead on a so-called null context, where speaker and hearer make no assumptions about each other. This is a dead end, however, because (as discussed by Nunberg, 1978a, pp. 92–95) there are no such null contexts in which utterances could be interpreted. As Crain and Steedman (1985, p. 338) put it, "the so-called null context is simply an *unknown* context." When we are asked to act as informants, and make judgements about expressions or their meanings "out of context" or "in a null context," we cannot help but imagine SOME context consisting of a speaker directing that expression as an utterance to some audience. We differ, as individuals, and on occasions, in how much context we import into the judgement task, and in what we are willing to imagine when we try to construe the expression as a sensible thing to utter on an occasion of the sort we assume.

In addition to normal uses, there are what Nunberg calls local uses: uses licensed by systems of beliefs generally considered rational in only a sub-part of the speech community (e.g., linguists, musicians, Roman Catholics, New Englanders, people who sail boats, surfers, MTV-watchers, and so on). Examples of local uses are (17a, 17b), among many others, and (29), where the name of a corporation is used to designate a representative of that corporation.

29. IBM was held up in traffic.

(Example (17c) is an example of a notice use, a use designed for a particular discourse, and conventional in an even narrower "community" than a local use.) Examining this distinction more closely, Nunberg suggested that the difference between normal uses and local uses is just the degree and/or extent to which a use is conventionalized. Starting from the assumption that "a word-use is predictable for a given speaker to the degree that he believes that normal beliefs provide its rationale" (p. 115), Nunberg distinguished several stages of conventionalization along parameters he outlined:

> Given a speaker S, who is aware both of a regular use R of a word w to refer to a, and of general conformity to another regular use R′ of w to refer to b, we can say that S can expect use R to be assumed if either I or II holds. (pp. 115–116):

Condition I requires, paraphrasing Nunberg, that S believe that it is normally believed that, given use R′ of w to refer to b, use R is licensed by normal beliefs. (The various uses of *newspaper* in (12) exemplify this condition. The relevant normal beliefs are that newspapers are produced with editorials, in regular editions, at manufacturing plants, by corporations which sell advertising, and so on.)

Condition II says that S must believe that it is normally believed that, given use R' of w to refer to b, use R is licensed by beliefs to which members of the community would normally conform, even if they don't themselves hold those beliefs. (This condition covers cases where only experts command all of the details needed to construct the appropriate referring functions (cf. Nunberg, 1978a, pp. 113–115 and Green, 1984 for discussion of Putnam (1975a, 1975b) on this topic). Examples are uses of trade jargon by lay people (as when a novice computer user asks, "How much memory does that computer have?"). Here it is assumed that there is a rational connection between the technical use and a more ordinary use, although the speaker need not know exactly what it is.)

Nunberg describes four progressively more conventionalized stages of word use, where S is less and less likely to expect a use R to be understood via a referring function generated from R'. That is, the more conventionalized a use is, the less reasonable it is to expect it to be correctly interpreted just by applying inferential processes to a more widely assumed use. Thus, in the first stage, S believes that it is normally believed that given use R' of w to refer to b, use R to refer to a is licensed by beliefs that are considered normal in some subgroup, but not in the community at large. (The example Nunberg gives of this condition is the use of *country* to refer to a kind of music, licensed by the belief of some speakers that that music has rural origins.)

In the next stage, S believes that it is normally believed that given use R' of w to refer to b, beliefs that license use R are normally reconstructable, although they are not necessarily assumed to be held by any members of the community. (Examples would be transparent idioms like *make book* or *book* (a suspect) which would involve belief in the existence of books in which bets or the names of accused criminals were entered.)

In a still more conventionalized stage, S believes that it is normally believed that given use R' of w to refer to b, there are beliefs which would license use R, though S may have no idea who might hold those beliefs. (This condition licenses the use of idioms which look analyzable, like *let the cat out of the bag* or *kick the bucket*, about which one can make up stories which are plausible, but which no one can actually verify.)

Complete conventionalization is characterized by S's belief that it is normally believed that given use R' of w to refer to b, there is no reason why w is used in use R to refer to a. (This condition covers purely arbitrary idioms, like *beef* for 'complaint.')

5. SUMMARY

When a speaker uses a word w to refer to some intended referent a, he must assume that his addressee will consider it rational to use w to refer to a in that context; he must assume that if he and his addressee don't in fact have the same assumptions about what beliefs are normal in the community at large, and in every relevant subgroup, at least the addressee will be able to tell what relevant beliefs the speaker imputes to the addressee, including reflexive beliefs, as described in chapter 1. Likewise, the interpreter must assume that she knows or can infer what beliefs the speaker will (reflexively) impute to the addressee about what is normal. For example, to interpret an utterance like *He bought IBM at 71 1/2*, the interpreter must assume (a) that the speaker assumes that it is normally considered rational to refer to shares of stock in a corporation by means of a referring function from the name of the corporation, or at least (b) that the speaker assumes that the addressee will assume it is rational to do so, or (c) that the speaker assumes that the addressee will assume that the speaker assumes it is rational to do so, and so on. Nunberg summed up the importance of this regressus when he concluded a discussion (pp. 81–86) of what is involved in our figuring out what he might mean by *jazz* when he says, *Do you like jazz?* with the observation, "My theory of jazz is relevant only insofar as it happens to coincide with the beliefs that somebody else might reasonably attribute to me."

CHAPTER 3 STUDY QUESTIONS

1. What is the difference between *sense (connotation, intension)* and *reference (denotation, extension, denomination)*?

2. What is the causal theory of names?

3. What is the difference between referential and attributive uses of referring expressions?

4. What is a possible world?

5. What is a rigid designator?

6. What is the problem of infinite polysemy?

7. How extensive is it?

8. How can the normal use of an expression be identified?

9. If the reference of referring expressions is not fixed by rules of grammar or semantics, how is the reference of a referring expression interpreted?

4 Non-truth-conditional Meaning: Interpreting the Packaging of Propositional Content

> *"I had an appointment at the lawyers," Gram announced. "At which I was told that you are now, legally and officially and permanently [. . .] my responsibility."*
>
> *"We're adopted?" James asked.*
>
> *"That's what I said."*
>
> *"No, it's not," he pointed out*
>
> *"Well it's what I meant and since you understood me it must be what I said."*
>
> —Cynthia Voigt, *Dicey's Song*, p. 150. (New York: Atheneum, 1983)

In this chapter and the two following, we turn our attention from the questions of the intended reference of referring expressions, which occupied us in chapters 2 and 3, to questions of what a speaker intends to accomplish in saying what she says, and saying it the way she says it and at the point in the discourse at which it is said.

We look first at the kinds of acts that are involved when one (merely) says something (speech acts and the illocutionary forces of utterances), and then turn to implications of a speaker's choice of word or phrase (presuppositions and connotations) and to the implications (technically, the implicatures) of saying something with particular propositional content and presuppositions. We consider implicatures in some detail in chapter 5, tracing how a single, general, non-linguistic principle provides the means to explain how people can mean (and convey) more than they say. This enables us to account for such conversational strategies as understatement, damning with faint praise, and intentional vagueness. At the same time, it provides the foundation for understanding the phenomenon of textual coherence—what makes individually comprehensible sentences into more or less coherent texts or discourses when they are strung together. Finally, applications of this principle are shown to provide solutions to a number of problematic questions in semantic and pragmatic theory that are treated in this chapter. We will see that implicature is far from being a rhetorical trick that only clever and accomplished writers and conversationalists use, as is sometimes thought, but rather is indispensable to an understanding of how even the simplest, most ordinary connected text is understood as intended.

1. SPEECH ACTS AND ILLOCUTIONARY FORCE

When James says, "We're adopted," in the passage quoted above, he performs, simultaneously, a number of different kinds of SPEECH ACTS, all of them intentional and goal-directed, although the execution of several is undoubtedly subconsciously controlled. At the most concrete level, he performs what the English philosopher J. L. Austin (1962) called a phonetic act—producing the articulation of tongue, jaw, diaphragm, larynx, and so on, that results in connected speech sounds. Presumably, the goal of the phonetic act is to produce an acoustic object that the addressee (Gram) will recognize as speech sounds (and not, e.g., as involuntary vocalizations such as belches or sneezes). Simultaneously, and by means of the phonetic act, James performs the act of uttering linguistic expressions, producing a series of tokens of forms according to the grammar of a certain language and with a certain intonation (Austin's "phatic act"), with the intention that it be recognized as belonging to that language. At the same time, in order that his utterance be recognized as connected discourse about some proposition, James performs the acts of referring (with *we*) and predicating (with *'re adopted*), intending the forms he uses to be taken as referring to individuals, actions, events, and so forth, according to the conventions of the language and culture of the community he shares with the addressee (Austin's "rhetic act").

Austin referred to these three kinds of acts as constituting a LOCUTIONARY ACT, an act of saying something. (In another influential work, the philosopher John Searle (1969) treated the first and second together as constituting an "utterance act," and used "propositional act" for Austin's "rhetic act".)

By means of the same utterance, James performs an ILLOCUTIONARY ACT, doing something by means of the locutionary act he has performed. In this case, James' illocutionary act is questioning, but in a different context and with a different intonation, the same utterance could have had the force of an assertion, an announcement, or an exclamation.[1]

---

[1] I do not know how many taxonomies of illocutionary acts list exclaiming, but I take declarative exclamations to be emotional expressions of conclusions, intended not so much to inform the addressee of their content, as to express (exploiting intonation and voice quality) the speaker's attitude toward it.

Finally, James performs this illocutionary act for some reason, and to the extent that he expects that reason to be recognized, he is performing a rhetorical act of implicating, a topic discussed in chapter 5. In principle, it could be that in or by asking Gram if they were adopted, James was intending to convey to Gram that she was speaking obscurely, although there is no particular reason to suspect that that is true in this case.

In addition, a speaker might, in performing a given illocutionary act, perform any number of PERLOCUTIONARY ACTS, acts which have an effect which is an intended, but not a necessary consequence of performing the illocutionary act. Thus, a person's committing himself to buying six shares of IBM is not a perlocutionary effect of his saying, "I hereby promise to buy six shares of IBM," because that commitment is entailed by his making that promise with those words. On the other hand, stating that an observed bear has cubs nearby would be a perlocutionary act of warning if it was intended to alert the addressee to a potential danger; addressing a question to an addressee unaware of the speaker's presence would be a perlocutionary act if intended to startle the addressee; a political candidate's utterance might have the perlocutionary effect of convincing the addressee that the speaker would make a good leader.

1.1 Performative Verbs

Sometimes linguistic properties of a sentence (e.g., particular forms or intonation) indicate the illocutionary force of the sentence. For example, *promise* in (1a) tells us that (1a) is a promise (and not, e.g., a prediction),[2] and *order* in (1b) tells us that (1b) is an order, and not a request, plea, or suggestion.

1a.   I promise I'll sit in the front row.
1b.   I order you to put out that cigarette.

By saying *I promise* or *I order*, we thereby promise or order, but only certain verbs, which Austin called PERFORMATIVES, have this property of allowing the speaker to do the action the verb names by using the verb in a certain way (hence Austin's title, *How to Do Things with Words*). Other verbs only name actions, and cannot be used in this way; by saying (2a), one does not thereby believe that it will snow; saying (2b) does not count as an act of driving a white car, but only as a report of one's driving; and although (2c) might be true on occasion, merely saying it cannot accomplish forcing anyone to do anything.

2a.   I believe that it will snow tomorrow.
2b.   I drive a white car.

---

[2]We need to ignore the interpretations available for any present tense verb which allow them to be used to assert habitual action, to assert that an action is scheduled, or to describe past action (historical present).

2c.   I force you to practice the piano.

While illocutionary acts can be performed by performative sentences like (1), perlocutionary effects cannot be accomplished by naming the act. Even a charismatic politician could not get people to vote for him by saying, "I convince you that I would make a good leader."

Performative sentences, although they look like ordinary declarative sentences, are not simply true or false the way declaratives like (2) are.[3] It does not make sense to ask whether the speaker of (1a) or (1b) is lying or telling the truth, even though the speaker of (1a) might or might not be sincere, and the speaker of (1b) might or might not have the authority to make the order, might or might not want the cigarette put out, and so on.

The performative expressions Austin mentioned cover a wide range, from *promise, assert* and *order* to *vote, nominate, deny, sentence, bet, resign, apologize, curse, bequeath* and *christen*. Austin and Searle devoted considerable attention to describing conditions (involving the sincerity of the speaker and various facts about the context) that have to be met in order for particular sorts of utterance acts to count as illocutionary acts of one kind or another. They and several others devoted considerable effort to classifying the verbs that could be used performatively (Austin, 1962; Fraser, 1973; Searle, 1975a, 1976a; McCawley, 1977), to the extent that in many people's minds, *speech act* became identified with *illocutionary act*, although in fact the former covers a much wider range of phenomena than the latter. Thus, any act performed through the production of speech is a speech act, including referring and predicating, as well as explaining, intimating, and nagging, but none of them can be performed by naming the act: saying "I refer to Mr. O'Neill" does not thereby refer to Mr. O'Neill, although it may indicate that a previous referring expression was intended to refer to him. Saying "I nag you to pick up your clothes" is not nagging.

1.2 The Performative Hypothesis

Austin noted that performative expressions only had performative force in the present tense, with first person singular subjects. Thus, utterances of (3a) and (3b) cannot be acts of promising or ordering, but only reports of acts of promising and ordering.

3a.   I promised I would sit in the front row.
3b.   She orders him to put out his cigarette.

And in general, the performative expression has to be the predicate of the main clause of the utterance, so uttering (4) does not count as a promise, even though

---

[3]In chapter 5, Section 4.2, we see that a case can be made for the claim that performative sentences like (1) are necessarily true, whether uttered sincerely or not.

it has a first person singular, present tense form of the performative verb *promise*, because *I promise* is in a subordinate clause.

4. My students are betting that I promise to sit in the front row.

In the late 1960's, linguists took note of these properties of performative expressions, and some argued (e.g., R. Lakoff, 1968; Ross, 1970; Sadock, 1974) that the underlying linguistic representation of every sentence contained as its highest clause, a performative verb with a first person singular subject. This clause could be overt as in (1), or "abstract" (i.e., invisible) as in (5).

5a. I'll sit in the front row.
5b. Put out that cigarette!

Thus, a declarative sentence like (5a) could have an underlying representation similar to (1a), and (3a) would have an underlying representation like (6).

6. I SAY TO YOU THAT I promised I would sit in the front row.

The Performative Hypothesis, as it was called, was offered to explain not only the different illocutionary force of sentences like (1) and sentences like (2), but also the ambiguity of sentences like (5a) (or (1)), which was attributed to the possibility of underlying performative verbs of predicting, promising, or announcing, and so on. As the Performative Hypothesis was a syntactic hypothesis, syntactic arguments were offered to support it. They generally hinged on the fact that certain linguistic expressions occurred only (a) in subordinate clauses which were introduced by a certain kind of verb referring to an illocutionary force, with an agreement relation holding between a noun phrase in the subordinate clause and a noun phrase in the introducing clause; or (b) in main clauses with a certain illocutionary force, and certain particular sorts of noun phrases.

For instance, it was argued that the idiomatic expression *be damned if*, as used to indicate emphatic negation, could occur in main clauses just in case its subject was first person and the sentence was declarative, as in (7). (The symbol "#" indicates unacceptability in the sense intended—here, emphatic refusal.)

7a. I'll be damned if I'll vote for that man.
7b. #You'll be damned if you'll vote for that man.
7c. #Will I be damned if I'll vote for that man?

It was claimed that *be damned if* with the emphatic negation reading could occur in a subordinate clause just in case it was in the complement of a verb of stating and its subject was coreferential to the subject of the verb of stating, as shown in (8).

8a. John says he'll be damned if he'll vote for that man.
8b. #John fears that he'll be damned if he'll vote for that man.
8c. #John says I'll be damned if I'll vote for that man.

If the Performative Hypothesis is correct, and a sentence like (7a) is (in its underlying structure) the object complement of a clause whose subject refers to the speaker of the sentence (i.e., is first person) and whose verb is a verb of stating, as in (9), then these conditions can be reduced to a single condition, stated as (10).

9. I say to you that I'll be damned if I'll vote for that man.

10. The idiom *be damned if*, with its sense of emphatic negation, can occur only embedded in the complement of a verb of stating, and the subject of the idiom must be identical in reference to that of the embedding verb.

Without the Performative Hypothesis, sentences (7c) and (11) are treated as anomalous for entirely unrelated reasons, since they violate entirely unrelated conditions; under the Performative Hypothesis, sentence (7c) has an underlying structure similar to (11), and thus they are anomalous for the same syntactic reason: both violate condition (10) in the same way.

11. #I ask you whether I'll be damned if I'll vote for that man.

The *be damned if* argument was only one of scores (cf. in addition to references given above, Peterson, 1969; Davison, 1970), and although the Performative Hypothesis quickly gained popularity, objections were raised, not only to the syntactic arguments, but to the assumptions and consequences of the theory itself. Linguists such as Anderson (1971) and Fraser (1971, 1974) pointed out that, contrary to the claim that performative verbs had to be main verbs, sometimes performative verbs occurred with performative force in subordinate clauses, as in (12), where (12a) appears to announce itself as a request, (12b) counts as an act of sentencing, and saying (12c) constitutes saying that one has no money.

12a. I'm afraid I must ask you to leave.
12b. Your behavior leaves me no alternative but to sentence you to 20 years.
12c. I regret to say that I have no money.

On another front, Morgan (1973a) showed that the Performative Hypothesis was inconsistent with other hypotheses about the syntactic representation of semantic properties of sentences. In addition, arguments began to appear that the hypothesis was also both unnecessary and empirically wrong (cf. Stampe, 1975; Searle, 1976b; Gazdar, 1979; Green & Morgan, 1980).

Linguists were also able to demonstrate that several of the phenomena that Ross (1970) had argued were conditioned by principles like (10) in fact occurred in syntactic contexts which those principles failed to predict. In fact, it can be shown (cf. Green & Morgan, 1976; Green, 1981) that many of the morphological or syntactic phenomena that were argued to imply an abstract performative on syntactic grounds are in fact conditioned by pragmatic considerations, not by semantic properties or syntactic contexts. Indeed, the use of *be damned if* is not, strictly speaking, sanctioned by being in the complement of a verb of stating. Rather, *be damned if* predicates refusal (by the referent of the subject of *be damned if*) to be responsible for the act[4] that the complement of *be damned if* refers to. Thus, although *know* is not a verb of stating, nor is *want you to know*, (13) could be uttered (and most likely would be) to inform the addressee that the speaker would not vote for a certain man.

13. I want you to know that I'll be damned if I'll vote for that man.

Similarly, the subject of *be damned if* does not have to be first person or coreferential to the subject of the embedding verb (as in (14)), as long as the utterance as a whole is being used to report or make a refusal, as it is if the speaker purports to be a spokesman for the individual named by the subject of *be damned if*, as in (14a) and (14b), but not (14c).

14a. John'll be damned if he'll vote for that man.
14b. I know John'll be damned if he'll vote for that man.
14c. #I wonder if John'll be damned if he'll vote for that man.

The correct condition on the occurrence of *be damned if* thus seems to be a pragmatic usage rule, not a syntactic condition. The idiom is used in verbal refusals to act, which may be conveyed directly, as in (7a), in reports of such refusals (8a),[5] or in refusals that are conveyed indirectly as in (13) and (14).

Ross (1970), unaware of facts like these and data like those cited by Fraser and Anderson, had considered a pragmatic analysis, and rejected it as premature, on the grounds that conditions like (10) were incapable in principle of being

---

[4]This includes acts by the speaker as well as acts by others for whom the speaker assumes responsibility. Thus (i) is acceptable:

  i. I'll be damned if she'll go out with greasers who drive souped-up convertibles.

  The reference to acts predicts that the complement of *be damned if* is not about a state:

  ii. ??I'll be damned if I like rutabagas.

[5]Thus it is even possible to use *be damned if* in the past tense. Sentence (i) is acceptable in an indirect free style narrative written from the subject's point of view.

  i. John was damned if he'd vote for that man.

extended to pragmatic objects like 'speaker' and 'speaking,' since they were not syntactic objects and could not stand in syntactic relations to genuine syntactic objects like verbs and subject noun phrases, any more than an actual piece of sports equipment could be part of a program for a computer simulation of a football game. We return to the issue of the possibility of a pragmatic analysis of illocutionary forces in chapter 5, section 4.2.

In retrospect, two facts doomed the Performative Hypothesis from the start. First, utterances often represent several acts at the same time, some relatively directly and some more indirectly. Thus, stating *I got it for you yesterday* might be an explanation, and by virtue of being an explanation, a rationalization or an excuse, or a refusal. In addition, any speech act can be accomplished by an unlimited variety of forms—typically, a few performative forms (like *I apologize*), a larger number of forms which are used to accomplish the act by conventionalized conversational implicature (like *I have to apologize, I'm afraid I have to apologize*—see chap. 5), and an unlimited number of forms the utterance of which implicates the goals and attitudes that characterize that particular speech act, for example, in the case of apologies: *I really feel awful about that, I hope you'll forgive me, It was really thoughtless of me to do that, Tell me what I can do to fix things, How can I make it up to you?* When cultural values make creativity of expression a hallmark of sincerity, it becomes virtually impossible to specify the class of utterances which are used to perform any speech act in terms of the words and syntax employed.

The literature on the analysis of illocutionary force is huge, and still growing. Useful bibliographies may be found in Verschuren (1976); Gazdar (1979); Searle, Kiefer, and Bierwisch (1980); and Sadock (1990).

2. PRESUPPOSITION

There is a rich and broad variety of phenomena that philosophers and linguists have discussed under the rubric PRESUPPOSITION. Briefly, this term is used to refer to propositions whose truth is taken for granted in the utterance of a linguistic expression, propositions without which the utterance cannot be evaluated. For example, it is said that the sentence *It's too bad that Carter lost the election* (or the utterance of *It's too bad that Carter lost the election*) presupposes the proposition 'Carter lost the election,' while *It's believed that Carter lost the election* does not presuppose this. This characterization of presupposition skirts all sorts of important issues. For example, taken by whom for granted? Granted by whom? Are the propositions implied by the linguistic object uttered, or by the act of uttering it? These questions will be addressed in more detail after a survey of the sorts of phenomena that have been called presupposition, and their common properties.

2.1 Some Representative Phenomena

Existence Presuppositions

The phenomenon that is probably most uniformly considered to represent cases of presupposition is the existence presupposition of definite descriptions, as in (15), where (saying) (15a) presupposes 'there is a movie on Channel 4,' and (saying) (15b) presupposes 'Jack has children.'

15a. The movie on Channel 4 is rated R.
15b. I've coached Jack's children.

Factive Presuppositions

A close second for the standard example of presupposition would be factive presuppositions (see Kiparsky & Kiparsky, 1971, for an early account), of which there are several sorts. One kind is associated with expressions that take a sentential subject or object. The object complements of such EPISTEMIC factives as *know* and *realize*, and the subject complements of *mean, prove,* and *be obvious* are considered to be presupposed true, as are the complements of such EMOTIVE factives as *regret, be glad, be surprised,* and *amaze.*[6] Thus the sentences in (16) all presuppose 'Taylor has a 42-inch vertical leap.'

16a. Jan knows that Taylor has a 42-inch vertical leap.
16b. That Taylor has a 42-inch vertical leap is obvious.
16c. Jan regrets that Taylor has a 42-inch vertical leap.
16d. That Taylor has a 42-inch vertical leap amazed the scouts.

---

[6]Implicative verbs, as described by Karttunen (1971), involve a presupposition that the proposition represented by the sentence as a whole is a necessary and/or sufficient condition for the truth of the proposition represented by the complement. Thus, (ia) expresses a necessary and sufficient condition for the proposition represented in (ib), which approximates the gist of the complement of *condescend* in (ia); (iia) represents a necessary condition for (iib), a representation of the complement of *be able* in (iia); and (iiia) represents a sufficient condition for the truth of the proposition which is the complement of *made* in (iiia), as approximated in (iiib).

ia. Sandy condescended to attend the party.
ib. 'Sandy attended the party'
iia. Jan was able to attend the party.
iib. 'Jan attended the party'
iiia. Sandy made Dana attend the party.
iiib. 'Dana attended the party'

There are negative implicative verbs of the three types as well, for example, *fail, refuse* and *prevent.* These verbs involve a presupposition that the proposition represented by the sentence as a whole is a necessary and/or sufficient condition for the negation of the proposition represented by the complement of the negative implicative verb.

Change of state, or inchoative verbs also have complements presupposed to be true, as in (17a,b), which both presuppose 'Ferd admires Frieda.'

17a. Jan discovered that Ferd admires Frieda.

17b. Jan forgot that Ferd admires Frieda.

Other constructions associated with factive presuppositions are cleft constructions, as in (18); constituent questions (called WH-questions by American linguists), as in (19); adverbial and relative clauses introduced by the corresponding subordinating particles, as in (20); and iterative particles, as in (21). Thus (18–21) all presuppose 'The Sixers beat the Lakers.'

18.   It was in Los Angeles that the Sixers beat the Lakers.

19a. When did the Sixers beat the Lakers?

19b. I don't know where the Sixers beat the Lakers.

20a. When the Sixers beat the Lakers, there was a power failure.

20b. The arena where the Sixers beat the Lakers needs to have the floor refinished.

21.   The Sixers beat the Lakers again.

In addition, there is a presupposition associated with the COUNTERFACTIVE verb *pretend*, that the complement is not true, as in example (22), and the COUNTERFACTUAL conditional has a presupposition that the proposition expressed by the *if*-clause is not true, as in (23). Thus (22) and (23) both presuppose that Germany did not invade Czechoslovakia.

22.   Sandy pretended that Germany had invaded Czechoslovakia.

23.   If Germany had invaded Czechoslovakia, England would still have entered the war.

Connotations

Many lexical items are used in only a subset of the class of situations in which they might conceivably apply, and the restrictions have been claimed to be (or reflect) presuppositions about the situation. For example, use of the transitive verb *play* normally implies the proposition that the referent of the subject is an organism capable of volitional action, and the proposition that the object noun phrase refers to a game or a musical instrument. Neither of these is likely in (24).

24.   Golf plays John.

The earliest descriptions of this phenomenon (cf. Chomsky, 1965) took this to be a matter of grammatical properties ("selectional restrictions") of the words involved, but McCawley (1968) showed that this phenomenon is not so much a function of the words themselves as it is a function of properties that language users attribute to the presumed intended referents of the words—in other words, that selectional restrictions were pragmatic, not syntactic.

A classic example of a connotation presupposition is *assassinate* (Gallagher, 1970; McCawley, 1975a). *Assassinate* is used to assert that the referent of its grammatical object is killed, but, as with *murder*, there is a presupposition that the killing was intended. Thus, the bizarreness of example (25).

25.   John accidentally assassinated the Prime Minister.

In addition, the use of *assassinate* presupposes that the victim had significant political power, from which his death removed him, and that removing that power was the motive for the lethal deed. Thus, powerful political figures, underworld leaders, and powerful charismatic leaders of any sort might be the victims of assassination attempts, but not movie stars or journalists, no matter how famous or threatening to an individual; the murder of a former chief of state who had retired from political activity would not be assassination, nor would murdering a chief of state for some perceived personal injustice.

Another well-discussed example of lexical presupposition is the verbs of judging discussed by Fillmore (1971a) and McCawley (1975b). Saying that A is accused of or blamed or criticized for doing B all involve the propositions 'A did B' and 'B is bad,' but, Fillmore claimed, using *accuse* involves attributing some act B to A and presupposing that B is bad, while using *criticize* involves a claim that B is bad and a presupposition that A is responsible for it. Similarly, the conventional wisdom is that use of German *fressen* 'eat' presupposes that the referent of its subject is an animal, while *essen* (also meaning 'eat') does not.[7]

Likewise, to refer to a government leader's *reign* could be said to presuppose that the government is a kingdom or empire, to his *regime* that the leader is a dictator, to his *administration* that he is chief executive in a state where real power is in other hands (e.g., the legislature), to his *government* that he is head of a (parliamentary) government where his tenure is a function of his support in the legislature. Thus, to refer to an elected governor's administration as *Governor Eks's regime* would imply that Governor Eks had a dictatorial administrative style, and to refer to it as *his reign* would imply that he acted as if the job was his for life (and maybe by divine right).

To stop (arbitrarily, because one could go on for volumes) with a final example, the quantifier *all* presupposes that the set it is applied to has at least three members. Thus (26a) implies that Jack has at least three children, and (26b) is a distinctly odd thing for a human being to say.

---

[7]If, on the other hand, *fressen* denotes 'eat crudely,' then a sentence that would translate to "The little pig [fressed] so neatly that I wanted to set a place for it at the table" should be a contradiction.

26a. All of Jack's children are bright.
26b. All of my legs hurt.

2.2 Properties of Presupposition

We have discussed a broad variety of cases that linguists have taken to represent examples of presupposition. In section 2.3, we take up the question of whether presuppositions are something inherent in linguistic objects like words and sentences, or whether they reflect properties of speakers (specifically, attitudes toward propositions) or properties of uses of sentences. The first alternative reflects an opinion held by many writers, especially in the period 1969–1975, that presupposition is a semantic phenomenon. The second reflects an opinion common among nonlogicians. Both the second and the third alternatives represent pragmatic approaches to the problem. Here we will just consider in more detail what the earmarks or identifying properties of presupposition have been taken to be.

First, as already mentioned, a presupposition is semantic material which is taken for granted, that is, entailed (semantic approach) or assumed (pragmatic approach) and not asserted in a declarative sentence, questioned in a question, or ordered in an imperative. A person who uttered one of the declarative sentences in (27) would be understood as taking for granted 'Mr. D. was late for class,' rather than asserting it, so objecting to the presupposition by simply denying it with (28) is not likely to meet with success. In contrast, the main assertion of the utterance is easily denied, as in (29).

27a. The students regret that Mr. D. was late for class.
27b. When Mr. D. was late for class, the students demanded an apology.
27c. If Mr. D. had not been late for class, the students would have done their work.

28.   No, he wasn't.

29.   No they don't/didn't/wouldn't.

Second, the presuppositions associated with a word or construction are constant when the clause containing that word or construction is negated or questioned. The presupposition 'Mr. D. was late,' linked to the factive verb, adverbial clause, or counterfactual conditional construction in examples (27a–c) is equally present in the negated and interrogative sentences in (30a–c).

30a. The students do not regret that Mr. D. was late to class.
30b. Did the students rejoice when Mr. D. was late to class?
30c. If Mr. D. had not been late for class, the students would not have done their work.

Similarly, (31a) still presupposes that Vader was emperor, and (31b) that Jack has children.

31a. Did Darth Vader's reign begin before the Jedi returned?
31b. Are Jack's children bright?

Third, presuppositions cannot be denied without evident self-contradiction, as illustrated in (32), although they can be suspended, as shown in (33).

32a. Jack's children are bright, but Jack has no children.
32b. The students regret that Mr. D. was late although Mr. D. was not late.
32c. The students rejoiced when the final score was posted, but it was never posted.
32d. If Mr. D. had been late, the students would have been disappointed, although Mr. D. was late.

33a. I'm sure that Jack's children are bright, if he has children.
33b. The students will regret that Mr. D. was late, if he was in fact late.
33c. I was in the locker room when the score was posted, if it was in fact ever posted.
33d. If Russia hadn't invaded Germany, Poland would be larger today, if Russia did in fact invade Germany.

Finally, presuppositions are relative to an assumed world. In all of the examples discussed here, it has been taken for granted that the relevant world is the real world (as presumed to be mutually known). However, certain world-creating verbs and constructions (cf. chap. 3, sec. 2; also, Morgan, 1969; McCawley, 1978c, 1993; Dinsmore, 1981; Fauconnier, 1985) can define other worlds as relevant for the evaluation of presupposition-involving constructions. For example, in (34) it is the world defined by a dream, a supposition, and a condition, respectively, where the relevant presuppositions must hold.[8]

34a. I dreamed that the earth was flat, and that a lot of people were glad when Columbus fell off the edge.
34b. Suppose Columbus discovered a passage to India: no one would criticize him for not landing in the West Indies.
34c. If pigs could fly, pork wings wouldn't taste any better than chicken wings.

Notice that *dream, suppose,* and *if* do not establish a new world for the presuppositions in (34) all by themselves; it takes a world-creating word and its

---

[8]The relevant presupposition in (34c) is the existence of such a thing as pork wings. Generic noun phrases in subject position have existential presuppositions (cf. Nunberg & Pan, 1975; Horn, 1986; and discussion of presupposition in sec. 4 of chap. 5).

complement to establish the world defined by the propositional content of the complement. This is why the presuppositions of (35) are all presuppositions relative to the real world, not to the worlds of dreams or suppositions.

35a. I dreamed that everyone regretted that Columbus fell off the edge of the earth.
35b. Suppose people had criticized Columbus for not landing in the West Indies.
35c. If pork wings don't taste good, don't eat them.

It is also important that the world-defining proposition does not have to be identical to the presupposition it warrants, as indeed it is not in the examples of (34). It is sufficient if the world-defining proposition provides a necessary or sufficient condition for the presupposed proposition, and in fact, not even this much is necessary; in (36) the world-defining propositions provide no more than a supporting context for the existential presuppositions of *their children* and *our house*.

36a. If Richard and Debra get married, their children will be beautiful.
36b. When we grow up, I hope we get married and move to the midwest—our house will have two stories and a front porch.

This property is the basis for one of the arguments (cf. Morgan, 1973b) that presupposition is not a semantic property inherent in lexical items, but a pragmatic property of utterances in context.

2.3 The Nature of Presupposition

A Property of Sentences or Utterances?

Presuppositions were originally described by logicians in semantic terms, as propositions associated with such linguistic objects as words or sentences (e.g., Strawson, 1950; cf. also Karttunen, 1973; Katz & Langendoen, 1976). In particular, they were defined as propositions that were entailed by a sentence and by its negation. (A proposition P is said to be ENTAILED by another proposition Q if whenever Q is true, P is also true.) However, problems with taking this description as a definition soon became evident (Morgan, 1973b). First, for non-controversial entailments, asserting a sentence and one of its entailments results in an argument that is intuitively valid, though trivial (as in (37)), but asserting a presupposed proposition in a context that presupposes it results in an argument which is intuitively invalid, as in (38).

37.   Jack has 5 children. Therefore Jack has more than 4 children.

38.   Dana regrets that Mr. D. was late. Therefore Mr. D. was late.

Second, the description of presuppositions as propositions entailed by a sentence and by its negation is inadequate as a definition of presupposition because it would fail to correctly characterize presuppositions of all the sentence types that do not have negations. There are no acceptable sentences which could be considered the negations of sentences like (39) or (40) in that they correspond to them in the same way that (30a) corresponds to (27a).

39a.   Drat/Damn the pork wings.
39b.   Long live the present king of France.

40a.   Here come the pork wings.
40b.   In waltzed the present king of France.

Furthermore, it is not clear what the logical negation of a polar question like (41a) would be, and while a constituent question like (41b) seems to presuppose 'someone ate my porridge,' its apparent negation (41c) presupposes 'someone didn't eat my porridge.'

41a.   Do you regret that you left your swim clothes at home?
41b.   Who ate my porridge?
41c   Who didn't eat my porridge?

Reformulating the definition to say that a sentence S presupposes a proposition P if whenever S is true, P is true, and whenever S is false, P is true does not resolve these problems, because sentences like (39–41) are not evaluatable as true or false. Even reformulating it in terms of satisfaction conditions for illocutionary acts, to avoid the problems posed by (41a), fails to distinguish presupposed "entailments" from the tautologies that are trivially entailed by every sentence: since tautologies like (42) are always true, they are true when sentences like (27) (or any other sentence, for that matter) are true and when those sentences are false.

42.   Things that are red are red.

But (42) is never involved in understanding (27) the way the proposition 'Mr. D was late for class' is. An adequate semantic definition of presupposition would therefore have to include the notion 'relevant'—a quintessentially context-bound and pragmatic notion.

Other arguments against a semantic treatment of presupposition are based on the fact that the context in which a supposed presupposition-involving sentence is used influences speakers' judgements of whether that sentence does or does not carry the presupposition in question. For instance, speakers agree that (43a) presupposes (43b), but that (43c), which contains (43a) as a coordinate part, does not.

43a. Jack's children have left home.
43b. Jack has children.
43c. Either Jack has no children, or Jack's children have left home.

And some inchoative factives, unlike the examples in (35), do not presuppose their complements in world-creating contexts. Sentences (44a–c) do not presuppose 'Dana had an appointment with the dean,' although (44d) in isolation is generally considered to.

44a. Maybe Dana realized he had an appointment with the dean.
44b. I bet Dana realized he had an appointment with the dean.
44c. I know. Dana realized he had an appointment with the dean! . . . No, that can't be it; the dean's out of town.
44d. Dana realized he had an appointment with the dean.

And while (45a) presupposes 'John got a parking ticket,' (45b) does not; it does not even presuppose 'John got a parking ticket or something.'

45a. John regrets getting a parking ticket.
45b. [Why is John so withdrawn?] Maybe he regrets getting a parking ticket or something.

Examples (34) and (36) illustrate the same point, and additional arguments against semantic presupposition may be found in Stalnaker (1974), Kempson (1975), Wilson (1975), Boer and Lycan (1976), and Gazdar (1979).

   Data such as (34–36, 43–45) exemplify what came to be known as the projection problem—the problem of stating when a presupposition of an embedded sentence is a presupposition of the sentence as a whole. A different aspect of the problem is provided by examples like (46), where (46a,b) do not presuppose that Jack has children, but only that Mary assumes (or presupposes) that he does.

46a. Mary asked to be introduced to Jack's children.
46b. Mary said that Dana realized that Jack had children.

Karttunen (1973) attempted a semantic treatment of the projection problem, but most analysts concluded that at least the projection problem, if not the phenomenon of presupposition itself, is a pragmatic phenomenon. Morgan (1973b) for example, characterized presuppositions relative to worlds (e.g., reality as perceived by the speaker, the world of a dream, the world of some individual's belief, or some hypothesized possible world), as propositions which could not be false in that world, and hypothesized a "free pass" principle for factive presuppositions. The "Free Pass" principle stated that for any sentence S, of the form *A F's that p* where F is a factive predicate (e.g., *Albert regrets that Sandy is 40*), p is true in any world where S is true or false. This principle predicted the necessary (nondefeatable) local projections (e.g., the fact that in any world where the sentence *Albert regrets that Sandy is 40* is either true or false, it is true that Sandy is 40). Projections to worlds not covered by this principle Morgan argued were contingent, subject to being overcome in contexts such as (36 and 44–46), and he showed how several could be accounted for as inferences from what was asserted, according to principles of the sort proposed by Grice (1975)[9] (see chap. 5 for detailed discussion).

Gazdar (1979) presents a formalization of this insight. He took presuppositions (in his terminology: pre-suppositions or potential presuppositions) to be conventionally associated with individual lexical items, and argued (1979: chap. 6) that they are filtered out by propositions assumed in the context of utterance of the sentence, by entailments (including what is asserted), and by clausal and scalar implicatures[10] of what is said, in that order, when they are inconsistent with them.

If one adopts an approach to lexical meaning in which ordinary lexical items are names for kinds of things (cf. Green, 1984, 1993), then it is hard to see how lexical presuppositions of the sort discussed in the third part of section 2.1 could be anything but pragmatic. If a word does not have a sense or definition, presuppositional aspects of meaning (e.g., *fressen* implying a non-human agent) could not be part of any semantic content, but would represent assumptions (not assertions) about what is referred to, namely that it has the properties in question.

Granted by Whom? Taken for Granted by Whom?

It is a simple task to show that it will not do to say that presuppositions have to be in fact true, rather than just assumed to be so, for this would treat sentences like (47) as ungrammatical or semantically anomalous, when in fact they are entirely grammatical and meaningful, and merely reflect their speaker's bizarre view of the world.

47.   Sandy doesn't realize that Tennyson wrote the King James Bible.

Similarly inadequate is the idea that the presupposed proposition must be assumed to be not only true, but common knowledge, because this would predict that sentences like (48) are self-contradictory, although in fact, they are not.

---

[9]Grice (1975) was circulated in pre-publication form as early as 1968. Grice's proposal was intended to account for the apparent nonstandard logic of ordinary language, but turned out, as we see in chapter 5, to have many other applications.

[10]The statement in (i) represents a clausal implicature of (ii); the statement in (iii) represents a scalar implicature of (iv) (cf. Horn, 1972, 1973).

    i. The proposition that Jack has children and the proposition that he does not are both consistent with all the speaker knows.
    ii. If Jack has children, Jack's children are bright.
    iii. Not all linguists like tofu.
    iv. Some linguists like tofu.

(

48.   Nobody realizes that Geralda is more qualified for the position than any
of the other candidates.

In the simplest pragmatic accounts of presupposition, the notion amounts to
no more than the speaker's *assumption* that the proposition said to be presupposed
is true. Some writers (e.g., Karttunen & Peters, 1979) have supposed that the
proposition must be mutually believed, that is, that both speaker and addressee
must assume it is true, and that the speaker must assume that the addressee
assumes it, etc. If this were correct, then a sentence like (49) would be an
unthinkably bizarre thing to say if the speaker did not think that the addressee
knew that the speaker had children, and (50) would never be appropriate, since
the addressee could not know that the speaker had a giraffe (cf. Hawkins, 1976;
McCawley, 1979; Gundel, 1985).

49.   Sorry I'm late—my children spilled milk on me, and I had to take the
time to change my clothes.

50.   Excuse me. You don't know me, but my giraffe has escaped into your
yard and is eating your eucalyptus.

But in fact, (49) is a pretty ordinary thing to say, and more likely than (50) only
because more people (are assumed to) have children than are assumed to have
giraffes.

Does the addressee have to take the presupposed proposition for granted in
order to understand and react appropriately to a sentence with a presupposition?
Of course not. She only has to be willing to infer that the speaker takes it for
granted, and that the speaker expects that she can reasonably infer that. This is
how sentences like (51a) can be used to convey to the addressee that her slip is
showing, why the utterance of (51b) flatters the audience as being assumed to
be among those who realize the enormity of the danger mentioned, and why
someone to whom (51c) is addressed may be annoyed if she believes that the
speaker could not have waded in a frozen creek.

51a.   Do you realize that your slip is showing?
51b.   Not everyone realizes that the passage of Senator Eks' amendment
would seriously jeopardize currently protected First Amendment rights.
51c.   Although the temperature never went above 15 degrees Fahrenheit, we
didn't regret wading in the creek.

In all cases, the explanation is that the speaker is treating the proposition in the
presupposition construction as noncontroversial, even though it may, in fact, be
controversial and not taken for granted by the addressee.

2.4 Some Other Phenomena That Have Been Called "Presupposition"

Felicity Conditions

One might think that felicity conditions on the successful performance of illocutionary acts are a sort of presupposition (also vice versa, that presuppositions are a sort of felicity condition). This would mean that the proposition 'Speaker is empowered to pass sentence on the addressee,' representing a felicity condition on (52a) has the same relation to it as the presupposition 'Jack has children' has to (52b).

52a. I sentence you to 10 years imprisonment.
52b. Jack's children are bright.

Similarly, the term *presupposition* has been used to refer to the sincerity and preparatory conditions (cf. Searle, 1969) on felicitous commands, e.g., the conditions that the speaker want the action being ordered, and that it be possible to perform the action (e.g., Fillmore, 1971b). Thus, sentences like (53) would be said to presuppose 'Speaker wants the door closed' and 'The door is not closed.'

53. Close the door.

Unlike other examples of presupposition, the requisite beliefs or attitudes in these cases are not linked to a particular linguistic form, but rather to the performance of an act of a certain type, an act which might be accomplished by a variety of forms, some or all of which systematically have other uses as well. Thus, any of the forms in (54) might be used to perform the sentencing which (52a) could be used to accomplish, as long as the speaker is empowered to pass sentence on the relevant addressee.

54a. The defendant is remanded to the custody of the Department of Corrections to serve a term of no less than 10 years.
54b. You're going to prison for 10 years.

And if 'Speaker wants the door closed' is a presupposition of *Close the door*, it ought to be equally a presupposition of its negation *Don't close the door*. But it isn't: the felicity condition for the latter is that the speaker wants the door not to be closed.

Pronoun Choice

Another set of phenomena referred to as presupposition involves pronoun choice. One of these phenomena is the assumption of coreference mentioned in chapter 2. A related phenomenon is the assumptions about sex and species that are necessary to choose the appropriate reflexive and relative pronouns, as in (55). Thus, in (55a) the use of *herself* reflects a presupposition that the neighbor is female, though the word *neighbor* neither carries nor invites any such presupposition; in (55b) we simply have no idea (or concern) what sex the neighbor is. And in (55c), the use of *which* reflects an assumption that Arotovignians (whatever they might be) are a nonhuman species.

55a.   My neighbor hurt herself mowing the lawn.
55b.   My neighbor mowed the lawn.
55c.   The Arotovignians, which eat chocolate, are sensitive to rotenone.

Although Postal (1970) referred to the phenomenon in (55a) as presupposed coreference, it appears he was using the term *presupposed* in a nontechnical way, and these phenomena are not included in descriptions of presupposition as a semantic phenomenon. These presuppositions are not suspendable the way garden-variety presuppositions are (cf. sec. 2.2), nor do they provoke a reaction of contradiction when explicitly denied. Thus, (56) is more a metalinguistic comment on the appropriateness of the word *him* (cf. Horn, 1985 and chap. 5, sec. 4.3), than a comment on the conditions under which it could be true or false, like (33a).

56.   I wrote him a letter, if he is in fact a male.

And (57a, 57b) do not sound contradictory, the way the sentences of (32) do.

57a.   The descendants which have simple eyes are human.
57b.   The descendants who have complex eyes are not human.

In both cases, the assumption reflected by the relative pronoun seems to be about as strong as the assertion; the speaker seems to think in (57a) that the descendants really are not quite human, in (57b), that they are almost as human as you can get.

Similarly, the choice of a so-called "familiar" second person pronoun[11] (French, Spanish *tu*, German *du*) over a "distant" form (French *vous*, Spanish *Usted*, German *Sie*) has been said (Levinson, 1983, pp. 89–92, 128–130, 166) to reflect a presupposition that the addressee is socially intimate with the speaker, or socially inferior (e.g., a young child), and it has been claimed that the use of

---

[11]This description oversimplifies the nature of the problem considerably. Thai, for instance, has a whole array of first and second person pronouns whose appropriate use depends on beliefs about the sex and pedigree of the referent (i.e., whether the referent is male or female, or a king, queen, or royalty) and on the speaker's relation to the addressee (i.e., parent–child, servant–master, monk–ordinary person), as well as on the degree of intimacy between speaker and addressee.

a vocative proper noun (e.g., *Judy* in (58)) presupposes that the person so addressed is called by that name.

58. Hey, Judy, give me a hand.

But again, the social relationship presuppositions are not suspendable; (59) does not succeed in suspending the assumption that the speaker considers the addressee to be an intimate.[12]

59. Je t'ai   vu   hier,   si nous nous   connaissons bien.
    I you-fam.-have seen yesterday if we   each-other know   well.
    I saw you-fam. yesterday, if we know each other well.

And using a vocative in a deductive-exclamative context does not cancel the vocative's presupposition, although garden variety presuppositions may be cancelled in such contexts (cf. 44c); in (60), the speaker using the vocative *Rumplestiltskin* still must presuppose the addressee's name is Rumplestiltskin.

60. ??I know, Rumplestiltskin! Your name is Rumplestiltskin![13]

In fact, there are certain proper nouns conventionally used to address individuals whose name is not known to the speaker: *Mac, Buster, Joe* (GIs). Thus, they are used to address individuals whose name they are assumed not to be. Consequently sentences like (61a) are not contradictory, and ones like (61b) are a little odd pragmatically.

61a. Hey, Mac! I know that's not your name, but your left rear tire's flat.
61b. Listen, Buster, if that's your name. Your truck is in my way.

Nonrestrictive Relative Clauses

It has been claimed (e.g., by Keenan, 1971) that sentences with nonrestrictive relative clauses as in (62) presuppose the truth of the relative clause, but almost all analysts agree that in fact nonrestrictive relative clauses are asserted rather than presupposed.

---

[12]It is possible to suspend a presupposition or speaker assumption that it is appropriate to use the familiar pronoun as in (i); both French and German have special verbs for referring to pronoun use.

i. Je t'ai   vu   hier,   si je peux te   tutoyer.
   I you-fam.-have seen yesterday, if I can you-fam. say-"tu"-to

[13]Compare (60) to (i), where the first instance of *Rumplestiltskin* is not a vocative, but the answer to a question.

i. I know! Rumplestiltskin! Your name is Rumplestiltskin!

62.   Taylor, who has a 42-inch vertical leap, will be a sophomore next year.

The rational speaker of (62) does not take it for granted that the addressee realizes (or even will infer that the speaker believes that it is common knowledge) that Taylor has a 42-inch vertical leap. Instead, the nonrestrictive relative clause in (62) offers a way of asserting that information, while not making it the main point of his utterance.

Further Remarks on Connotations

It is not always clear what connotations should be analyzed as presuppositions lexically tied to a word. For example, as McCawley (1975b) points out, the presuppositional properties of *accuse* and *criticize* are not quite as straightforward as Fillmore's analysis suggests. Most importantly, the 'X is bad' presupposition is more accurately characterized as 'Accuser thinks X is bad,' and the 'Defendant is responsible for X' presupposition is more accurately characterized as an assumption that the criticizer thinks X happened and that the defendant is responsible for X. Thus, they are more like sincerity conditions on illocutionary acts (i.e., acts of saying that someone did something that is bad, and of saying that what someone did is bad) than they are like more standard kinds of presuppositions, in that denying the supposed presupposition does not result in a contradiction, as it does for undisputed presuppositions. Thus, (63a, 63b) report an insincere accusation and an insincere or mistaken criticism, not impossible events, just as (64a, 64b) are merely blatantly insincere, and not contradictory like the examples in (32).

63a.   The students accused Mr. D. of being late, although they liked his being late.
63b.   The students criticized Mr. D. for being late, although they knew he was not late.

64a.   It's snowing, although I don't believe that it is.
64b.   I hereby reluctantly order you to close the door, even though it is already closed.

Conclusions

The phenomena discussed in section 2.4 involve, even more clearly than those discussed in preceding sections, the assumptions of speaker and addressee, as well as, in some cases, those of agents named in the utterance. Indeed, in certain speech interactions, it might be more important that the speaker assumes he stands in a social relation to the addressee which licenses the use of a certain pronoun, than whether some factive presupposition of a sentence or utterance is in fact true. A comprehensive theory of utterance interpretation must provide an account of all of these phenomena. Chapter 5 sketches some proposals for the foundations of such a theory.

CHAPTER 4 STUDY QUESTIONS

1. What is a locutionary act?

2. What is an illocutionary act?

3. What is a perlocutionary act?

4. What is a performative verb?

5. What is the performative analysis?

6. What is the source of inadequacies of the performative analysis?

7. What is a presupposition?

8. What constructions are universally acknowledged to involve presuppositions?

9. What properties distinguish presupposition from entailment?

10. What is the projection problem?

11. To what extent is presupposition now considered to be a semantic phenomenon?

12. To what extent is presupposition now considered to be a pragmatic phenomenon?

13. Why is presupposition considered to be at least partially pragmatic?

5 Implicature

> Capt. Renault: *Rick, do you have those letters of transit?*
> Rick: *Louis! Are you Pro-Vichy or Free French?*
> Capt. Renault: *Ha-ha! Serves me right for asking a direct question.*
> *The subject is closed.*

The reader may recognize the dialog reproduced above from the movie *Casablanca.* Captain Louis Renault (Claude Rains) suspects cafe-owner Rick (Humphrey Bogart) of having some stolen letters of transit which will enable a suspected Free French spy to escape from Vichy-controlled Casablanca. Captain Renault asks Rick a straightforward question, no doubt with utter sincerity. Rick responds with another question, and we can believe he does not know the answer to it any more than the captain knows the answer to the question he asked Rick. The captain responds to Rick's question as if Rick has rebuked him for asking about the letters of transit. Why isn't this dialog incoherent? Why, in fact, is Rick's question many times more eloquent than a plainspoken "You shouldn't ask me that; if I answer, it will destroy our ability to get along here"? The first section of this chapter describes a theory of discourse which provides means to answer these questions. Subsequent sections show how this theory has been or can be used in resolving a number of problematical issues in pragmatics, including coherence, indirect speech acts, the range of illocutionary forces, and the nature of presupposition, metaphor, and reference.

1. THE COOPERATIVE PRINCIPLE

In 1967, the philosopher H. P. Grice argued that it was unnecessary to consider the differences noted by logicians between such logical operators as $\wedge$, $\vee$, $\exists$, $\sim$, $\supset$, and their natural language counterparts (i.e., *and, or, some, not, if . . . then*) to be differences in meaning. Grice proposed that the differences were just differences in use, and arose from the fact that the ordinary kinds of discourse (his term was *conversation*) in which the natural language expressions are used are governed by principles irrelevant to the use of the corresponding operators in formal logical proofs. Grice argued that the extra baggage that goes along with the natural language terms compared to their counterparts in formal logic follows from the fact that instances of natural language are situated acts as well as forms.

Briefly, Grice proposed that more could be conveyed than was said if one assumed that in conversing (indeed, in behaving rationally[1] (Grice, 1975,[2] p. 47)), human beings follow a behavioral dictum, which he called the Cooperative Principle:

> Make your conversational contribution such as is required, at the stage at which it occurs, by the accepted purpose or direction of the talk exchange in which you are engaged. (p. 45)

The reference to "the accepted purpose or direction of the talk exchange" implies that speaker and hearer are constantly involved in the interpretation of each other's goals in saying what they say.[3] Since Grice was explicit about the Principle not being restricted to linguistic acts, and because the imperative formulation has led to a lot of misunderstanding, it may be more useful to rephrase it more generally, and declaratively, where it amounts to this:

> Individuals act in accordance with their goals.

Grice described four categories (Quantity, Quality, Relation, and Manner) of special cases of this principle, that is, applications of it to particular kinds of requirements, and gave examples of their application in both linguistic and non-linguistic domains. It is instructive to translate these into general, declarative formulations as well:

QUANTITY: I. An agent will do as much as is required for the achievement of the current goal.

II. An agent will not do more than is required.[4]

---

[1]In fact, one could take adherence to the Cooperative Principle as (part of) the definition of rational behavior.

[2]Dittoed copies of the text of the seven 1967 lectures circulated "underground" among linguists and philosophers for several years. In 1975, Lecture II was published (Grice, 1975), and in 1978, Lecture III (Grice, 1978). All seven lectures are published in Grice, 1989.

[3]Parts of the following discussion first appeared in Green, 1990.

[4]Grice expressed some doubt regarding the necessity of the second maxim of Quantity, pointing to the possibility of subsuming it under the maxim of Relevance. One might also argue that it is at least an implicature (see following footnote), if not an entailment, of the first maxim of Quantity.

QUALITY: Agents will not deceive co-agents.
Consequently, an agent will try to make any assertion one that is true.
I. Agents will not say what they believe to be false.
II. Agents will not say that for which they lack adequate evidence.

RELATION: An agent's action will be relevant to and relative to an intention of the agent.

MANNER: Agents will make their actions perspicuous to others who share a joint intention.[5]
I. Agents will not disguise actions from co-agents. Consequently, agents will not speak obscurely in attempting to communicate.
II. Agents will act so that intentions they intend to communicate are unambiguously reconstructible.
III. Agents will spend no more energy on actions than is necessary.
IV. Agents will execute sub-parts of a plan in an order that will maximize the perceived likelihood of achieving the goal.

The special cases, which Grice called maxims, tend to strike the naive reader variously as common sense, wishful thinking, or composition teachers' futile rules, but the attraction of Grice's theory is its ability to explain how in being honored as much in the (apparent) breach as in the observance, the maxims provide explanations for otherwise puzzling phenomena. That is, Grice showed that as long as participants in a mutual enterprise such as a conversation each assume that the other is behaving in accordance with the Cooperative Principle, meanings that are conveyed without being made explicit follow as inferences

---

[5]Grice's formulation of this maxim is "Be perspicuous." I have always thought that he was indulging in a private joke in the formulation of this maxim and submaxims (3) and (4), which he formulated as "Be brief (avoid unnecessary prolixity)" and "Be orderly." Insofar as *perspicuous* and *prolixity* are unnecessarily obscure expressions (compared to *clear* and *verbosity* or *too many words*), the statement of the maxim and its third submaxim violate the first submaxim; submaxim (3) violates itself as well with the obscure and repetitious paraphrase; and submaxim (4) is not ordered well with the others, bringing to mind infuriating recipes like that in (i).

i.   MATZO BALLS

2 tablespoons fat	1 teaspoon salt
2 eggs, slightly beaten	2 tablespoons soup stock or water
1/2 cup matzo meal	

Mix fat and eggs together. Add matzo meal and salt, which were first mixed together. When well blended, . . . [Manischevitz Matzo Meal package] from the fact that some particular maxim appears to be being violated. Grice noted that speakers value the maxim of Quality much more highly than the other maxims[6]—violating it amounts to a moral offense, whereas violating the others is at worst inconsiderate or rude.

As mentioned, the Cooperative Principle derives its explanatory power from what happens when behavior appears not to conform to it. Grice noted (1975, p. 49) that a maxim can fail to be observed in several different ways. A maxim may be just ignored, or quietly violated, in which case hearers will be misled. Telling a lie, for instance, is a quiet violation of the first maxim of Quality.

A speaker may be unable to make her behavior satisfy all of the maxims at once; if two are in conflict, she may have to sacrifice one to the other. It may be impossible in some situation, for example, to say as much as is necessary without saying things for which one does not have adequate evidence. Similarly, a speaker who thinks her audience may not have as much background knowledge as she has may have to sacrifice the maxim of Manner and be prolix or obscure, or risk violating the first maxim of Quality by saying something that will be understood as something she believes to be false. The strong claim is that the Cooperative Principle governs conversational interaction, and rational speakers behave according to the maxims insofar as they are able, and expect their interlocutors to. Consequently, in cases where a speaker cannot honor one maxim without ignoring the requirements of another, hearers may be misled into thinking that all maxims are being observed if the speaker does not explicitly opt out of conforming to a maxim, by informing her interlocutor, either explicitly as in (1) or implicitly as in (2), that she is not conforming to that maxim.

1a.	I am not at liberty to say any more.	[Quantity I]
1b.	I probably don't need to say this . . .	[Quantity II]
1c.	I'm not sure if it's true, but . . .	[Quality I]
1d.	I have no evidence for this, but . . .	[Quality II]
1e.	I know this is irrelevant, but . . .	[Relation]
2a.	As you know, . . .	[Quantity II]
2b.	This may be just a rumor, but . . .	[Quality II]
2c.	By the way, . . .	[Relation]

The consequence of assuming that behavior conforms to the Cooperative Principle is that even when speech behavior appears inconsistent with these maxims, hearers assume that the speaker is behaving in accordance with the Cooperative Principle—to do otherwise would be to assume that the speaker is irrational and unpredictable, and cannot be expected to participate in rational discourse. Assuming then that the speaker is behaving rationally, and expecting

---

[6]In some cultures, anyway. Things may well be different in contexts or subcultures where narrative style is more highly valued than accuracy.

to be perceived that way, the hearer must adopt a strategy of assuming that the speaker's behavior is in maximal conformance with the maxims, and considering what propositions must be accepted in order to justify the assumption that the behavior conforms to the Cooperative Principle and the maxims.

As a speaker–hearer of a natural language spoken in a society, the speaker expects the hearer to adopt this strategy for interpreting speech behavior. Consequently, speakers are free to exploit it, and speak in such a way that their behavior must be interpreted according to it. Speakers must know that if their remark seems irrelevant, hearers will seek to construct a sequence of inferences which make it relevant to some assumed goal. This exploitation of the maxims is the basic mechanism by which utterances are used to convey more than they literally denote, and Grice gave it the name IMPLICATURE. In this section, we first examine some examples showing how implicature works, then examine the notion of implicature more closely, and illustrate the varieties of implicature with more examples.

Implicatures are likely to arise or be intended whenever a maxim appears to be conspicuously violated. For example, in the dialog in (3), adapted from Grice (1975, p. 51), B's response to A's remark about Smitty appears on the surface to violate the maxim of Relation.

3.   A: Smitty doesn't seem to have a girlfriend these days.
     B: He's been driving to New York every weekend.

But if A assumes that B is behaving in accordance with the Cooperative Principle, he must assume that B's response is as relevant, truthful, complete, and clear as B considers appropriate. B may intend A to infer (i.e., B may implicate) that (B believes that) Smitty has a girlfriend in New York, or has too many business obligations in New York to have time for a girlfriend, or has so much to do in New York he finds no need for a girlfriend, or some other comment on or explanation for Smitty's apparent girlfriendlessness which preserves the assumption that B is conforming to the maxim of relation. The implicated proposition might be one which B does not have adequate evidence for, or one which B has adequate evidence for, but does not want to explain how he got it (which would sacrifice Quantity I in order to conform to the maxims of Quality). By implicating his comment rather than asserting it, B observes Quality I and Relation, without violating Quality II.

In the dialog in (4), D would be violating Relation and Quantity I if he didn't expect C to be able to interpret his reply as one which recognized and temporarily adopted a goal he imputes to C.[7]

---

[7]Apparently, as speakers we assume that our addressees provisionally adopt the goals that they infer we have, unless we have evidence to the contrary. This would follow as a consequence from the plausible conversational strategy of assuming that if S conveys some proposition P to A, and A doesn't deny P, then A accepts P.

4.   C: Have you seen my stubby screwdriver?
      D: Look in the red toolbox.

But D expects C to infer that D believes the screwdriver is in the red tool box, that the toolbox is accessible, and so on. By responding as he does, D implicates that the screwdriver is in the toolbox and accessible to C. Indeed, to respond directly with *yes* (meaning 'In my lifetime, I have seen it') would be distinctly unhelpful. If D infers, as most of us do in such cases, that what C really wants is to know where the screwdriver is, and that he is implicating that he wants that, then answering "yes" implicates that D does not want or intend to cooperate with C in this enterprise.

As the ordinariness of example (4) suggests, conversational implicature is an absolutely unremarkable and mundane conversational strategy. Examples (5–7) all exploit the assumption that the utterance conforms to the relevance maxim. With (5b) and (5c), the speaker implicates an answer to a question (given as (5a)) which she might feel social taboos prevent her from answering directly.

5a.   Q: What would you like for your birthday?
5b.   A: I need a new camera.
5c.   A: Well, my camera's broken.[8]

One ordinarily understands an utterance like (6) as implicating that the proposition expressed by the second sentence is relevant to the proposition expressed by the first, probably by representing an intended effect of the state of affairs which the first sentence describes.

6.   I will rake the leaves that have fallen on Toad's lawn. He will be surprised.

And in (7), B's answer exploits the assumption that she is speaking in accordance with the relevance maxim, to implicate that because her car is not working, she cannot provide a ride for A.

7a.   A: Can I get a ride with you?
7b.   B: My car's not working.

A speaker may also exhibit behavior which blatantly and conspicuously fails to conform to a maxim with the intention that her behavior be recognized as failing to conform to that maxim, and interpreted as nonetheless being cooperative (i.e., rational, goal-directed, relevant) in the overall scheme of things. For example, a speaker might say much more than clearly is necessary, or say something obviously false or irrelevant, obscure, ambiguous, or prolix. If the hearer assumes

---

[8]As discussed in chapter 6, the initial particle *well* often indicates that not everything relevant is being made explicit. Cf. also Lakoff (1973a) and Schourup (1982).

that the speaker is behaving rationally, is able to conform to the maxim so clearly ignored, and so is not opting out or sacrificing the observance of one maxim to preserve that of another, he will have to reconcile this assumption with the fact that a maxim appears to have been violated.

Examples (3–7) illustrate the generation of implicatures. The next example (after Grice, 1975, p. 52) illustrates in more detail how failing conspicuously to conform to a maxim exploits that maxim to generate implicature. Suppose Professor A is asked by his professional colleague Professor B to evaluate for a position at an American university, candidate Smith, a former student of A's. Professor A writes a letter of recommendation consisting of the paragraph in (8).

8.   Mr. Smith's command of English is excellent, and he always attended class regularly.

A regular kiss of death recommendation—but how? Since A has responded to the request to write, he is not opting out of the interaction. Since Smith was his student, A is in a position to abide by Quantity, Quality, and Relation, and provide a considerable amount (Quantity) of adequately warranted (Quality II) relevant (Relation) information about Smith of the sort that he knows his colleague B wants. But all A says is that Smith speaks English well and attended class regularly. Since A can be assumed to realize (a) that his saying only this obviously violates Quantity I, and (b) that B will recognize this, A must intend for B to recognize it. However, if A is alert, he must also realize that B will try to interpret A's behavior as cooperating with the request, by concluding that it is significant that A did not say more. Therefore, A must intend B to conclude this. A logical reason for A not to say more is that there is nothing to recommend Smith beyond what A wrote. Since this is obviously an inadequate recommendation for an academic position, if A is rational and alert, he must have intended to implicate that Smith's qualifications for the position in question are inadequate.

Now that we have some clear examples of the sort of phenomena Grice had in mind, it may be helpful to examine his characterization (1975, pp. 49–50) of implicature. In, by, and when saying "P," a speaker implicates 'q,' provided that:

a.   the speaker is presumed to be observing the maxims, or at least the Cooperative Principle,
b.   in order to make the speaker's uttering "P" consistent with (a), it is necessary to assume that the speaker believes that 'q,'
c.   the speaker reflexively expects (cf. chap. 1, sec. 6) that the addressee is able to grasp intuitively or actively infer (b).

The description of the maxims as just special cases of the Cooperative Principle is quite deliberate. They are not (contra Lycan, 1984, p. 75) logical consequences (corollaries), because they do not follow as necessary consequences in all possible worlds. They are not additional stipulations. They are not necessarily an exhaustive list of special cases. Rather, they are just particular ways of being cooperative; all other things being equal, conforming to the Cooperative Principle involves conforming to all of them. When speakers cannot conform to all of them, as Grice discusses, they conform to as many as they can.

It is important to understand also that the maxims do not *constitute* the Cooperative Principle, as some writers have thought (e.g., Sperber & Wilson, 1986, p. 36). On the contrary, the Cooperative Principle is a very general principle which determines, depending on the values shared by participants, any number of maxims instantiating ways of conforming to it. The more that can be said about what values are shared, the more maxims can be articulated as explaining behavior.

Equally important, the maxims are not rules or norms that are taught or learned, as some writers would have it (e.g., Pratt, 1981, p. 11; Brown & Yule, 1983, p. 32; Blum-Kulka & Olshtain, 1986, p. 175; Allwood et al., 1977, p. 37; Ruhl, 1989, p. 96; Sperber & Wilson, 1986, p. 162). Regardless of whether *norms* is understood as referring to prescriptive rules (cf. Brown & Yule, 1983, p. 32) or to social customs (cf. Brown & Yule, 1983, p. 83), norms are not what Grice was referring to. Nothing in "Logic and Conversation" suggests that Grice thought of the maxims as statistical principles that people tend to conform to, or as ideals that people aspire to conform to. Rather, they are articulations of consequences of the assumption that individuals act in accordance with their goals—the Cooperative Principle. It is this assumption that allowed Grice to suggest that the Cooperative Principle constitutes a definition of what it means to be rational (Grice, 1975, pp. 45, 47, 48–49). Thus, if X's goal is to get Y to do some act A, or believe some proposition P, X will want to speak in such a way that A or P is clearly identifiable (Maxims of Quality, Quantity, Manner), and X will not say things that will distract Y from getting the point (Maxim of Relation). Furthermore, X will most likely not want to antagonize Y (numerous writers' Maxim of Politeness).

That the maxims are just obvious ways of behaving in accordance with the Cooperative Principle, and not rules we have to learn, suggests that they may only come to our attention when we encounter speech which is difficult to reconcile with the assumption that speech behavior is consistent with them. This seems to be the case, as can be seen by examining what we might make of an apparently irrelevant speech act. Suppose a stranger were to approach us in a public place, and after introducing himself, ask the time. We would think this very strange, and wonder why he introduced himself.

9.   Excuse me, I'm Sterling Ryznich. Can you tell me the time?

Why would he think we would want to know who he was? Why should he think we would care who he was if all he wanted was the time? Knowledge of time of day is not, in a case like this at least, a precious commodity to be shared only with those who have proper credentials. It is only when we come across an utterance whose relevance is not easily inferred that we notice that we expect every utterance in a discourse to be relevant to some participant's goal which is at least mutually accessible, if not truly shared.

That is, speakers assume that other speakers do what they do, say what they say, on purpose, intentionally, and for a reason (cf. Brown & Levinson, 1978, p. 63). In other words, they assume that speech behavior, and indeed, all behavior that isn't involuntary, is goal-directed. Speakers "know" the maxims as rules of thumb for efficiently achieving goals, especially through speech. A person's behavior will be interpreted as conforming to the maxims, even when it appears not to, because of the assumption of rationality (goal-directedness). Implicature arises when novel (that is, previously unassumed) propositions have to be introduced into the context to make the assumption of rationality and the assumption of conformity with the maxims consistent with the behavior. If no such propositions can be imagined, the speaker will be judged irrational, but irrationality will consist in believing the unbelievable, or believing something unfathomable, not in having imperfect knowledge of the maxims, or in not observing the maxims.

In the case of (9), we have two choices: either (a) assume that the introduction is truly irrelevant to any purpose of speaker or hearer, in which case we should consider the stranger truly deranged, or (b) assume that there is some goal to which the stranger's identity is relevant. Maybe it is a goal of his: maybe he wants to use us as an alibi (we would certainly remember bizarre behavior like uttering (9)). Maybe he is trying to terrorize us psychologically, and just wants us to worry about why he said what he said. On the other hand, maybe it is relevant to some goal he imputes to us. Maybe he (mistakenly) thinks we were supposed to meet him. Maybe he thinks he is such a celebrity that even though he never expects to see us again, we would want to know whom we had befriended. Maybe he just wants to know the time, but believes that the injunction against speaking to strangers will inhibit us from answering him unless he introduces himself, making him no longer a stranger. Only our imagination limits the goals, and beliefs about the addressee's goals, that we might attribute to the speaker. The point is that if we reject the assumption that the speaker is irrational, then we must at the very least assume that there is some goal to which his introduction is relevant in the context of asking the time, even if we can't figure out what it is. Thus, the purposes which the Cooperative Principle refers to are not so much shared or mutual as they are mutually modelled (Cohen & Perrault, 1979; Cohen & Levesque, 1980; Green, 1982; Appelt, 1985; Cohen & Levesque, 1990; Perrault, 1990): for George to understand Martha's utterance of some sentence to him, George must have beliefs about Martha which include Martha's purpose in uttering that sentence to him, which in turn includes Martha's model of George, including George's model of Martha, and so on. Grice's assertion (1975, p. 48) that "in characteristic talk-exchanges, there is a common aim even if . . . it is a second-order one, namely, that each party should, for the time being, identify himself with the transitory conversational interests of the other" is an under-noticed expression of this view. The idea that participants will at least temporarily identify with each other's interests, i.e., infer what each other is trying to do, is what allows quarrels,[9] monologues, etc. (Pratt (1981) and Schauber and Spolsky (1986) notwithstanding) to be included in the talk exchanges that the Cooperative Principle governs. The participants may have different values and agendas, but given Grice's (1957) characterization of conventional meaning, for any communication to occur, for each participant to understand what the other meant, each must make assumptions about the other's goals, at least the low-level communicative goals. This is the sense in which participants recognize a common goal. When the assumptions participants make about each other's goals are incorrect, and this affects non-trivial beliefs about each other, we say they are talking at cross-purposes, precisely because of the mismatch between actual goals and beliefs, and attributed goals and beliefs.

Grice distinguished between CONVERSATIONAL implicatures, which must be capable of being worked out, even if they are short-circuited and grasped intuitively (cf. Morgan, 1978), and CONVENTIONAL implicatures, which can only be "grasped intuitively." Grice (1975) gave only one example of a conventional implicature, the implicature of causality associated with *therefore* in (10).

10.   He is an Englishman; he is, therefore, brave.

According to his analysis, *therefore* differs from *because* in that *A because B* is used to assert that B is the cause of A, while *B, therefore A* only implicates, takes for granted, or presupposes that B is the cause of A.[10] Indeed, presuppositions associated locally by convention with the use of particular forms (the "pre-suppositions" of Gazdar, 1979) are now customarily referred to as conventional implicatures rather than as presuppositions.

Conventional implicatures also differ from conversational implicatures in that conventional implicatures do not depend crucially on assuming the speaker to be observing the Cooperative Principle. The particular conversational implicature that a particular utterance generates in a particular context is a function of the addressee's estimate of the speaker's reflexive estimate of what the addressee assumes and will conclude. Since there is ample room for error here, what is conversationally implicated is somewhat indeterminate: what is potentially conversationally implicated is a large, perhaps indefinitely large, disjunction of

---

[9]Careful reading of "Logic and Conversation" shows that Grice cited quarrels and letter-writing as instances that did not fit an interpretation of the Cooperative Principle that he rejected (Grice, 1975, p. 48), not one that he supported.

[10]The causal connection to some previously mentioned circumstance is thus similar to the implication connected with the use of pronouns. Just as *he* doesn't assert 'masculine and singular', but rather presupposes it, so the "pro-conjunction" (cf. chap. 2, sec. 5) *therefore* presupposes rather than asserts a causal relation.

propositions (recall example (3)), and the speaker is in a position to rationally deny that any particular one was intended. Thus, it might be a little disingenuous to respond to A's observation in (3) that Smitty doesn't seem to have a girlfriend by saying *I don't mean to contradict you, but he's been driving to New York every weekend*, but it is not contradictory. The conventional implicature of a linguistic expression, on the other hand, is quite specific, and so not CANCELLABLE; you cannot deny that you meant them without involving yourself in a contradiction. Consequently, a sentence like *He is an Englishman; therefore he is brave— but I'm not implying that being an Englishman makes a person brave* is a foolish contradiction.

Grice also distinguished a class of implicatures as generalized conversational implicatures (1975, p. 56). These are implicatures that in normal (nonspecial) circumstances are regularly associated with a linguistic expression. For example, Grice describes a generalized conversational implicature associated with the indefinite article *a*, that the referent of the noun it modifies is not closely associated "with some [contextually] identifiable person."[11] This is why (11a) implicates that the woman is not the wife, girlfriend, sister, or mother of John or the speaker or the addressee, and why (11b) implicates that it was neither John's car, nor the speaker's or the addressee's, that was involved.

11a. John is meeting a woman this evening.
11b. A car ran over John's cat.

Generalized conversational implicature differs from conventional implicature in that, as conversational implicature, it is cancellable, context-dependent, and not strictly determinate. As Hirschberg (1985) pointed out, the difference between generalized conversational implicature and particularized conversational implicature is only a matter of the degree of dependence on context, and thus, not a categorical distinction.

The reader is cautioned not to take these characterizations of conversational, conventional, and generalized conversational implicatures as defining criteria. Grice did not intend them that way (Grice, 1978, pp. 114–115), and Sadock (1978) outlines serious problems with taking them that way. Kempson (1975),

---

[11]With entities that are inalienably connected with an identified referent, *a* implicates, as Grice notes, the reverse. We would infer from the utterance of (i) that it was Smitty's own finger that he broke, unless we made the (special) assumption that Smitty was (known to be) a gangster or other sort of brute, or such a clutz that it was not unusual for him to injure others.

i. Smitty broke a finger yesterday.

Naturally, the inalienably connected entity has to be of the sort that individuals typically have more than one of. Example (ii) works more like (11a) than like (i).

ii. John broke a nose yesterday.

Cf. Horn (1984a) for extended discussion of this phenomenon.

Wilson (1975), Gazdar (1979), and Wilson and Sperber (1979), among others, offer more explicit accounts, based on Grice's principles or extensions of them.

In talking about the observance of the Cooperative Principle as rational, Grice (1975, pp. 47, 49) hinted that he took it and the maxims to represent values universally assumed in human society. Grice did not actually claim universality for the Cooperative Principle and the maxims (which he took to be special cases of the Cooperative Principle)[12] but it is clear that the value of the Cooperative Principle and the maxims in explaining linguistic phenomena is much greater if they are universal (and hence potentially a consequence of some property of human nature or human society) than if they are not. Thus, it is worthwhile to examine Keenan's (1976) frequently cited argument that the maxims do not universally govern human talk exchanges. Keenan claimed that Malagasy speakers regularly withhold information from their conversational partners, and concluded from this that they must lack the first maxim of Quantity, and that therefore, the maxims are not universal. In her discussion, Keenan indicates that it is not uncommon for speakers to withhold information in answering a question. For example, a question amounting to something like (12a) might be answered with the equivalent of (12b), even when the respondent is in a position to give a more precise answer.

12a. A: Where is your mother?
12b. B: She is either in the house or at the market.

But as Prince (1982) noted, Keenan's account indicates that among the Malagasy, information that is not readily available is a highly prized commodity which confers prestige on those who have it. Furthermore, there are cultural taboos about making statements which turn out to be incorrect, or that assign blame. But information that the speaker is not the unique possessor of is readily imparted, as is information whose publication would not make the speaker guilty of a cultural infraction. Thus, when B knows where his mother is, and saying where would not amount to blaming her for anything, interchanges like (12) involve either opting out of the first maxim of Quantity, to preserve one's status, or flouting the maxim, to flaunt it. Either way, the existence of the maxim of Quantity among the Malagasy is entailed; it could not be exploited if it did not exist. Keenan's account confirms this in revealing (1976, pp. 76–78) that when providing the information sought does not threaten the speaker's position in the community, even uniquely possessed information is not withheld. Thus, Malagasy speakers are just like Western Europeans in abiding by the Cooperative Principle and observing even the questioned first maxim of Quantity, although it is readily sacrificed to Quality (II), and to a Malagasy prohibition against assigning blame.

---

[12]Actually, since Grice took the maxims to be only special cases, and not corollaries, discovering that one of the maxims was not universal would not invalidate claims that the Cooperative Principle was universal.

Indeed, they exploit it when maintaining membership in an information elite is valued more highly than other interpersonal goals.

This case should make it clear how the value of the maxims as an explanatory tool lies in what they induce a rational hearer to infer when she assumes that a speaker is abiding by them, even when what is said appears not to conform. Grice's contribution was thus not the claim that discourse should conform to the maxims, or that a very particular sort of discourse does conform to them, but the observation that assuming that conversation is governed by the maxims explains how uses which appear illogical when taken at face value can be taken as rational contributions to a conversation, and convey much more than is said. This assumption, put as the Cooperative Principle, is in essence the eminently reasonable claim that man is a social animal. As section 4 details, other scholars saw that this same assumption could help to resolve troubling puzzles in syntax, semantics, and discourse theory.

To give the reader some idea of the scope of the phenomena that implicature can be invoked to explain, the next section provides a variety of examples of the exploitation of various maxims to make implicatures.

2. EXPLOITING THE MAXIMS

Probably most of the implicatures we commonly make involve apparent violations of the maxim of Relation, that is, cases where the maxim 'Be relevant' looks like it has been disregarded, but where what is said is correctly understood only by assuming that what is apparently irrelevant is, in fact, relevant.[13] A typical example is the use of a question to respond to a question as in the example from *Casablanca* above, and in example (13).

13.

© 1984 United Feature Syndicate, Inc.

---

[13]Indeed, Sperber & Wilson (1982, 1986) have taken the maxim of Relation as central and attempted to show how the implicatures Grice derived from violations of the other maxims could be derived without them.

Here Garfield, widely known to love food above all else, responds to Arlene's question with an apparently irrelevant question. His question is one whose true answer is negative and obviously negative. Arlene realizes this, and apparently infers (as intended) that the relevance of that is that the true answer to her question is likewise obviously negative. Thus Garfield's question implicates not only "No," but also "as you ought to know." Novel rhetorical questions work as well as clichéd ones like this (and their positive counterparts like *Is the Pope Catholic?*). Garfield could have achieved the same effect with *Do alligators grow geraniums?*

But we are all also probably familiar with cases where implicatures are intended to arise from recognition that the maxim of Relation is being conspicuously disregarded. Someone may change the subject abruptly to indicate to the other conversant(s) that what was being said could put its speaker in an awkward situation (or worse), because the referent of uncomplimentary remarks has just walked into overhearing range, because the room might be bugged by spies or political opponents, or the like. It is usually safer, quicker, and more effective to implicate 'Don't say any more about that. What you said was a faux pas' (or: 'Don't say anymore about it. Doing so could endanger our plans') than to openly try to persuade the other conversant(s) of it.

In most cases where a speech acts appears not to conform with all of the maxims, the addressee is intended to assume that it is in conformity with all of them, and interpret it in that light. In cases of genuinely disregarding a maxim, however, the addressee is intended to infer that the speaker is not conforming to a maxim, and to figure out why. This generally induces an implicature which is a metalinguistic comment about the discourse. For example, the violation of Quantity I in (8) implicates 'What I am not saying is significant'; changing the subject abruptly (violating Relation) implicates, 'This subject is dangerous.' Such comments disrupt the discourse, and so appear not to further the goals of the discourse in progress, although if the speaker is assumed to be rational and cooperative, they will be taken as cooperative with respect to some broader, more global enterprise involving speaker and addressee, for example, maintaining appearances (for instance, that everyone is nice and good, that no one is inferior), or just keeping a private conversation from being overheard.

One can simultaneously openly violate Relation and the first maxim of Quality for effects similar to Garfield's above. In (14), B utters an obviously and outrageously false statement which has no apparent relation to A's remark.

14.   A: You know, I can crush rocks with my bare hands.
       B: Yeah, and I'm Marie of Rumania.
       [Or: Yeah, and the sun rises in the west.]

But if A assumes that B means to be conveying something not false that is relevant, B may be successful in implicating that A's assertion is equally false.

Grice cited understatement, hyperbole, and sarcasm as also being cases where Quality is apparently violated to implicate something true and relevant while avoiding "going on record" (for whatever reason). Thus, uttering *That was smart!* implicates 'That was stupid!' just in case the addressee can be expected to realize that the speaker believes that the literally expressed proposition is relevant, but doesn't believe it is true (Grice, 1975, p. 53; cf. also Sperber & Wilson, 1981, 1986). By treating it as relevant, despite obviously not being true, the speaker may implicate that someone apparently thinks that it is true, and therefore, that it is relevant and necessary to mention it, in order to draw the addressee's attention to its obvious falsity.

Purporting to blatantly violate the first maxim of Quantity (Say as much as is required . . .) is fairly commonplace as well, implicating, as in (15), that the speaker is unwilling to say more.

    15a. A: Where've you been?
            B: Out.
    15b. A: Where do you live?
            B: Somewhere.

If speaker B is not intending to be understood as unwilling to participate in the conversation altogether, she may intend the addressee to infer further that the contribution he sought is none of his business, or should not have been requested in public, or was rudely requested, or something of that nature. Equally commonplace are apparent violations which, like the example of the letter of recommendation cited earlier, implicate 'There is nothing more positive I can say.'[14] Other familiar examples include the evaluation *It was interesting* of a scholarly paper or an artistic performance.

Examples of the blatant violation of the second maxim of Quantity (Say no more than is necessary) are not so easy to find. It is common enough for a participant in a conversation to contribute much more detail than is relevant (usually simultaneously violating Relation and the Manner sub-maxim against prolixity) in order to show off his knowledge (the opposite of the Malagasy case), but since the violator does not ordinarily intend his intention to be recognized, this is not an example of implicature arising from flouting the second maxim of Quantity, but of boorishness.

However, it is not too hard to imagine a context (involving espionage and intrigue, say) where someone who is known to be a person of few words deliberately monopolizes the conversation, in order to keep a certain participant from talking (because that person might give the game away, say), with the intention that this ploy be recognized (and abetted) by other participants. This

---

[14]This gloss is ambiguous between 'nothing else positive' and 'nothing with greater positiveness.' Either suits my meaning.

would be a case of implicature arising from blatant violation because the speaker's talking "too much" would be intentional, and intended to be recognized as both intentional and significant.

As with all the other cases of blatantly flouting a maxim, when the maxim of Manner is flouted, the implicature is a metalinguistic comment about the discourse in progress. Thus conversants may be intentionally obscure, communicating in stylistically inappropriate polysyllables, even in a foreign language that neither of them knows well, in order to implicate 'What I am saying is not for the ears of those who may overhear us' (e.g., the children playing at our feet, the subordinate at the coffeepot over there, and so on).

Speakers are also intentionally prolix or obscure (sometimes the two co-occur) to implicate that a shorter, more direct manner of speaking would be inaccurate, as in example (16a), or inconsiderate, impolitic, or the like, as in (17a). All of the examples in (16–17) are from "Walter Scott's *Personality Parade*"; the examples in (16b) and (17b) addressing the same issues show that this feature is not uniformly obscure about certain topics, and support the hypothesis that the implicatures of (16a) and (17a) are intentional.

16a. Q: Now that he's hit the big time, is it true that Don Johnson of the "Miami Vice" TV show has dumped Patti D'Arbanville, the mother of his 3-year-old boy?

A: At this writing, Johnson and his longtime live-in are reportedly not as compatible as they once were. Johnson has been working and residing in Miami, while Patti has been holding down the fort and caring for their son, Jesse, in Los Angeles. (6Apr86)

16b. Q: How about the rumor that, after she gives birth to her second child in August, Princess Caroline of Monaco plans to drop her young husband for the Argentine tennis star Guillermo Vilas?

A: Caroline, 29, had a fling with Vilas in the South Pacific several years ago, before marrying Italian heir Stefano Casiraghi, but there's little or no chance she would dump Stefano. (6Apr86)

17a. Q: Is Don Regan, the White House chief of staff, a feudist? [. . .]

A: [. . .] Don Regan, 66, is not a feudist, but he is not as well liked as his predecessor, [James] Baker. Somehow, the adjective "ruthless" invariably arises when Regan is discussed. (8Dec85)

17b. Q: [. . .] Did Maria [Shriver] get that ["CBS Morning News"] job because she is a Kennedy family member?

A: Maria Shriver, 30, replaced Phyllis George on "The CBS Morning News" not because she happens to be a daughter of Eunice Kennedy and Sargent Shriver but because CBS executives believed her well-qualified for the job. A 1977 graduate of Georgetown University, Shriver worked at [. . .] (6Apr86)[15]

The injunction against ambiguity is often quietly ignored in the service of politics and politeness, as we saw in chapter 1. But it is also flouted, by every speaker who makes a (good) pun. In the example below, Bea's remark is only funny if the ambiguities of *racing* and *running* ('beating rapidly' versus 'good for racing,' and 'dripping' versus 'good for running') are recognized.

18.   Abe: You're in bed with a cold, and you're still planning to run in the marathon tomorrow?
        Bea: Why not? I've got a racing pulse and a running nose.

3. COHERENCE

One consequence of the Cooperative Principle, and of the relevance maxim in particular, that Grice never discussed, is that it provides the basis for a natural account of the problem of the coherence of texts, that is, of elucidating what it is that makes (19a) a plausible discourse, in contrast to (19b), which appears to be just a string of sentences related only by temporal or spatial order.[16]

19a.   The following days were unlike any that had gone before. There wasn't a man on the ranch who didn't know of Saturday's race and the conditions under which it would be run. They gave any excuses to get near the black stallion's corral.
        (Walter Farley, *The Black Stallion*, p. 199. (New York: Random House, 1953))
19b.   The sun climbed higher, and with its ascent the desert changed. There was nothing Lucy liked so much as the smell and feel of fur. One evening, after dark, she crept away and tried to open the first gate, but swing and tug as she might she could not budge the pin.[17]

---

[15]The observant reader will have noticed that the answers in these examples do not conform to the maxims the same way answers in face to face oral conversations do. Specifically, if these were personal, oral answers, they would be considered disorderly and overly informative. However, the apparent violation of the second maxim of Quantity is motivated by the fact that the real addressee is not the person who asked the question (whose initials and city I have left out), but the entire readership of *Parade* magazine, so journalistic values and assumptions regarding optimal discourse structure enter into the writer's notion of "required by the purpose of the talk exchange." See Green (1979) for further discussion of unique pragmatic features of journalistic prose.

[16]I use *discourse* to refer to either spoken or written language, and *text* to refer to any written language segment, whether transcribed from speech or not.

[17]These sentences are from Walter Farley's *The Black Stallion Revolts* (New York: Random House, 1953), C. S. Lewis's *The Lion, the Witch, and the Wardrobe* (New York: MacMillan, 1950),

Some theorists (e.g., Halliday & Hasan, 1976) have claimed that what makes a sequence of sentences hang together to be a text that is more than just a sequence of sentences is LINGUISTIC properties of those sentences: whether they exhibit (a) anaphoric expressions which (could be taken to) refer to (the same entities, properties, and so forth as) previous expressions, and (b) whether the same or related[18] lexical items appear across sentences in the text. The reader can see, however, that as far as such linguistic properties go, (19a) and (19b) do not differ significantly. The sentences are structurally similar, pairwise across examples. The third sentence in each contains a pronominal subject whose intended referent is plausibly indicated or evoked by a phrase in the second sentence. In both texts, the lexical items in each individual sentence have nothing inherently to do with the lexical items in any other sentence. And in both, there is no cohesive linguistic link between the first and the second sentence at all. In any case, Halliday & Hasan insisted that the linguistic properties of a text (termed by them *cohesion*) that contribute to coherence are not a function of the reference of the words in the text, but of the forms themselves and their histories of occurrence. It is difficult to see how a theory like this could account for the striking difference between (19a) and (19b).

There are also theories (e.g., Prince, 1973; Rumelhart, 1975; van Dijk, 1972, 1977) which treat the coherence of text as reflecting a (defining) property comparable to grammaticality for sentences, which all genuine texts have, but random collections of sentences don't have. Morgan & Sellner (1980) and Morgan (1981) critique these theories in some detail.

A more promising approach to what connects individual sentences in a genuine text but not a spurious one is based on the assumption that the sequence of sentences at issue is produced by an individual in accordance with the Cooperative Principle, and that as a consequence, each sentence is intended to say something necessary, true, and relevant to accomplishing some objective in which the text-producer and the intended audience mutually believe there is interest. A coherent text is one where the interpreter can readily reconstruct the speaker's plan with reasonable certainty, by inferring the relations among the sentences, and their individual relations to the various subgoals in the inferred plan for an enterprise understood to be at hand.

With this in mind, let us examine (19a) and (19b) once more. The first sentence of (19a) tells us that certain days were unique. We expect subsequent sentences to tell us what was unique about them, or perhaps, what that uniqueness led to, and we are not disappointed. The second sentence tells us that there was universal interest in a race, and we infer that this is what is extraordinary. We take the

---

and Mary Norton's *The Borrowers* (New York: Harcourt, Brace and World, 1952), respectively. They were chosen to match the excerpt in (19a) for syntax, anaphora, and introduction of noun phrases with definite articles.

[18]It is not clear what criterion of relatedness Halliday & Hasan had in mind, but from their examples, it seems to be topical rather than formal, despite being described by them as formal.

days to be days experienced by men on a ranch anticipating a race which will take place under unusual conditions on the next Saturday. We take the *they* in the third sentence to refer to the men, and take the sentence as a whole to be intended to provide an additional example of what was unique about the days mentioned in the first sentence. Finally, we infer from the reference to a black stallion that the race is a horse race and not, say, a road race or a drag race.

In (19b), on the other hand, the first sentence describes a desert sunrise. We expect the next sentence to elaborate on that description, or maybe to begin a narration of an event in the desert, or perhaps to state a cause or an effect of the conditions of this particular sunrise. From the descriptive *there*-construction (cf. Milsark, 1977), a guess that the second sentence is an elaboration seems to be the best bet, but it is hard to imagine how a cooperative writer could expect us to infer what Lucy's attraction to fur has to do with a desert sunrise. Maybe (although this is pushing it) Lucy regrets the sunrise, because after sunrise, fur-bearing desert animals will disappear into burrows to keep cool, so maybe a narration will ensue. This inference allows us to infer that the third sentence refers to Lucy's attempt to go out at night in an effort to find some furry animals, but whether it is taken as the beginning of a narrative, or as an exemplification of Lucy's love of fur, I still cannot think of a rational way to connect the third sentence with the first one. Since (19b) is composed of sentences from three different books (cf. footnote 17), it is not surprising that they seem to have nothing to do with each other.

Coherence, in this approach, depends not on properties of the text components themselves, either individually or in relation to each other, but on the extent to which effort is required to construct a reasonable plan to attribute to the text-producer in producing the text. This in turn depends on how hard or easy it is to take each sentence as representing a true, necessary, and relevant contribution to that plan.

Examination of one more example may prove instructive. In example (20), the first paragraph of a bona fide text by a professional writer, the nature of the connection between the first and the second sentence is not immediately obvious.

20. One afternoon last fall I found myself unable to leave my car when I arrived at the grocery store. On "All Things Considered" there was an excerpt from a series called "Breakdown and Back," the story of a mental breakdown as experienced by one woman, Annie.
(Jeanie Cheeseman, "Breakdown and back." *Patterns* (WILL AM, FM and TV programming guide) Feb. 1986, p. [4]. (Urbana, Illinois, 1986))

The writer of this paragraph has taken it for granted that the reader will recognize "All Things Considered" as the name of a radio program and understand that the writer was listening to it over a radio. Still, that is not enough to understand what the two sentences have to do with each other.

Asked about this paragraph, some respondents assume that the relation is just that of contemporaneousness of events, and that the two sentences together set the stage for a narration of what happened to the writer in the car. Others agree that the second sentence is relevant to the first in that it represents the proximate cause of the writer's inability to get out of the car, but vary widely in their interpretations of the ultimate cause. Some infer that the writer was paralyzed by the recall of a breakdown she herself experienced, some infer (correctly, as is clear from subsequent paragraphs) that the excerpts were so fascinating that the writer did not want to miss the rest (by moving out of the range of the radio's speaker). Others might infer that the writer was afraid to hear the rest of the program in the grocery store, and no doubt there are still other plausible reasons one might infer.

In any case, the variation in understanding provoked by examples like this provides strong evidence that the coherence of text is not a matter of properties exclusively of the text, but of the likelihood that the text's audience will be able to make whatever inferences are necessary to relate the content of the individual sentences to each other in such a way that they support the inference of an orderly execution of an inferred plan to achieve an inferred objective.

It is a mistake, however, to think that since easily inferable connections among sentences contribute to making a text coherent, then increasing the number of explicit connections will make any text better and easier to understand correctly. For example, understanding the passage in (21) requires a certain amount of inferencing.

21. Suddenly Mrs. Reilly remembered the horrible night that she and Mr. Reilly had gone to the Prytania to see Clark Gable and Jean Harlow in *Red Dust*. In the heat and confusion that had followed their return home, nice Mr. Reilly had tried one of his indirect approaches, and Ignatius was conceived. Poor Mr. Reilly. He had never gone to another movie as long as he lived.
     (John Kennedy Toole, *A Confederacy of Dunces*, p. 103. (New York: Grove Press, 1982))

We have to infer what was horrible about the night. What, if anything, did Ignatius' being conceived have to do with the horribleness? What did it have to do with Mr. Reilly approaching something? Who or what did he approach? Why should we feel sorry for Mr. Reilly? Why didn't he ever go to another movie? I doubt that the average adult reader has difficulty understanding this paragraph in its context, but suppose we spell out some of these inferences, as in (22).

22. Suddenly Mrs. Reilly remembered the horrible night that she and Mr. Reilly had gone to the Prytania to see Clark Gable and Jean Harlow in *Red Dust*. It was horrible because it resulted in Ignatius being conceived. It happened like this. They had gone home after the show. Mr. Reilly

wanted to have intercourse with Mrs. Reilly. This had caused heat and confusion. In the heat and confusion that had followed their return home, nice Mr. Reilly had tried one of his indirect approaches to her. He succeeded, and Ignatius was conceived. Poor Mr. Reilly. He so regretted conceiving Ignatius that he was afraid to go to the movies again because he feared that if he went to the movies he might get carried away by passion. He feared that if he got carried away by passion, he might father another child and suffer as he did with Ignatius. Consequently he had never gone to another movie as long as he lived.

The paragraph in (22) is more explicit than (21), but it does not seem to be any easier to understand, and it certainly is not better writing. In fact, in spelling out the relations among the propositions entailed and asserted by the sentences in (21), (22) raises other questions. If the writer is abiding by the Cooperative Principle, then everything he says should be relevant to the goal of the discourse and necessary for its achievement. Therefore everything he says must be noteworthy. Is it noteworthy that the Reillys had gone home after the show? Should they have been expected to go elsewhere? Noteworthy that Mr. Reilly succeeded in achieving intercourse? Didn't he usually? Noteworthy that Ignatius' existence was regrettable? The author has provided ample evidence that Ignatius is an extremely unpleasant person in the previous 90 pages. Should it be reinterpreted in light of the fact that he finds it necessary to inform us of this now? Are the details of Mr. Reilly's logic so unlikely that they need to be spelled out in such detail? Or does the author think that we readers are so dim-witted that we would not be able to figure out why Mr. Reilly would attribute the conception of Ignatius to viewing a romantic movie?

Far from making the passage more coherent, spelling out the connections that we have to make in order to account for why the author of the original appears to have left things out distracts our attention from the author's point and directs it toward tangential issues, even toward ourselves and his opinion of us. If a reader makes even one of these inferences, the passage is thereby less coherent and more difficult to appreciate properly than it would have been without the unnecessary explicit connections.

This points up again the degree to which coherence is a function not of the properties of the text, but rather of the text-producer's estimate of his audience's beliefs and inferencing capacity, and of his acting appropriately on that estimate.[19]

---

[19]This is not a new observation, though perhaps it is a long-forgotten one. The following passage, written over a hundred years ago, presages in its reference to "common sense and good faith" Grice's Cooperative Principle, and in references to the interpreter's knowledge and to usual customs, the notion of normal belief.

Suppose a housekeeper says to a domestic: "fetch me some soupmeat," accompanying the act with giving some money to the latter; he will be unable to execute the order without interpretation, however easy and, consequently rapid the performance of the process may be.

4. PRAGMATIC ALTERNATIVES TO SYNTACTIC AND SEMANTIC ACCOUNTS OF SOME PHENOMENA

As Morgan (1975b) pointed out, the possibility of accounting for meaning properties and syntactic distributions of uses of linguistic expressions in terms of conversational inferences rather than semantic entailments or grammatical rules was welcomed by many linguists as a means of avoiding redundant analyses on the one hand, and analyses which entail rampant ambiguity on the other. The program of resolving syntactic and semantic puzzles via implicature was not without its own problems, but it will be worthwhile to examine some of those puzzles, and the contribution which implicature makes to their solution.

4.1 Indirect Speech Acts

Investigation of the performative hypothesis brought the attention of linguists (e.g., Sadock, 1970, 1972) to a class of utterances whose syntactic form did not match their apparent illocutionary force. These INDIRECT SPEECH ACTS, illustrated in (23), posed a problem for the performative hypothesis.

23a. Will you please pass the salad. = Please pass the salad.
       [Question form, imperative force]
23b. Why don't you pass the salad. = Pass the salad.
       [Question form, imperative force]
23c. I'd like you to set the table now. = Set the table now.
       [Declarative form, imperative force]
23d. Is that good! = That is good!
       [Question form, declarative force]

Common sense and good faith tell the domestic, that the housekeeper's meaning was this: 1. He should go immediately, or as soon as his other occupations are finished; or, if he be directed to do so in the evening, that he should go next day at the *usual* hour; 2. that the money handed him by the housekeeper is intended to pay for the meat thus ordered, and not as a present to him; 3. that he should buy such meat and of such part of the animal, as, to his knowledge, has commonly been used in the house he stays at, for making soups; 4. that he buy the best meat he can obtain, for a fair price; 5. that he go to that butcher who usually provides the family, with whom the domestic resides, with meat, or to some convenient stall, and not to any unnecessarily distant place; 6. that he return the rest of the money; 7. that he bring home the meat in good faith, neither adding anything disagreeable nor injurious; 8. that he fetch the meat for the use of the family and not for himself. Suppose, on the other hand, the housekeeper, afraid of being misunderstood, had mentioned these eight specifications, she would not have obtained her object, if it were to exclude all *possibility* of misunderstanding. For, the various specifications would have required new ones. Where would be the end? We are constrained then, always, to leave a considerable part of our meaning to be found out by interpretation, which, in many cases must necessarily cause greater or less obscurity with regard to the exact meaning, which our words were intended to convey. (Lieber, 1880, pp. 17–19)

Adherents of the performative hypothesis maintained (a) that illocutionary force was uniformly represented in (underlying) syntactic structure, and (b) that surface form was related in a regular way to illocutionary force. Faced with phenomena like those in (23), they attempted to construct syntactic analyses of these constructions that would be consistent with the performative hypothesis, but found themselves with baroque analyses that had little in the way of syntactic support (Sadock, 1970; Heringer, 1972). Sadock (1972) and Searle (1975b) thus proposed that sentences like those in (23) represented speech act idioms, forms whose illocutionary force was arbitrarily connected to their syntactic form; in this analysis, utterances of the form *Can/Could/Would/Will/Won't you* VERB PHRASE and *Why don't you* VERB PHRASE have the force of the corresponding imperative-form (verb phrase) utterances, simply by convention.

Gordon and Lakoff (1975), on the other hand, proposed to account for the imperative senses of these question forms as implicatures arising from the fact that the question forms (interpreted as questions) suggest that one or another of the various sincerity conditions involving the addressee of a request is not met. (As Searle (1969) had shown, the maker of a sincere request assumes that the addressee is able to perform the requested act, would be willing to do so if asked, and has no standing plans to do it.) Thus, asking if the addressee can do something implies a belief that he might not be able to, and asking why he does not do something implies a belief that he intends not to do it. Similarly, they treated cases like (23c) as an implicature arising from the assertion of a sincerity condition involving the speaker—the maker of a sincere request wants the requested act performed. Gordon and Lakoff's analysis accounts not only for the fact that (23a–23c) have the illocutionary force of imperatives, but also for the fact that (24a) and (24b) can be understood as (or, in their terms, entail) requests to close a window (Gordon & Lakoff, 1975, pp. 84, 86).

24a. It's cold in here.
24b. I assume you can close the window.

This generality, however, is a weakness as well as a strength of the analysis, for it is unable to distinguish between indirect speech acts that seem at worst ambiguous, like those of (23), and ones whose purposes, being inexplicit, are unclear, as in (24a) and (25).

25. I left my watch at home.

A sentence like (24a) may be understood as hinting at a request to open a window, close a window, turn up the heat, find the speaker a sweater—generally, to do whatever would make the speaker more comfortable if she is assumed, because of the utterance of (24a), to be uncomfortable; (25) could be an excuse for being late (or early), or a request for the time, for a watch, for the location of a clock, for notification of the time at some future point, and so forth. Furthermore, forms like (23a, 23c) convey requests much more directly (in English, anyway) than forms like (24) or (25), and curiously, there seems to be much more cross-linguistic agreement about the potential for sentences like (24a) and (25) to be used as hints than there is about the directness with which sentences like (23a, 23c) convey requests (Green, 1975).

Finally, in order to account for the fact that question forms with certain stigmata such as preverbal *please* (as in (23a)) are always understood as requests, Gordon and Lakoff were forced to introduce a novel kind of grammatical rule, one which was conditioned by utterance context. (Cf. Green, 1975, and Morgan, 1977, for more detailed discussion of these and other issues, and Clark, 1979, for demonstration of the psychological reality of distinctions of the sort made here.)

The situation with indirect speech acts typifies the problems that Morgan (1975b) outlined: A purely syntactic analysis neutralizes pragmatically relevant semantic distinctions (like the difference between declarative and interrogative clauses), but distinct syntactic properties of forms that appear to be semantically equivalent complicate a purely pragmatic analysis. Morgan (1978) attempts to cut through this Gordian knot by demonstrating that linguistic expression is governed by two different kinds of convention: (a) conventions of language, like language-specific rules for constituent order in syntax, and meaning postulates for words and idioms, and (b) conventions of use, such as culture-specific rules for the use of expressions for answering the phone, or for the use of forms like *God bless you*, or, according to Morgan, for the use of forms like (23), which in his analysis SHORT-CIRCUIT an implicature. A short-circuited implicature is a kind of conversational implicature. As with other conversational implicatures, what is intended to be conveyed is readily derivable from the assumption that it was uttered in conformity with the Cooperative Principle and the maxims. However, because of known conventions of usage (including even known idiosyncratic habits of the speaker), the intended effect can be recognized immediately, although it can also still be calculated.

Morgan's (1978) description of short-circuited implicature involved the elaboration and subsequent reduction over time of means–ends chains of the sort schematized in (26).

26a. In situation X, one does Y.
26b. In situation X, one does Y by indicating Z, which one does by expressing A, by saying, "P."
26c. In situation X, one does Y by saying "P."
26d. In situation X, one says "P."

Assuming that the means in (26) are implicatures, (26c) represents a short-circuiting of the implicature represented in (26b), while (26d) is an arbitrary convention of use. The fact that *dog* is an English word while *dgo* is not, and the fact that yes–no questions begin with an auxiliary verb in English are conventions of English; the fact that Americans answer the phone by saying *Hello* or by identifying themselves by saying the name of some unit they represent, like *Cognitive Science Program*, and the fact that we regularly use forms like (23a–23c) to implicate requests are conventions of the use of English.

4.2 Illocutionary Force

One effect of linguists being introduced to Austin's ideas and the performative hypothesis was to focus attention on performative verbs and on classification into their various kinds. In many quarters there was an identification of the general notion 'speech act,' with 'illocutionary act'[20] (or even with 'illocutionary force'), and one wondered whether there were as many distinct illocutionary forces as there were distinct performative verbs. After all, an utterance like (5a) in chapter 4 (repeated here as (27a)) can have the force of a promise or a prediction, and an utterance like (27b) seems to have a different force when it is understood as intended to remind the addressee than it has when understood as intended to straightforwardly inform the addressee; the TAG *you know* can only follow the reminder.[21]

27a. I'll sit in the front row.
27b. You have an appointment with Dean Brown at 3:00.

Does the performative hypothesis imply that these two uses have distinct illocutionary forces and distinct underlying forms?

In a paper that seems to have been about 10 years ahead of its time, Stampe (1975) argued against the conventionalism of the Searle–Austin performative hypothesis on the grounds that it was not by virtue of any rules, linguistic or otherwise, or Illocutionary-Force-Indicating Devices, overt or abstract, that promises, for example, were promises, and when uttered sincerely, required or entailed an intention on the part of the speaker to act accordingly. Rather, Stampe argued, it is the speaker's intending an utterance as a promise, reminder, suggestion, or request that makes it one; whether it will be so understood depends on the addressee's ability to infer that it was so intended. Sometimes parenthetical tags like *you know, why don't you*, and *please* will be present and provide a sufficient clue to the speaker's intention; overt main clauses of the sort Austin called

---

[20]To my mind, the identification is mistaken. Searle took 'speech act' to include a variety of acts accomplished with language, including uttering, referring, and predicating. I would include also implicating, reciting, imitating, and other such complex acts.

[21]Naturally, a speaker can use *you know* with a sentence intended to inform, *implicating* that the sentence is a reminder rather than new information. A speaker might do this in order to appear not to know more than his addressee. See chapter 7 for a discussion of the values and assumptions involved in this sort of choice.

performative, in Stampe's view, reflect metalinguistic comments about the discourse, in which the speaker asserts the intended force of the utterance (1975, p. 29)[22] so the addressee can make no mistake. But in many cases, the addressee will have only her estimate of the speaker's goals and plans to base her inference of the intended illocutionary force on. In this view (suggested also in Morgan, 1976, and formalized in Cohen & Levesque, 1990), the number of potential illocutionary forces is not limited (to around four) by the number of basic sentence types, or (to a couple of thousand) by the number of verbs in a language that can be used "performatively," but only by the number of different kinds of intentions which a speaker might have (in saying what she says) and which an addressee assuming that the speaker is abiding by the Cooperative Principle could be intended and expected, given the utterance in its context, to infer that the speaker has. Probably there are an infinite number of such intentions. Thus, in this view, there are illocutionary forces for which we do not have conventional names, such as those intended in utterances like those in (28), suggested by Larkin and O'Malley (1973).

28a. Gotcha! [said as Speaker tags Addressee]
28b. Hello?/Cognitive Science. [picking up the receiver of a ringing telephone]
28c. You put the shirt with the check in it in the washing machine?!
28d. She's your mother, not mine.
28e. Hey, you reached over the net!
28f. Well, that's done. [to co-worker, finishing a difficult task]

Another set of data which support the claim that illocutionary force is conveyed as an inference the addressee is expected to make from the utterance of a form with some ostensible literal meaning and the mutually assumed context in which it is uttered is to be found in the analysis of forms like those in (29), which were described by Yanofsky (1978, 1980) as NOUN PHRASE UTTERANCES.

29a. Police!
29b. Lunchtime!
29c. The laundry!
29d. My car!

While what is intended to be conveyed by the utterance of just a noun phrase is generally clear in context, in principle there is no limit to what a speaker could reasonably expect one of them to convey. Thus, in different contexts (29c) might successfully convey what any of the more explicit expressions in (30) could be depended on to convey.

---

[22]And so, contra Austin, have a truth value.

30a. That thunderstorm is wetting my laundry that's hanging out to dry!
30b. I/You have to pick up the laundry before the cleaner closes in 15 minutes!
30c. I/You have to remember to do the laundry today.
30d. I forgot to do the laundry!
30e. What have you done to the laundry!?
30f. We can't have the leading lady exit with her arms folded; that will leave the laundry onstage, and it will seem very strange when Sir Richard comes on stage and doesn't say anything about it.

Under the performative hypothesis, utterances like (29), if they have any illocutionary force at all, have an indefinitely large number of them. The pragmatic alternative is to say that the noun phrase utterance merely MENTIONS its referent. The noun phrase itself has no inherent illocutionary force, but as long as the hearer assumes that the speaker is behaving rationally, uttering a noun phrase will implicate that its referent is relevant to the speaker's and/or addressee's goals (whether or not these goals correspond to goals of the ongoing conversation). Unless the speaker has misjudged the addressee, the addressee will be able to infer how merely mentioning the referent of the noun phrase is relevant in the context.

Similarly, one could argue (along the lines of Clark, 1993) that the fact that a certain syntactic form represents an imperative is merely an inference derived from the mention of a kind of action.[23] The fact that utterances consisting of tenseless verb phrases are just as ambiguous or vague as (27a) or (27b) would follow as a consequence of such an analysis. Thus (31) could be a directive[24] to give Eks the keys to the city, but it could also be an expression of disgust at the

---

[23]It is also, of course, vague or ambiguous as to what kind of directive it might be, it could be a command, a demand, a plea, a request, a suggestion, etc. Cf. Green (1975) for some discussion of these different types.

[24]Similarly both (i) and (ii) could be used to indicate glee, or disgust.

   i. give Eks the key to the city
   ii. giving Eks the key to the city

The fact that (i) is more readily understood as a directive than (ii) would have to be taken as a reflection of the fact that its implicature is regularly short-circuited, and it is understood directly, like *Can you please pass the salt.*

The validity of such an analysis, however, depends on the existence of cases where (ii) is clearly used to implicate a directive. While (iii) might provide such a context, since both (i) and (ii) would be acceptable and essentially equivalent responses, uses of forms like (ii) as directives are limited to cases where -*ing* phrases are licensed as subject or object of a salient expression in the immediately preceding context, and this diminishes the significance of their interchangeability with forms like (i) in contexts like (iii).

   iii. What do you think would induce Eks to locate his factory here?

Thus (ii) is not nearly so good an answer to (iv) as it is to (iii), and this suggests that it represents a reduced sentence, rather than the mere mention of an action (cf. Morgan, 1973c).

   iv. How can we get Eks to locate his factory here?

absurdity of the suggestion that someone give Eks the keys to the city, or dismay or astonishment or glee that plans are in effect to do that, and so on.

31.   Give Eks the keys to the city.

Which one of these will be inferred would depend on what the speaker and addressee mutually assume about plans to bestow the city keys, and what they mutually believe about the speaker's attitudes toward Eks, among other things (cf. also Cohen & Levesque, 1990), although there may be use conventions which favor imperative interpretations for verb-phrase utterances, interrogative interpretations for inverted sentence constructions, and so forth.

A genuinely explanatory account of illocutionary force will place the analysis of speech acts within a more general theory of action, treating so-called speech acts as acts which like any other are intentionally undertaken with the belief that their performance is necessary for the achievement of some desired goal.[25] Thus, an act of uttering a sentence has an expositive force when a speaker S does it with the intention that addressee A recognize S's intention that A believe that S believes its content. Promises are made with the intention that A recognize S's intention that A believe that S will be responsible for the realization (i.e., factualization) of their content. Interrogatives are uttered with the belief that A will recognize S's intention that A provide information which S indicates. The set of possible goals of an act of uttering a sentence also includes the essentially unlimited class of possible perlocutionary effects that an utterance might be intended to have. So, reminders are expositives uttered with the intention that A will recognize that S believes A has believed what S wants A to believe. Warnings are utterances the uttering of which is intended to be recognized as intended to inform A that some imminent or contingent state of affairs will be bad for A. An insult is made with the intention that A recognize S's intent to represent A as having properties normally believed to be bad. It is crucially important that for inferring a speaker's goal, the particular form of an utterance is only significant in connection with the act of uttering it. An utterance is a warning just in case S intends A to recognize THE UTTERING OF IT as intended to cause A to recognize that some situation may result in a state which A would consider bad.

For some early results along the lines suggested here, see Cohen and Perrault, 1979; Cohen and Levesque, 1980, 1985; Perrault and Allen, 1980.

4.3 Presupposition

The question of whether presupposition is pragmatic or semantic in nature seems no longer to be a live one. There seems to be agreement on the one hand, that

---

[25]Cf. Sorenson (1990) for discussion of some consequences of the process/product ambiguity of *speech act*.

by convention, all other things being equal, the use of certain expressions of a language implies a state of knowledge or justified true belief on the part of the utterer concerning the propositional complements of certain predicates or the referents of noun phrases that are introduced by certain articles.[26]

On the other hand, because sentences are instruments used intentionally by agents in the context of the execution of particular plans relative to particular addressees presumed to have particular beliefs and attitudes, all other things are not equal, and there is general agreement that there is a conditional, pragmatic, conversational, discourse structural aspect to what has been described as presupposition also. Thus, Gazdar (1979, pp. 129–135) articulated a means by which potential presuppositions of a sentence (his "pre-suppositions") are projected as actual presuppositions of an utterance of that sentence only if they are consistent with entailments of the sentence and implicatures of its utterance in its context. Similarly, McCawley (1978a, 1978b) showed how supposed presuppositions of particular lexical items are better analyzed as involving implicatures from the maxim of quantity, and Horn (1978, 1984a) elaborated on this theme more generally.

On another front, a pragmatic approach offers an account of what is going on in negative sentences which deny propositions they allegedly presuppose, like (32).

32a.   The king of France isn't bald; there is no king of France.
32b.   John doesn't regret failing the exam, because in fact he passed.

The fact that such sentences are acceptable, interpretable, and not nonsensical had plagued adherents of semantic presupposition, but Horn (1984b, 1985, 1989; Horn & Bayer, 1984) accounts for the negation in (32) as not linguistic negation, which denies a proposition, but as a METALINGUISTIC device, which denies the appropriateness of the way something was said. Horn showed that metalinguistic negation can be used to register objection to an utterance on any grounds whatever, including the way it was pronounced, as in (33c).

33a.   I'm not his daughter; he's my father.
33b.   I don't like coffee; I love it.
33c.   I didn't [míyəni̵j] to read it; I [mǽni̵jd] to read it.

Finally, to take one last example of work elucidating the pragmatic nature of the presuppositions of utterances, Horn (1986) demonstrated that the discourse

---

[26]Thus Karttunen and Peters (1979) identified epistemic factive, counterfactual, and focus factive presuppositions (e.g., *too/either* (cf. Green, 1973; Karttunen, 1973), *also, even, only* (cf. Horn, 1972), clefts and pseudo-clefts) with Grice's conventional implicatures, and proposed apparatus, including projection principles, for incorporating them into the framework of Montague semantics. Similarly, Gazdar (1979, p. 124) codified them as pre-suppositions, propositions associated by convention with particular lexical items.

role of the content of an expression affects whether or not presuppositions are associated with that expression in a given utterance. He presents an account of why definite noun phrases are more likely to convey a presupposition of the existence of their referent when in subject position, as the contrast in (34) shows, and why the complements of factive verbs are more likely to be interpreted as presupposed true when in subject position, as in (35), than when extraposed to the end of the sentence or in object position, as in (36).

34a.   But for the grace of God, the first king of the U.S.A. would have been Nixon.

34b.   But for the grace of God, Nixon would have been the first king of the U.S.A.

35a.   That Kim is a vegetarian is obvious.

35b.   That her guests are vegetarians may be worrying her.

35c.   That Pat was involved hasn't yet been discovered by Lee.

36a.   It's obvious that Kim is a vegetarian.

36b.   She may be worrying that her guests are vegetarians.

36c.   Lee hasn't yet discovered that Pat was involved.

The relevant factor, Horn showed, is not actually subject position, but whether or not the clause or phrase in sentence-initial position represents what the sentence is about (i.e., represents the theme, or topic, of the sentence); when the initial phrase or subordinate clause is not a topic, then it is not necessarily presupposed, as in (37).

37a.   The king of France does not exist.[27]

37b.   ??That apartheid is doomed, Ed was muttering.[28]

Since sentence topics are typically material familiar to both speaker and addressee, and preferentially either salient or presupposed, sentence interpreters will tend to

---

[27]The following passage provides a contextualized example of the same phenomenon, a nontopic definite noun phrase (italicized) failing to presuppose the existence of a referent. The narrator is a female detective investigating the death of her cousin Boom-Boom, a hockey player for the Chicago Blackhawks. The passage describes her contemplation of a calendar she has found in his desk, with certain dates circled each month.

I ... stared fixedly at the dates circled in the front of the book. I keep track of my period by circling the dates when I get it in my desk calendar, but that wouldn't be true in my cousin's case. I grinned to myself, picturing Boom-Boom's reaction if I'd suggested that to him.

The dates might not track *Boom-Boom's menstrual cycle*, but maybe they indicated some other periodic occurrence.

(Sara Paretsky, *Deadlock*, p. 97. (New York: Ballantine Books, 1984))

[28]Sentence (37b) is odd because the clausal complement of a manner-of-speaking verb like *mutter, whisper, shout*, etc. is always predicated, and thus is always the point or focus (or comment) of a sentence, never the topic or theme.

take initial subjects (and other initial phrases, as in (37b)—cf. chap. 6) as presupposed if they can be interpreted as representing sentence topics. Some early psychological studies suggesting this are reported in Clark and Haviland (1977).

4.4 Reference, Compositionality, and Metaphor

It was claimed in chapter 3 that most ordinary predicative expressions (e.g., nouns, verbs, adjectives, prepositions) exhibit an extensive multiplicity of uses, or intended senses, and the question was posed, how do language users ever figure out what is being referred to by the use of such expressions? As mentioned in that chapter, the problem of reference is to determine which of the vast number of referring functions is to be used to identify the speaker's intended referent from the referring expression she used on some occasion of utterance. This section demonstrates that inferences which depend on the Cooperative Principle and the maxims (mostly Quality and Relation) are instrumental in making this determination. A natural conclusion from this is that metaphorical uses of language are basically just more extreme examples of the same phenomenon (cf. Rumelhart, 1979; Nunberg, 1978b).

Reference

How does a hearer tell which of the several normal uses of a referring expression a speaker intended? And how does he get from an intended use to an intended referent? To answer these questions, we must assume that the hearer (H) assumes that the speaker (S) is acting according to the Cooperative Principle. If he fails to make this assumption, he must assume that the connections between what S says and what she means are arbitrary, and not rationally inferable—rather like the child who believes he has the right to call a marking pen with permanent ink a *pregnant marker* if he chooses.

Let us take a relatively simple case first. Suppose that faced with the task of interpreting (38), H assumes that utterance of it respects the Cooperative Principle.

38.   Sandy bought IBM at 71.

Now, what can H infer about what S meant by *IBM*? H must assume that S assumes that the initials *IBM* abbreviate the same thing he assumes they abbreviate. It might be International Business Machines, or it might be Indiana Building Materials, or Idaho Bulk Minerals, and so on. This is essentially the same problem as guessing or inferring which Sandy that H might know is intended by S's utterance of *Sandy*, or what a gesture indicates (recall the problem posed in the introduction to chap. 2). H must also identify what referring function for *IBM* S assumes H will assume S assumes (etc.): 'corporation called x,' 'share of stock in corporation called x,' 'goods produced by corporation called x,' and so on. In addition, H must infer what the number 71 refers to. Probably a quantity, but a quantity of what: dollars? thousands or millions of dollars? percentage points (as in *They got their mortgage at 8 1/2*)? years of age (as in *At 46, Phil Niekro is the oldest active player*)? home runs (as in *Roger Maris got in the record books at 61*)? Importantly, while H must come to conclusions on all of these issues, there is no factor determining a priori which one must be resolved first, and in some cases the resolution may need to be simultaneous. Let us look in more detail at how this might work.

Given the assumption that the utterance respects the Cooperative Principle, and the fact that S has chosen to use the cryptic/vague/ambiguous referring expression *IBM*, H infers that the explicit expression those initials are supposed to invoke is assumed by S to be salient enough for S to say that little. In other words, H utilizes the belief that S is saying as much as is necessary (abiding by the maxim of Relation and the first maxim of Quantity) to infer that the most likely explicit expression is the intended one. If H has no reason to believe S is concerned with Indiana Building Materials or Idaho Bulk Minerals (or to believe that S believes that H is so concerned), H will be rational in assuming that *IBM* refers to the corporation that makes computers and other office machines. (Otherwise, of course, S's utterance may be functionally ambiguous, and H will want to seek clarification if he realizes this, and may be misled if he does not.)

Suppose S meant International Business Machines, and H took her to mean this. What is S claiming Sandy bought? Suppose further that S and H mutually know that Sandy wants to take control of the IBM corporation, and that this is a matter that is on their minds. Considerations of relevance and quantity (or avoiding ambiguity) similar to those cited above will make such referring functions as 'goods produced by' and 'a spokesman for' less likely candidates. But does S mean that Sandy bought shares of stock in IBM for $71 a share, or that Sandy bought the whole corporation for $71 billion (overbidding Lee by, say, $2 billion)? How could H narrow down the choices to just these? If H knows that both Sandy and IBM are under 71 years of age, and can safely assume that S knows this and knows that H knows it, and H assumes further that S is acting according to the maxim of Quality, and telling the truth, H can assume that *at 71* is not a temporal phrase locating the event in time by referring to the age at the time of the purchase of the purchaser or the purchasee. H may infer then that *at 71* refers to the compensation necessary to effect the transfer of ownership that *bought* entails. Because H takes it for granted (and takes it for granted that S believes H takes it for granted) that the usual sort of compensation is monetary, he can infer from the fact that S didn't specify 71 of what that *71* represents some sum of money; if S had meant percentage points, or years of servitude, or home run obligations or possessions, she would have said so under the circumstances if she was acting rationally and according to the maxim of Quantity, and so saying as much as was necessary to communicate what she wanted to communicate. Thus, the use of a minimally specified expression implicates that the action was effected by the means assumed most likely. If some other form of payment than money was involved, it would have been relevant to say so; if S was acting according to the Cooperative Principle and the maxim of relevance, she would have said so. Since she did not specify the form of payment, it must be what H would (be expected to) take as normal: money.

Now, shares of stock for $71 per share, or a whole corporation for $71 billion? (H can assume it was $71 per share and not $71,000 or more, and $71 billion and not $71,000 or less for reasons similar to those adduced in inferring that the consideration was monetary; H assumes that shares of stock are not normally assumed to sell for more than $1,000 per share, or huge corporations for less than 100 million dollars.) In addition to knowledge that H may have about Sandy's financial resources, S's using the preposition *at* rather than *for* in this discussion of a purchase provides a clue. Because the price per share of regularly traded stocks fluctuates in a regulated and regularly charted way, it is conventional to use the preposition *at* in naming the price per share. Strictly speaking, a sentence like (39) must mean that the subject bought 31 shares of stock when it was at $71 per share. Sentence (39) merely implicates that Lee bought the stock for $71 per share—with a shady broker, he might have actually paid more or less than that.

39. Lee bought 31 shares of IBM at 71.

Since referring to the sale of a corporation as if it had a price that fluctuated publicly in response to pressures other than what the owners decided to ask or demand would provoke implicatures that this was indeed the case, in the absence of any independent evidence that it was a corporation that Sandy would be purchasing (and not stock in one), or that the price of the corporation did indeed fluctuate publicly, H can assume that it was stock that S is saying Sandy bought.

Again, H cannot reach this conclusion without assuming that what S says is all relevant, true, and necessary to inferring what S means to convey. The mental processes involved in interpreting an ordinary utterance like this are not necessarily exclusively inferential ones; obviously inference is not the only mechanism involved in understanding what must have been meant by an utterance of an ordinary sentence like (38). Salience and attention, and assumptions about them, are intrinsic to the process as well, as described above. Nonetheless, the interpretation process is governed, limited, and especially, made tractable, by the assumption that the making of utterances respects the Cooperative Principle and the maxims. The reader is referred to Horn (1984a) for a comprehensive discussion of a wide variety of discourse consequences of the interaction between the assumption that the speaker is saying as much as is necessary and the assumption that what she intends to convey is relevant.

The interpretation of example (38) illustrates a very important fact about natural language understanding: parsing, determination of the sense and reference of uses of linguistic expressions, and evaluation of the truth of the propositions that an utterance expresses, entails, and implicates are interdependent processes, in that the information which represents the resolution of an indeterminacy in one area may equally well be crucial for, or dependent on, the resolution of an indeterminacy in another. How human beings or efficient machines actually manage the necessary integration is an open question.

Compositionality

It was observed in footnote 5 to chapter 1 that the interpretation of complex noun-like constructions poses a problem for compositionality. For example, *public beaches* is ordinarily taken to refer to beaches open to the public and not beaches which concern the public, while *religious affairs* is ordinarily taken to refer to affairs which concern religion and not affairs open to the/a religion; *public intoxication* is taken to refer to intoxication in public, and not intoxication concerning the public; and *religious person* to a person who observes a religion, and not to a person concerning religion. Either these forms are idioms, and not compositional at all, or the usual interpretation is an inference from a compositional but vague sense, or an inference disambiguates (as with *IBM* and *71* above) among a disjunction of precisely distinguishable compositional senses.[29] Aspects of this general issue are discussed in some detail by Downing (1977) and Levi (1978), with respect to complex nominals like *corporation lawyer, student protest*, and *avocado shampoo*, and by Clark and Clark (1979), who deal with denominal verbs like *to hammer, to party*, and *to bench*.

On the one hand, expressions such as *religious affairs* differ from compound nouns like *flea collar, kitchen carpet*, or *Illinois shirt* only in the superficial syntactic category of the first word,[30] and compound nouns represent an infinitely large class, because they are formed recursively by the addition of a noun (or compound) to the right of a noun (or compound) which modifies it, thus: *rug shampoo, rug shampoo container, rug shampoo container cleaner, rug shampoo container cleaner law education*, and so on. This means that in general, they cannot be treated as idiomatic, that is, lexicalized and conventional, because they are productive. Because they represent a potentially infinite set of expressions, their senses cannot be exhaustively listed. And if their ranges of senses are not determined compositionally, we cannot explain how they are interpreted at all.

---

[29]For convenience, I am using *sense* here (idiosyncratically) to refer to the relation between a word and the kind it is taken to name.

[30]Nouns in complex nominals can only have adjectival form when they are initial in the compound; [[*criminal* [*legal education*] is not a complex nominal, which explains why a criminal legal education is not the same as an education in criminal law, and *corporation legal education* does not have a parse like that of [[*corporate law*] *education*]. It seems that in medial position, adjectival forms force a predicating interpretation on the preceding constituent. Cf. Levi (1978, pp. 15–39) for discussion of difference between non-predicating adjectives like *religious* in *religious affairs* and predicating adjectives like *red* in *red Porsche*.

On the other hand, we do want to say that some expressions have a conventional, lexicalized interpretation. *Sonic boom* refers to a noise heard when a noisy object travels faster than the speed of sound, and not just to a boom which is from or concerns or has sound, and *water bed* is conventionally used to refer to a bed with a water-filled mattress, not to a bed for water, or a bed which is water, etc. The senses normally associated with *water, bed, sonic,* and *boom* are discernible in descriptions of the normal referents of these expressions, but the contribution of those senses to the sense of the referring expression as a whole is no longer regular and predictable, although it may once have been. This is what it means to say that a meaning of a complex form has become lexicalized and conventional (cf. Morgan, 1978).

Let us assume then, that some complex nominals (i.e., Adjective–Noun and Noun–Noun compounds) may have lexicalized and conventional senses. In general, however, complex nominals are productively constructed expressions whose reference is a function of the references of their parts. This leaves us with the question of whether they are (a) vague, or (b) ambiguous, their parts related by a finite and relatively small number of distinct semantic functions. Levi's position was that such expressions are multiply ambiguous; there is a small number (12) of distinct semantic functions relating the parts of a complex nominal construction, in addition to (a) lexicalized, conventionalized, idiomatic meanings for some complex nominals (e.g., *venereal disease, blackboard, eggplant*) and (b) metaphorical uses of complex nominals (e.g., *wind bag, coffin nails*) which must be interpreted by strategies that exploit the assumption of the Cooperative Principle.

The Clarks, on the other hand, treated novel ("innovative") constructions not as ambiguous, but as vague (or in their words, as having "an indefinite number of potential senses" (Clark & Clark, 1979, p. 783)). They maintained that "their interpretation depends on the context, especially the cooperation of speaker and listener" (p. 783), and that for this reason, innovative expressions "must be dealt with differently from both purely denotational and indexical expressions" (p. 783).

We have seen, however, in chapter 3 and earlier in this chapter, that under Nunberg's approach, (a) "purely denotational" expressions are generally indefinitely many ways "ambiguous" in that, in principle, nothing limits the range or complexity of the referring functions a speaker might choose to use[31] in referring to a particular object with a particular expression, and (b) "purely denotational" expressions must be interpreted via strategies very similar to those needed for interpreting indexical expressions[32] (as described in chap. 2 and 3). That is, there is nothing particularly unique about the wide range of interpretations intended for novel complex nominals or denominal verbs; they simply represent a more extreme case of the general principles for using words of the language to refer

---

[31]This is why Nunberg refers to his description of what others might call "word meaning" as "the pragmatics of reference."

[32]See Green, 1995, for further discussion of this issue.

to objects and classes of objects in the universe. In this view, Levi's 12 semantic functions are neither necessary nor sufficient, and the Clarks' claim that "innovative" or "contextual" uses are interpreted by principles distinct from those used for regular uses is mistaken.

Indeed, it is generally the case that, whether we call it disambiguation or interpretation, understanding the intended reference of a linguistic expression involves comparing a candidate interpretation of a speaker's utterance of that expression with the goals and beliefs imputed to that speaker, and either rejecting interpretations which, given those goals and beliefs, are less plausibly relevant, or revising our assessment of the speaker's goals and beliefs.

In fact, the notion of normal belief provides a framework for pragmatic interpretation generally: the analysis of some expression E as intended to denote some referent r, or evoke some proposition P, predicts that in contexts where reference to r or evocation of P would normally be believed to be unexpected, E should not occur (that is, it should be normally believed to be unlikely or impossible), but if E does occur, its occurrence will induce (whether intentionally or not) beliefs about the situation being referred to that are in fact abnormal in that context (for example, that E is being used to refer to something other than r, or that, contrary to expectation, the speaker considers P to be true).

Metaphor

The most extreme case of so-called contextually determined meaning is figurative language, or metaphor (construed broadly enough to include metonymy and synecdoche). The interpretation of standard, clichéd, or stored metaphors like those cited in (40) appears to depend on principles not significantly different from those Nunberg used to define analyzable idioms.

40a. Hedley is a *pig*.
40b. That's a *half-baked* idea.
40c. x *shot down/shot holes in/poked holes in* y's argument
40d. x *stabbed* y *in the back* in his review of her book
40e. The Mets *jumped on/rocked* the Cards for 11 hits.
40f. They have given this program a real[33] *shot in the arm.*

These principles, described in chapter 3, section 4, characterize cases where the speaker believes that given some fairly standard use R′ of an expression *e*, there are beliefs which would license use R, though the speaker might not know who might hold those beliefs. The difference is that the beliefs licensing metaphorical uses such as those in (40) are recognized to be fanciful, nonrational beliefs; the speaker does not assume that (anyone assumes that) anyone actually believes them. That is, no one has to believe that anyone believes that ideas are explored

---

[33]I.e., metaphorical—cf. G. Lakoff, 1972.

and developed by baking them, or that arguments have mass and can be physically damaged, to expect success in communicating with expressions like (40b) or (40c). Rather, it is assumed that there are beliefs that in some significant way the development of an idea is *like* the cooking of a cake (or in other metaphors, like the cultivation of a crop) or that the construction or structure[34] of an argument is like a structure or organism that will collapse if its vital parts are damaged. Thus the referring functions inferred in the interpretation of metaphors involve the same referring function 'like x' (cf. Miller, 1979) that is invoked in so many entries in reference dictionaries.

Indeed, Nunberg defined poetic metaphor (1978a, pp. 150–151) as cases where a speaker (a) uses an expression *e* to refer to A in context C even though there is another expression (*e'*) which the speaker expects the addressee is more likely to be successful in interpreting as referring to A, and (b) realizes that the use of *e* to refer to A is not rational, and expects the addressee to recognize that the speaker realizes this, and so on, and despite this, (c) is acting in accord with the Cooperative Principle and expects to be understood as so acting. Nunberg argued (1978a, p. 152) that there is no need to make the rhetorician's distinctions between metaphor, metonymy, synecdoche, etc., since they are simply reflections of the use of different referring functions (viz. 'similar to', 'entity with', 'part of') in the same general process. Nunberg analyzed in some detail (1978a, pp. 153–163) the beliefs that license an expectation of interpretability for Byron's metaphorical use of *frown* in the lines "The castled crag of Drachenfels/frowns o'er the wide and winding Rhine." These involve beliefs that (a) the crag has a face, i.e., a front side, as when we speak of the face of a clock, or a building facing a street, (b) the face faces the Rhine, (c) the face has a brow, and (d) the face expresses an attitude. Belief (a) involves a metaphor (and a referring function) so common that we hardly notice it; belief (b) is the prosaic point of the sentence; belief (c) involves a straightforward similarity function; belief (d) is the irrational belief that licenses the metaphor which, I take it, is supposed to convey that the crag does not merely overlook the Rhine, but has a somewhat threatening appearance.[35] This is not really an unusual irrational belief; Nunberg cited comparable clichéd expressions such as *raging stream, threatening clouds,* and *oppressive heat.*

Although I have suggested that metaphors are understood by means of strategies that involve the same mechanisms as are used for understanding implicatures, and in fact, the same mechanisms as are used for so-called literal uses of language, indicating just how all (or most) meaning is metaphorical,[36] it would be misleading to imply that there are no differences between indirect speech, poetic metaphor,

---

[34]It is probably impossible to talk about abstract ideas without expressions that are (at least ultimately) metaphorical.

[35]Or, as Nunberg pointed out (1978a, p. 155), a bemused or worried appearance, though this seems less likely in this context.

[36]Cf. Lakoff and Johnson (1980) for evidence of the pervasiveness of such metaphor in ordinary language.

and ordinary mechanisms of reference. There are at least two dimensions on which the use of metaphor differs from the use of more conventional referring expressions, and from the use of indirect speech (implicature). First, as mentioned, the beliefs that license a clearly metaphorical use are not rational beliefs. Consequently, the referring function ultimately derived will not be the "best" referring function for that referent, compared to other referring functions for other expressions to indicate the same referent, but it will be the best one for that expression for that referent. With a novel metaphor like the ones in (41), the hearer will have to do some work to infer the intended referent.

> 41a. Sheathe thine impatience.
> 41b. Eks's mind is a meadow in winter.

If the metaphor is a good one, he will be rewarded with a rich set of consistent associations and the security of having made a (most likely) correct inference. Thus, (41a) implies that (in the context) impatience is dangerous, like a sword or dagger, and (41b) implies that Eks's mind is either barren, or dormant and awaiting a (metaphorically) environmental event to awaken it to (metaphorical) growth, blossoming, and fruition. The speaker is aware of all this, and thus aware that the hearer must pay a price in mental effort for the speaker's economy of words in conveying all that she chooses to convey with her metaphor.

Second, and this is not unrelated, metaphor as ordinarily understood is an art form. Part of a speaker's motivation in choosing to use metaphor over more literal language is to display his talent or virtuosity with words, a sort of verbal athleticism. But Nunberg pointed out (1978a, pp. 163–171) that the expressions that constitute slang frequently involve metaphors as recherché as those of poets, although the purpose of being potentially obscure in using slang may be not so much pure aesthetics as it is a desire to display membership in an exclusive subculture. Like a secret handshake, it identifies the speaker to other members, and can be used as a filter to exclude nonmembers.

Metaphors differ from hints conveyed by conversational implicature in another way as well. At a superficial level, a metaphor often involves a proposition that is intended to be recognized as literally false. At the level of what is intended to be conveyed, however, it presumably represents a proposition that is intended to be taken as uttered in conformance with the maxim of quality. (Both metaphors and hints may, however, appear to violate the maxim of relevance at the superficial level, while conforming to it at the level of what is intended to be conveyed.)

Sadock (1979, pp. 61–62) suggested that conventionalization or not of the means and strategies that Morgan (1978) described could be used to define four categories of linguistic convention. Elaborating on this idea, it may be helpful to look at conventionalization of the analogic means and directness of the communicative strategy (cf. Morgan, 1979) as situating referring expressions of the sorts we have considered in a somewhat richer constellation, perhaps as in Figure 5.1. The vertical axis in Figure 5.1 represents the conventionality of the metaphor (i.e., of the analogy), while the horizontal dimension refers to the transparency of the connection between what is said and what is intended to be conveyed.

STRATEGY: DIRECT ←

MEANS:

CONVENTIONAL

SO-CALLED LITERAL MEANINGS AND GENUINE IDIOMS	SHORT-CIRCUITED IMPLICATURES	CONVERSATIONAL IMPLICATURE
a. Fido is a *dog*	c. *Can you pass the salad.*	d. *Is the Pope Catholic?*
b. Eks *gave* me *the cold shoulder.*		e. Do you know the time?
		f. *when hell freezes over*
		PROVERBS [cf. Green, 1975b]
		g. *Birds of a feather flock together.*

FROZEN METAPHORS AND CLICHES

h. Eks is a *pig*, 'selfish'; 'slovenly'
i. *half-baked* idea 'poorly thought-out'
j. *stab* someone *in the back* 'betray'
k. references to facts/ arguments as *swords, daggers, bullets; shooting* or *poking holes in* an argument
l. *cruel frost, oppressive heat*
m. He has been *cool/warm* 'unfriendly/friendly'
n. *Mickey-Mouse* 'non-serious'
o. *Familiarity breeds contempt.*
p. *Beauty is in the eye of the beholder.*

r. [Q: How can I make John feel at home?]
A: *Buy him some Purina Hog Chow.*
[Morgan, 1979, p. 139]

EXTENSIONS OF FROZEN METAPHORS

q. He suspected that most of his listeners were sympathetic to the position that *selection restrictions* were totally inadequate. But he attacked the *sputtering tyrant* once again, if only to place his *little penknife* alongside the *daggers* of his companions. [Reddy 1969, p. 242]

NOVEL METAPHORS

	INDIRECT REFERENCE TO NOVEL METAPHOR	IMPLICATURE OF NOVEL METAPHOR
s. Her souffle is *death,* 'awful'	x. On arriving home, I found I had been *sentenced* by She Who Must Be Obeyed to the eggplant souffle promoted in last month's "Gourmet Anglais," for what *capital crime,* I never knew.	y. [Q: How do you like the souffle?] A: *On the whole, I'd rather be in Philadelphia.* [Morgan, 1979, p. 145]

t. *Sheathe* thine impatience!
u. Eks' mind is a *meadow in winter.* [Morgan 1979, p. 140]
v. *plastic, Wonder Bread* 'non-genuine'
w. The castled crag . . . *frowns* . . .
UNCONVENTIONAL

FIGURE 5.1

Cutting across the categories defined by the points on these orthogonal parameters[37] are motives for being indirect; one might indulge in indirectness because one enjoys word play, or as a sign of subgroup membership (cf. chap. 7), or to be diplomatic, avoiding confrontation, or to be politic, and intentionally vague or ambiguous, or for any of a number of other reasons.

Examples (h & r), (s, x, & y), and (k & q) illustrate how metaphors may be recycled into more indirect or less conventional forms. A final example illustrates how a sentential cliché may be reinterpreted as containing an independent metaphor. The football player Richard Dent was interviewed after his team was victorious in the Super Bowl. Alluding to the sportcasters' cliché "It isn't over until you hear the fat lady sing" (itself an allusion to the belief that in the 1940s and 1950s, the end of many events broadcast by American radio and television was marked by the late Kate Smith singing "God Bless America"), and probably equating that cliché with related ones, "It isn't over until the final gun" and "It isn't over until it's over," Dent referred to the opponents trailing 23–3 at halftime, saying:

> It was over at the half. When you're going in with those points, and you're facing such a great defense—you know, *the fat lady began to sing*.

making *the fat lady begin to sing* into a metaphor for 'the game be over'.[38]

4.5 Multiple Explanations: Killing One Bird With Two Stones

Sadock's (1970) syntactic analysis of indirect requests like *Can you pass the salad*, referred to at the beginning of this section, is partially redundant in the face of an independently motivated pragmatic analysis. Some of the phenomena discussed in the previous section may be equally susceptible to more than one analysis. It is important to understand that in general, the fact that an explanation provided by analysis is redundant is not a reason to reject that analysis out of

---

[37]I have not taken a position on whether these parameters are discrete or continuous, although I suspect the latter is the case.

[38]Similarly, *hear the fat lady sing* is taken as a metaphorical reference to victory in the battle with flies in this jingle for fly repellent:

Didn't have the strength to cope
And ward off a nasty sting
Until he bought Irving's Fly Dope
And heard the fat lady sing.
[*Yankee* May, 1986, p. 16]

hand. There is reason to believe that it is natural for linguistic systems to tolerate a certain amount of redundancy. Hankamer (1977), Sadock (1983), and Green (1985a) argue that in many cases, linguistic principles overlap to provide two different but non-contradictory explanations for a single phenomenon (e.g., number agreement between subject and verb), and are both necessary; overlapping may be avoidable only at the cost of arbitrariness. Furthermore, it seems clear that a system which offers more than one principle to motivate the use of a linguistic expression, expression type, or construction type would be easier to learn than one which does not, since one kind of support for an analysis might be easily inferred in a particular situation when the other kind would not. Consequently, it should not bother us too much if we can motivate an analysis as governed both by convention and by very general rules and principles of cooperative communication, as long as we can account for the regularity of form-use correspondences. Where the correspondence is partially irregular, only one of the analyses may be adequate. This is the case, for example, with the imperative-like syntax of *Can you please pass the salt*,[39] and for Gordon and Lakoff (1975), the unpredicted indirectness of *Are you able to pass the salt* and the ungrammaticality of ??*Are you able to please pass the salt*. But where either makes correct predictions, the question of which one a flesh-and-blood language user actually employs (or employs on a given occasion) will be a very subtle, and often inconsequential one.

---

[39]Bach and Harnish's reaction to this form is to call it ungrammatical but acceptable to speakers anyway (Bach & Harnish, 1979, p. 199). For commentary on this strategy, see Green, 1983.

CHAPTER 5 STUDY QUESTIONS

1. What is Grice's Cooperative Principle?

2. How do the maxims relate to the Cooperative Principle?

3. In what ways do they constrain behavior?

4. How is it that they constrain behavior?

5. Under what sorts of conditions, or for what reasons, might individual maxims be ignored?

6. What is the difference between conversational and conventional implicature?

7. How can the Cooperative Principle and/or the maxims be invoked to explain the coherence of texts?

8. How can the Cooperative Principle and/or the maxims be invoked to explain indirect speech acts?

9. How can the Cooperative Principle and/or the maxims be invoked to explain how a hearer infers what a referring expression is used to refer to?

10. How can the Cooperative Principle and/or the maxims be invoked to explain how hearers cope with the wide variety of likely potential interpretations for compound nouns?

11. How can the Cooperative Principle and/or the maxims be invoked to account for the interpretation of metaphors?

6 Pragmatics and Syntax

In chapter 5, we discussed how what people said reflected, and was more or less consciously intended to reflect, their intentions and beliefs, especially beliefs about their interlocutors' beliefs. The focus of this chapter is how the way in which something is said reflects speakers' attitudes toward and beliefs about the topics and referents of an ongoing discourse. The aspect of how something is said that we will focus on is the choice of a syntactic construction from among the many which the grammar of the language makes available for the proposition to be expressed, although intonational choices (Schmerling, 1976; Cutler, 1977; Ward & Hirschberg, 1985; Olsen, 1986) and phonological choices (Cutler, 1974, p. 117; Zwicky & Sadock, 1975, pp. 26–27) have also been discussed, as well as the choice of which language to use (Gumperz, 1976; Burt, 1990). Section 1 treats syntactic devices which reflect the speaker's assumptions about the structure of the discourse. In section 2, we examine some constructions which differ from their truth-conditionally equivalent counterparts in various other ways. Some differ in rhetorical function (i.e., in what gets asserted and what is presupposed), but most reflect different beliefs about or attitudes toward referents of linguistic expressions that are part of the utterance. Section 3 deals with syntactic constructions which enable a speaker to compensate for (perceived) difficulties in producing or parsing a complex utterance. Many of the constructions have more than one use or function, and show up in more than one category.

1. REFLECTIONS OF DISCOURSE STRUCTURE

Language scholars have recognized for some time that there are correlations between the order of syntactic constituents in a sentence and the discourse role of the information which a particular constituent represents (Mathesius, 1928;

Firbas, 1964; Halliday, 1967; Kuno, 1972).[1] In general, and all other things being equal, the first phrase in a sentence tends to be intended to denote familiar (or TOPICAL, or GIVEN, or OLD, or presupposed, or predictable, or THEMATIC) material, while phrases toward the end of the sentence tend to denote NEW (or asserted, or RHEMATIC) material. Other things are not always equal, however, Sentence stress or intonational accent (higher pitch which falls off rapidly and is perceived as louder) also correlates with information being treated as new (Schmerling, 1976), and new information may be expressed in phrases that occur toward or at the beginning of a sentence if they bear the main sentence stress, as in (1) (Olsen, 1986).

1.   *John* ate the cookies.

Furthermore, as Prince (1981b) demonstrated, *familiar, predictable, given, old, theme,* and *sentence topic* do not denote interchangeable notions, and different writers have used the same term to refer to rather different categories. Yet the various writers seem to have been trying to get at the same point, summarized by Horn's observation that the initial slot in a sentence tends to be reserved for material taken to refer to the discourse theme or sentence topic (i.e., what the sentence is about). Typically, this is material that the speaker (reflexively) assumes to be familiar to the addressee, and preferentially, it is material which is either salient (assumed by the speaker to be in the addressee's consciousness) or presupposed (taken as noncontroversial) (Horn, 1986, p. 171). It is not surprising, then, that syntactic rules of languages provide for numerous alternative constructions which differ in the order of phrases while preserving truth-conditional semantics and illocutionary force. This is true even in a "fixed word order" language like English,[2] as illustrated by the incomplete list of options for English declarative sentences given in examples (2–5).

2a.   Eks delivered a rug to Aitchberg.
2b.   A rug was delivered to Aitchberg by Eks. [PASSIVE][3]
2c.   There was a rug delivered (to Aitchberg) (by Eks). [THERE-INSERTION]
2d.   A rug, Eks delivered to Aitchberg. [TOPICALIZATION]
2e.   It was a rug that Eks delivered to Aitchberg. [CLEFT]
2f.   What Eks delivered to Aitchberg was a rug. [PSEUDO-CLEFT]
2g.   . . . and deliver a rug to Aitchberg, Eks did. [VERB PHRASE PREPOSING]

---

[1]For more recent treatments, see Prince (1981b), Zaenen (1982), Van Oosten (1986), and Horn (1986).

[2]The writers have generally not claimed that the Old Information First principle is a universal principle, though it may be. Most of the illustrations have come from Czech, English, French, and Japanese.

[3]The construction names given here are those familiar in modern generative grammar. See Green and Morgan (in prep.) for further references.

3a. Finding typographical errors is never simple.
3b. It is never simple to find typographical errors. [EXTRAPOSITION]
3c. Typographical errors are never simple to find. [TOUGH-MOVEMENT]
3d. Simple to find, typographical errors are not. [ADJECTIVE PHRASE PREPOS-ING]

4a. Eks met a woman who said she was the Princess Anastasia's governess at Treno's.
4b. At Treno's, Eks met a woman who said she was the Princess Anastasia's governess. [ADVERB PREPOSING]
4c. Eks met at Treno's a woman who said she was the Princess Anastasia's governess. [HEAVY NOUN PHRASE SHIFT]
4d. Eks met her at Treno's, a woman who said she was the Princess Anastasia's governess. [RIGHT DISLOCATION]
4e. A woman who said she was the Princess Anastasia's governess, Eks met her at Treno's. [LEFT DISLOCATION]

5a. The little bunny scampered into its hole.
5b. Into its hole, the little bunny scampered. [LOCATIVE PREPOSING]
5c. Into its hole scampered the little bunny. [INVERSION]

Of course, old information does not tend to go first just because it is old, or become old just because it is first. Sometimes none of the material in a sentence represents "old information," and as noted above, new information sometimes goes first; generally, speakers have more particular reasons (not necessarily conscious reasons) for making a particular constituent first or last in a sentence (cf. Green, 1982a). Such functions of word order have been explored in some detail for a number of constructions. We look at two examples here.

1.1 Preposing

Ward's (1985) analysis of preposings like those in (2d), (2g), (3d) and (5b) indicated that while they may serve a variety of discourse functions, which he described in detail, they have two properties in common. In Ward's terminology, they first of all mark the preposed element as referring to an entity which is related in a certain way (as a BACKWARD-LOOKING CENTER) to entities previously evoked in the discourse (the set of FORWARD-LOOKING CENTERS).[4] Second, they

---

[4]Specifically, the backward-looking center must stand in a salient scalar relation to the partially ordered set constituting the forward-looking centers. A partially ordered set is a set whose members are all related by some ordering relation which is transitive, and either reflexive and antisymmetric, like 'is as tall as or taller than,' or irreflexive and asymmetric, like 'is taller than' (cf. Hirschberg, 1985; Ward, 1985, p. 64). Salient scalar relationships include any where one element is higher or lower than another on some scale, or they are incomparable alternative values, but there are values higher or lower than both. Some examples are the set/subset relation, part/whole, type/subtype, entity/attribute, and of course, 'greater-than' and 'less-than'.

mark the unstressed, presupposed part of the sentence (its OPEN PROPOSITION) as salient in the discourse. Viewed from a different perspective, these properties represent conditions that must be fulfilled for the utterance of a sentence with a preposed phrase to be acceptable in its context. Thus, a sentence like (2d) might be used in a context like (6a), where the referent of *one of these rugs* is very obviously in a subset relation to the previously mentioned set {rugs to be given as rewards} and the open proposition is 'Eks deliver a rug to someone.' It might also be used in a context like (6b), where *one of these rugs* is a member of the set {rugs concealing cocaine}, and the open proposition 'Eks delivered something to Aitchberg' is salient in the discourse. But a sentence like (2d) could not be used in a context like (6c), where neither of these conditions holds.

6a.   An Eastern bloc embassy official gave Eks six full-size oriental rugs, and directed him to give them to the senators who had been most cooperative. One of these rugs Eks delivered to Sen. Aitchberg.[5]

6b.   FBI agents suspected both Eks and Aitchberg of trafficking in cocaine, and had been tailing them for months. In March, they learned from an informant that six oriental rugs concealing 20 pounds of cocaine each had come through JFK airport, and as Exhibit B indicates, one of these rugs Eks delivered to Aitchberg.

6c.   Eks and Aitchberg played golf together regularly.
       ??An oriental rug Eks delivered to Aitchberg one day.

1.2 Inversion

English is graced with a number of inversion constructions which, like (5c) allow the subject noun phrase to appear after the main verb instead of before it (Green, 1980, 1982b, 1985b; Birner, 1992, 1994). The inversions begin with a preposed adjective phrase, participial phrase, or locative or directional adverbial phrase. Because of this, they can be called into service to perform any of a number of functions which exploit this phrase order (Green, 1980; Birner, 1992, 1994). For example, a writer[6] may use an inversion with a preposed phrase which refers to a previously established or implied referent to describe how information following it relates to previous discourse, as in the examples in (7), where the initial phrase is explicitly ((7a), (7b)) or implicitly ((7c)) anaphoric to something preceding in the discourse.

7a.   Attached to it, as always, is an application blank for next year's license.

7b.   Jerome and Rita Arkoff and Tom and Fanny Irwin were in the front row
       . . . Back of the Arkoffs and Irwins were William Lesser and Patrick

---

[5]The example is adapted from a passage in Nixon's *Six Crises* cited by Ward, 1985, p. 71.

[6]Or speaker, but these inversions are more typical of writing than of colloquial speech. Cf. Green, 1982b.

Degan, and between them and slightly to the rear was Saul Panzer. (Rex Stout, *Might as Well Be Dead*, p. 180. (New York: Viking Books, 1956))

7c. At issue is Section 1401(a) of the Controlled Substances Act.

In other instances, what is exploited is the fact that the inversion construction puts a subject noun phrase in the sentence final position, which is typically reserved for focused, new information. This enables a writer to introduce a new discourse element (e.g., an important character or object or an element of the setting) in a focused position, as in (8).[7] Travelog-style descriptions exploit this extensively, as in (8c).

8a. In a little white house lived two rabbits. (Dick Bruna, *Miffy*. (New York: Two Continents (1975))

8b. Competing with the screamers for popularity are the phone-in programs, an adaptation of two rural American pastimes—listening in on the party-line and speaking at the town meeting. (Robert Dye, "The Death of Silence." *Journal of Broadcasting*, 12, 3 (1968). Reprinted in *Subject and Strategy*, ed. by Paul Escholz and Alfred Rosa, pp. 169–172, p. 170. (New York: St. Martins, 1978))

8c. The grounds were lavishly furnished with ceramic, stone, and wrought-metal sculpture. There were an enormous stainless steel frog and two tiny elves in the foyer of the guest house, and outside stood a little angel.

A related use of inversions is to describe an event or locative relationship which resolves some puzzle in a narrative as it has been established up to that point. It might be the whereabouts of an important character as in the second inversion in (9a) or the identity of the previously unknown agent of some significant action, as in (9b), or an event significant in the protagonist's execution of his plans, as in the second inversion in (9c) (the first introduces a new discourse element).

9a. Then at the darkest hour dawned deliverance. *Through the revolving doors swept Tom Pulsifer.* (S. J. Perelman, "The Customer is Always Wrong". *The Most of S. J. Perelman*, p. 227. (New York: Simon & Schuster, 1958))

---

[7]This common function of inversions may be what has misled some writers (e.g., Longuet-Higgins, 1976) into thinking that inversions after directional phrases must describe a character coming into (the narrator's) view. Inversions have other uses, and we do find such inversions as (i–iii), which describe a character going out of view.

  i. Then off marched the little tailor, cocky as could be, with his thumbs thrust through his boasting belt.
  ii. Into the forest ran the four, and soon they could be seen no more.
  iii. Off across the grass ran the three little girls.

Examples (i) and (iii) are from children's books whose exact titles I cannot locate.

9b. One night there was a tap on the window. Mrs. Rabbit peeped through the window. *Outside stood a little angel.* (Bruna)

9c. . . . Dumble vanished and in his place rose a dark, angry cloud of bees. They flew straight at the soldiers' faces, and *from the soldiers came yells of anguish, of sorrow, and of despair.* (Jay Williams, *The King with Six Friends.* (New York: Parents' Magazine Press, 1968))

The particular discourse values of several other of the constructions in (2–5) have been explored in some detail (cf. for example, Prince, 1981c, 1984—Topicalization and Left Dislocation; Prince, 1978b—Cleft and Pseudo-cleft; Milsark, 1977; Napoli & Rando 1978; Aissen 1975—*There*-insertion).

2. REFLECTION OF BELIEFS AND ATTITUDES ABOUT CONTENT

Another kind of "stylistic variant" exhibiting a difference in rhetorical value involves constructions with sentential complements as in (10) and (11), or adjuncts as in (12). The (a) sentences in these examples differ from the (b) sentences in that the italicized subordinate clause represents a presupposed or otherwise subordinate proposition in the (a) sentences, but has its own illocutionary force in the (b) sentences.

10a. I bet *it'll float if you throw it in the lake.*

10b. It'll float if you throw it in the lake, I bet. [SLIFTING]

11a. That *Sandy thought it was Tuesday* is obvious/clear.

11b. It's obvious/clear that Sandy thought it was Tuesday. [EXTRAPOSITION]

12a. Someone *who said the girls were supposed to bring two quarts of potato salad* called.

12b. Someone called who said the girls were supposed to bring two quarts of potato salad. [RELATIVE CLAUSE EXTRAPOSITION]

Thus, depending on the sense intended for *bet* in (10a), (10a) is either a bet or a speculation, but (10b) can only be a speculation—*bet* does not have a performative interpretation in that construction (Ross, 1975; Horn, 1986). And while both (11a) and (11b) could be used to assert something about the claim that Sandy had some belief about the identity of a day, only (11b) could be used to make the claim that Sandy had that belief (Morgan, 1975b; Horn, 1986). In the case of (12), the (a) sentence reports who called, while the (b) sentence reports what someone said the girls were supposed to bring (Ziv, 1976).

Other constructions reflect particular kinds of beliefs speakers have about the objects of their discourse. For example, use of the INTERNAL DATIVE construction with animate indirect object noun phrase (Green, 1974) in (13b) implies that the speaker believes that the referents of the subject and indirect object noun phrases were alive at the same time.

13a. Win this one for the Gipper/me.
13b. Win me/!the Gipper this one.

Wierzbicka (1986) argued, more generally, that use of the internal dative construction reflects the speaker's greater interest in the referent of the indirect object noun phrase. The accusative-infinitive construction in (14b, 14d–14f) (Borkin, 1974; Postal, 1974; Steever, 1977; Schmerling, 1978) reflects the speaker's assumption that the (implied) experiencer (MacArthur in (14b)) or agent (Eks in (14d–f)) would be capable of interaction with the referent of the object phrase (Caesar, Sandy, Dale) at the time referred to by the main verb.

14a. It seemed to MacArthur that Patton/Julius Caesar was the greatest general in history.
14b. Patton/!Julius Caesar seemed to MacArthur to be the greatest general in history.
14c. Eks asked that Sandy leave.
14d. Eks asked Sandy to leave.
14e. Eks allowed Dale to examine Dana.
14f. Eks allowed Dale to be examined by Dana.

A slightly different case involves the use of the present tense to refer to future time in sentences like (15) (G. Lakoff, 1971).

15a. The Celtics are going to play the Bucks tomorrow.
15b. The Celtics play the Bucks tomorrow.

If the event is not (mutually) understood to be prearranged or scheduled, simple present tense cannot be used for future time. Thus, the use of (16) would imply that the speaker (and the addressee, in the speaker's estimate) either (a) knew that the game was fixed, or (b) were staunch believers in predestination and believed that the speaker had an inside line on the Omnipotent's plans for basketball games.

16.   The Celtics win tomorrow.

R. Lakoff (1969a) and Horn (1971, 1978b, 1989) have described the NEGATIVE TRANSPORTATION phenomenon illustrated in (17a), where with a certain class of verbs and adjectives, a negative occurs one or more clauses away from the clause it conversationally negates. Thus (17a) would communicate the same as (17b), and (18a) would be conversationally ambiguous between a report that Dana lacks the desire to wash dishes, and a report like (18b), that Dana desires not to wash dishes.

17a. I don't think Sandy will arrive until Monday.
17b. I think Sandy won't arrive until Monday.

18a. Dana doesn't want to wash dishes.
18b. Dana wants to not wash dishes.

The difference between the (a) sentences and the (b) sentences in (17–18) is that the (a) sentences, with transported negatives, are hedged—they represent weaker claims, apparently by implicating rather than asserting the relevant negative proposition (cf. Horn, 1978b, pp. 131–136, 177–216 and Horn, 1989 for discussion). A similar phenomenon is evident in the fact that the morphologically incorporated negative in (19b) is stronger than the unincorporated negative in (19a) (Sheintuch & Wise, 1976).

19a. I didn't see anyone there.
19b. I saw no one there.

The use of *some* or *any* described by R. Lakoff (1969b) provides a very clear reflection of speakers' attitudes. As Lakoff showed, although *some* and *any* have the same truth conditions, the use of *some* in interrogative, conditional, and hypothetical constructions indicates a positive attitude toward the situation described by the proposition it is part of, while *any* reflects a neutral or negative attitude. Thus, *if there are some apples on the table* is satisfied by the same states of affairs as *if there are any apples on the table*, but implies a different attitude towards the likelihood or desirability of that state of affairs, and the question in (20a) reflects the hope that Bill wants spinach, while (20b) may reflect the hope that he does not.

20a. Does Bill want some spinach?
20b. Does Bill want any spinach?

And (21a) could be a bribe, intended to get the addressee to eat bread (treating cooking hamburgers all week as a reward), while (21b) would be a threat, intended to keep the addressee from eating bread (and treating cooking hamburgers all week as an undesirable event).

21a. If you eat some bread, I'll cook hamburgers all week.
21b. If you eat any bread, I'll cook hamburgers all week.

Other NEGATIVE POLARITY ITEMS (cf. Baker, 1970; Horn, 1971, 1989; Schmerling, 1971), as in (22), reflect attitudes similar to those which *any* reflects:

22.   Do you think Sandy has $\left\{\begin{array}{l}\text{a red cent?}\\\text{eaten a bite?}\\\text{bothered to RSVP?}\end{array}\right\}$

Similarly, both the inversion of subject and auxiliary verb in embedded questions, and truncation of embedded questions (SLUICING) imply that the individual to whom the answer is implied or assumed to be relevant is in fact ignorant of the answer. Thus the (a) sentences in (23) and (24) are more acceptable than the (b) sentences, which have contradictory implications which their acceptable, and uninverted or unreduced (c) counterparts lack. This property of sluicing and subject-auxiliary inversion explains why the (d) sentences induce the implicature that the speaker does not know the answer to the question.

23a.   She wants to know who did I appoint.
23b.   !She already knows who did I appoint.
23c.   She already knows who I appointed.
23d.   It never occurred to me to wonder who did she appoint.

24a.   John broke something, but he won't say what.
24b.   !John broke something, and he said what.
24c.   John broke something, and he said what he broke.
24d.   John went somewhere with my car, and you know where.

Many languages have special particle words or morphemes whose use indicates an attitude toward the content or referent of some adjacent sentence constituent, or toward the addressee. For example, Japanese and Korean have a variety of honorific morphemes which indicate the degree of respect the speaker has for the addressee or some entity referred to in the sentence (Kuno, 1973; Harada, 1976; Levinson, 1979). Some languages have particles that indicate the speaker's degree of certainty about the utterance (Whorf, 1950; Matthews, 1965; Corum, 1975; Kendall, 1985). Even familiar languages like English have eloquent little particles. The use of *ah!* for instance, indicates (James, 1972, 1973) that the following material represents information that is news to the speaker, as in (25).

25a.   Ah, it says in the paper that Kissinger is a vegetarian.[8]
25b.   Mr. Eks will arrive at, ah, 3:35.

---

[8]Sentence (25a) is conversationally ambiguous between an understanding that Kissinger's eating habits are news, and an understanding that their being reported in the paper is news. The first interpretation involves a very ordinary implicature from the second, whereby the subordinate clause is what is most relevant to the goals of the discourse, and a "prefix" like *It says in the paper* or *My father says* or *Dr. Kramer thinks* indicates the basis for the speaker's giving credence to the proposition expressed in the subordinate clause. In this way, the speaker can make a relevant contribution without violating the maxim of quality even when he has no direct evidence for the truth of the relevant proposition.

James also describes the use of *oh*— with high, level intonation as indicating that the following material represents a choice made with the knowledge that at least one other choice would have been equally correct or cooperative, as illustrated in (26).

26a.   A: What'll we do when our cousins get here?
       B: Oh—we'll have a picnic. Or maybe we'll go to the movies.
26b.   A: When are we going to get to Chicago?
       B: Be ready to leave at, oh—2:00, and we'll be there by 6:00.

Similarly, the particle *well* is used (R. Lakoff, 1973a; Schourup, 1982) to indicate that something in the immediately preceding discourse is hard to reconcile with the speaker's model of the world (that is, it indicates a perception that speaker and hearer don't share the same beliefs about something relevant). Its use implies that the speaker knows more than she is saying. Thus, B's response in (27b) implies that B is not certain of her watch's accuracy; B's response in (27c) is odd unless B has reason to believe that the answer "2:30" would be misleading (as it would if B thought A really wanted to know what time it was in a nearby city which, unbeknownst to A, was in a different time zone, or if B thought that A really wanted to know if some TV program had started yet, and assumed that A didn't know it had been postponed).

27a.   A: What time is it?
27b.   B: Well, my watch says 2:30.
27c.   B: Well, 2:30.

Using the particle *why*, on the other hand, indicates that the speaker believes that she is not telling the addressee anything he didn't already know. Consequently, when it precedes the answer to a question, its use implies that the questioner should not have needed to ask the question. Thus, B's response in (28b) implies that A ought to have known the answer, while the response in (28c) indicates that she may believe someone besides Grant is buried in Grant's tomb.

28a.   A: Who is buried in Grant's tomb?
28b.   B: Why, General Grant is.
28c.   B: Well, General Grant is.

Likewise, when *why* precedes statements, its use implies that the content is news more to the speaker than to the addressee, as in (29a), and it precedes questions to which both speaker and addressee know the answer (i.e., rhetorical questions), like (29b).

29a.   Why, you're Clyde's little girl!
29b.   Why, how should I know?

3. REFLECTIONS OF PERCEIVED DIFFICULTY

Finally, speakers may take advantage of constructions like Extraposition (30b) and Heavy Noun Phrase Shift (31b) which allow a constituent to appear at the end of the sentence to put the longest or most conversationally significant constituent last. It is not clear whether this serves to make the sentence easier to articulate (cf. Olsen, 1986) or simply easier to keep track of, or whether the motivation is altruistic—accommodating the addressee's likely strategies or difficulties in parsing, or some combination of these.

30a. Whether Kim will visit museums in France and Dana will go to concerts in Vienna, or Dana will visit museums in France and Kim will go to concerts in Vienna is unclear.

30b. It is unclear whether Kim will visit museums in France and Dana will go to concerts in Vienna, or . . .

31a. Dana attributed a poem in which intuitions were compared to anemones and academic theories were described as battlements to Coleridge.

31b. Dana attributed to Coleridge a poem in which intuitions were compared to anemones and academic theories were described as battlements.

Length and discourse significance seem to be at least partially independent factors. Longer postposed noun phrases tend to sound better, as in (32a), even if they have no more semantic content, as in (32b), but of two noun phrases of equal length the more significant-sounding sounds better, as (32c) shows.

32a. But they attributed to Blake *The Rise and Fall of the Roman Empire/?Typee.*

32b. The district attorney considers indictable Montgomery J. Jingleheimer-Smith III/?Rose Budd.

32c. The committee has attributed to Margaret Thatcher an extraordinary poem/?the 27-line poem.

4. SOME OTHER CASES

This chapter has only sketched some of the kinds of pragmatic factors which may be reflected in the speaker's choice of syntactic construction. It did not examine all of the factors which might enter into the choice to use a passive construction, for example. These include ensuring that the phrase describing the agent is at the end rather than the beginning of the sentence (33a), and, where there is no agent phrase, accommodating the fact that the agent is not known (33b) or suppressing the fact that the agent is known (33c). The use of a passive also commonly implies that the event described had a particular effect on the speaker or some other explicitly mentioned affected person (R. Lakoff, 1971; Davison, 1980; Fukada, 1986).

33a. The car was stolen by two young men wearing designer jogging suits.
33b. My bike was taken between 3:00 and 5:30 on Monday.
33c. This idea has been attacked as simplistic and naive.

In fact, there are truth-conditionally equivalent alternatives to practically every describable construction,[9] and to the extent that this is true, the alternatives will tend to have different pragmatic values.[10] It would not be too surprising to discover that even constructions as similar as the (a) and (b) examples in (34) and (35) (cf. Bolinger, 1972) really differed systematically in their use, reflecting different assumptions of the speakers, for example, that the (b) examples imply a stronger conviction on the part of the subject.

34a. He expects that he will win.
34b. He expects to win.

35a. I know that it's raining.
35b. I know it's raining.

In this chapter we have diverged from the pervasive emphasis on the hearer's need to make on-line inferences from what the speaker has said and the way it was said, to what was intended to be conveyed. This chapter draws attention to a variety of cases where potential inferences from the way something is said have been grammaticized. In these cases, the connection between the way something is said and what is intended to be conveyed is automatic, suggesting an analysis as fossilized conversational implicatures, according to the following logic. With "live" conversational implicature, and even with short-circuited conversational implicature, it is often reasonable to deny that an implicature was intended, as in (36) since implicatures exploit (assumed) literal meanings.

36.   The committee money disappeared from the safe that day, and Lee came home with a new jacket that night, but I don't believe or intend to imply that the two events have anything to do with each other.

---

[9]In English, anyway, and probably in other languages.

[10]Even verb agreement (Morgan, 1972a, 1972b) as in (i) and (ii) induces inferences from the fact that one choice was made rather than another, in fact, inferences that affect the truth conditions, not just "mere" pragmatic differences. Thus, (i) would be used to extol the virtues of two foods, while (ii) is about a single somewhat bizarre dish.

i. Pickles and ice cream taste good.
ii. Pickles and ice cream tastes good.

But in the cases considered here, use conditions which refer to beliefs or attitudes of the speaker are so strongly linked to the syntactic construction that it sounds irrational to use such constructions and then deny that the conditions hold, as in (37).

37.   !The Celtics win tomorrow, but it's not preordained or fixed; there's an off chance the Pistons might beat them.

In the following chapter, we diverge from our previous approach in a different direction, and look at ways in which speakers manipulate what they say to manage conversation and maintain and change social relations.

CHAPTER 6 STUDY QUESTIONS

1. What are some ways in which the choice of syntactic construction reflects the speaker's beliefs about the relation of an expressed proposition to the ongoing discourse?

2. What are some ways in which the choice of syntactic construction reflects the speaker's attitudes about referents of the ongoing discourse?

3. What are some examples of syntactic constructions where phrase order may reflect language-processing considerations?

7 Conversational Interaction

In chapter 1, the point was made that particular communicative acts are performed to further plans for specific, possibly nested, goals. Most of the goals we have assumed in subsequent discussions have involved getting the addressee to have a certain belief or attitude (including a desire to do something) about events or entities in the real world. In a simple case, A says "X" to B in order to tell B 'Y,' with the purpose of getting B to believe 'Y,' and therefore, to want to accomplish Z. In this chapter, we focus on how language is used to further other sorts of goals. Section 1 deals with politeness phenomena: strategies for maintaining or changing interpersonal relations. Such goals are sometimes an end in themselves, as in purely social conversation ("small talk"); other times they are a link in a chain of goals whose ultimate end is to influence someone's behavior or attitude. In the most direct cases, it is the addressee's attitude or behavior which is the target, but it could be the attitude or behavior of an individual linked to the addressee in a series or hierarchy of interacting plans. In section 2, we look briefly at strategies for managing the mechanics of conversation—the lowest level of goals: getting to speak and getting the addressee to respond. The final section provides a cross-sectional view of the functions of one sentence type: the sorts of goals a speaker might use a question to accomplish.

1. POLITENESS

R. Lakoff (1972) asked why it is that it is considered polite for an English-speaking hostess to offer a guest something to eat with (1a), that if she used (1b) it would be accounted familiar, and that use of (1c) for the same purpose would be considered downright rude.

147

1a.   You must have some of this fruitcake.
1b.   You should have some of this fruitcake.
1c.   You may have some of this fruitcake.

After all, on the face of it, (1a) would appear to be more overbearing, and (1c) less imposing. Why isn't (1c) the more polite offer? In this section, we examine a couple of approaches to the question of what makes one utterance act more polite than another, and how to explain the phenomena of (1).

The obvious difference between polite behavior and rude behavior is that polite behavior makes people feel comfortable and rude behavior makes them feel uncomfortable. If we consider to be polite any behavior whereby a person shows regard for another person by trying to make that person feel comfortable or by making an obvious effort to avoid making that person feel uncomfortable, then politeness is a property of any kind of interpersonal behavior, including completely non-linguistic acts (e.g., opening a door, clearing a place for someone), and also acts of consideration accomplished by linguistic means (offering food or drink, apologizing for an injury), as well as strictly linguistic acts of uttering special "polite" expressions. Lakoff (1973b) described three different rules[1] a speaker might follow in choosing to be polite.

The most formal politeness rule, Lakoff's Rule 1: Don't Impose, is described as appropriate to situations where there is an acknowledged difference in power and status between the participants, such as between a student and a dean, or between a factory worker and the vice-president in charge of personnel. Imposing on someone means impeding their desires to act as they please; refraining from imposing means not impeding these desires. A speaker (S) who is being polite according to this rule will avoid, mitigate, or ask permission or apologize for making the addressee (A) do anything which A does not want to do. This includes acts which distract A from whatever A may be doing or thinking about when S addresses him or her.

Formal politeness is impersonal; S will also choose his acts so as to minimize the extent to which he imposes on A by forcing A to acknowledge that he and A are human beings with human foibles and shared experiences. Thus, formal politeness will favor treating addressees as if they were objects and had no feelings. Consequently, not imposing means not giving or seeking personal opinions, avoiding personal reference, avoiding reference to family, personal problems, habits, and the like—in short, upholding a pretense that participants have no personhood or shared experience. At the most superficial level, this means avoiding earthy, slangy, and even merely emotional language, and also whatever topics of conversation are taboo because they are considered too personal to discuss in

---

[1]These are descriptive rules (principles), of course, not injunctions. Although behavior appears to conform to them, people are generally not consciously aware of them any more than they are of rules of grammar.

public: love, sex, politics, religion, economic difficulties, the human body, and the like. In most English-speaking cultures, avoiding personal reference means using titles (e.g., *Mr., Dr., Professor, Captain*). In some cultures (e.g., Japan), both participants may use special words or particles which mark their speech as formal.

A more informal politeness rule, Lakoff's Rule 2: Offer Options, is described as appropriate to situations where the participants have approximately equal status and power, but are not socially close, for example, the relationship between a businessperson and a new client in a business, or the relationship between two strangers sharing a semi-private room in a hospital. Offering options means expressing oneself in such a way that one's opinion or request can be ignored without being contradicted or rejected, for example, saying "I wonder if it would help to get a haircut" or "Maybe you should get a haircut," instead of "You should get a haircut." Generally, if S wishes to persuade A of some view or course of action, S will phrase his speech so that A does not have to acknowledge S's intent, statements and requests will be hedged or implicated as in (2) and (3).

2a. It *looks like* you and I got into the wrong line.
2b. This style comes in a size 14 also. [implicates: The size you're trying on is too small (or too large) for you]

3a. Could you *perhaps* let me see that newspaper *for a few seconds*?
3b. Are you done reading that newspaper? [implicates: Please let me have that newspaper, if you're finished with it]

Utterances which (the speaker recognizes) might be interpreted as imposing the speaker's will or opinion (and thereby not offering the addressee any options for their interpretation) are likely to be phrased in a pragmatically ambiguous way so as to give A a graceful out if she prefers not to agree, comply, or answer, as in (4).

4a. Some people think buying a Japanese car is an insult to all the unemployed American autoworkers. [indirect assertion about buying Japanese cars]
4b. I was wondering if it would inconvenience you if I asked to use your telephone. [indirect request to use a telephone]
4c. I don't suppose the number 2 bus stops here. [indirect question about the bus]

Lakoff's Rule 3 for friendly or intimate politeness: Encourage Feelings of Camaraderie, is appropriate to intimates or close friends. Even lovers have to abide by certain "politeness" norms with each other, or their relationship will come unstuck, as evidenced by the fact that if a spouse or lover or best friend chose to display formal politeness behavior, the significant other would interpret it as implying that signs of intimacy were inappropriate and wonder what had caused the relationship to change. In intimate politeness, almost any topic of conversation is fair game, on the grounds that with a close friend, one should be able to discuss anything, though there may still be some propositions that "even your best friend won't tell you,"[2] and which will have to be broached with all of the informal politeness devices a soul can muster.

Generally, however, participants are expected not to mince words; to speak indirectly implies that participants do not know each other well enough to risk speaking their minds freely. Consequently, forgoing the strategies for avoiding direct communication conversationally implicates that what one did not say is significant; the presence of straightforward statements and requests in place of hedges and hints implicates that the speaker believes that the relationship between participants is so strong that truths do not need to be disguised or softened. In contrast to informal politeness, the governing principle here is not only to show an active interest in the other, by asking personal questions and making personal remarks, but also to show regard and trust by being open about the details of one's own life, experiences, feelings, and the like. Participants use intimate forms of address, including nicknames and in some contexts, abusive epithets.

Brown and Levinson (1978, 1987) provide a somewhat deeper analysis of politeness phenomena. In their highly detailed and profusely exemplified account, politeness is seen as trade in a commodity they call *face*. FACE is defined as consisting of the freedom to act unimpeded (autonomy) and the satisfaction of having one's values approved of (approbation) (Brown & Levinson, 1987, p. 62).[3] To engage in normal interaction is to risk losing face, for example, being asked to do something or to change your opinion of something. Maintaining face requires the cooperation of others, since it is defined in terms of others' actions and value systems, so interactants trade in face, paying face whenever they must perform a face-threatening act in the course of accomplishing their goals. According to Brown and Levinson, when S contemplates an act which he believes may threaten A's face, S is confronted with calculating how much he is risking in performing the face-threatening act. According to Brown and Levinson, the factors that enter into this calculation are S's estimates of how close a relationship S and A have, the social power of S relative to A, and the extent to which A will consider the act that is contemplated to be an imposition on him. On the basis of this calculation, S determines whether he can (a) dispense with trading in face and perform the act without apology or mitigation ("baldly on record"), or whether he should (b) choose a POSITIVE POLITENESS strategy of making A feel good, and feel that her values are shared, or, in more extreme cases, (c) choose a NEGATIVE POLITENESS strategy of hedging, apologizing, offering options, or asserting a desire to avoid interfering with A's freedom of action. In cases where the risk of face loss is greater still, S may decide to (d) perform the face-threatening act by implicature ("off record"), giving A the option of not acknowledging whatever face-threatening act is

---

[2]This slogan was part of an advertising campaign in the 1950s for a product that purported to cure or prevent body odor, bad breath, dandruff, or some other social liability.

[3]Brown and Levinson refer to these components of face as negative and positive face, respectively.

intended. If the act is sufficiently face-threatening, S might even decide to (e) forego performing the face-threatening act altogether.

Although many people associate the notion of politeness exclusively with formal (Don't Impose) or informal (Offer Options) behavior, both Lakoff and Brown and Levinson take the ways in which intimates are expected to show their regard for each other as a natural extension of the formal and informal politeness principles that govern interpersonal interactions between non-intimates. I have followed this usage in using *politeness* to refer to whatever means are employed to display consideration for one's addressee's feelings (or face), regardless of the social distance between the speaker and addressee.

In a very rough way, Brown and Levinson's strategy (a) (Bald on Record) corresponds to Lakoff's Rule 3 politeness (Promote Camaraderie): mincing no words implicates that S and A share so much that what might threaten an outsider's face is no threat to them. However, the bald-on-record strategy is also predicted in their account to be appropriate for someone who is not concerned with the addressee's face, for example, a king addressing a commoner. The correspondence between Lakoff's Rule 3 and Brown and Levinson's strategy (b) (positive politeness) is obvious. Strategies (c) (negative politeness) and (d) (implicating) correspond roughly to Rule 2 (Offer Options), since implicating and all of the various tactics for accomplishing negative politeness involve either offering A a range of interpretations for an utterance, or attempting to mitigate any impositions that are unavoidable from S's point of view. Brown and Levinson's strategy (e) (refraining from the act) corresponds to Lakoff's Rule 1 (Don't Impose).

There are two main differences between the two approaches. First, Brown and Levinson attempt to characterize the factors which make one rule or strategy more appropriate than the others, allowing a large power, small distance relationship (e.g., parent–child) to count the same as medium power, medium distance (e.g., doctor–patient) in determining that the informal, negative politeness strategy of offering options is called for. Second, Brown and Levinson's scheme predicts that in situations where there is a large power differential between participants, they will use different politeness strategies (cf. Brown & Levinson (1987, pp. 17–22) for discussion).

Obviously, cultural values will affect how polite a particular act will be deemed to be in a particular culture, but it is also important to note that within a culture, individual speakers may vary somewhat in employing conversational devices to execute politeness strategies. Speakers, even a particular speaker and addressee, may differ in their respective estimates of the social distance between them. In addition, speakers apply the various politeness strategies and tactics in different ways according to their desire to change that social distance, their beliefs about what kind of situation a certain behavior is appropriate to (that is, the degree to which they evaluate a contemplated act as face-threatening), and finally, according to their personal style. For example, speakers differ on what kinds of facts are inviolably private, so that some people believe that asking personal questions like "What were you in the hospital for?" or "How much did your TV cost?" is a good way to show interest, and thus conform to the conventions for positive, intimate politeness, while their conversational partners may feel threatened by this opportunity to reveal personal weakness, or may feel that they don't know each other well enough for this sort of talk, and take such questions as implying a greater intimacy than exists or is desirable. Another example: as Tannen (1979) showed, some people believe that contributing relevant remarks while someone else is talking shows interest in what the other person is talking about; other people feel that it shows utter disregard for the interrupted speaker.

It may be helpful here to offer a wider range of linguistic examples[4] of politeness choices than has been provided so far. For example, as Lakoff (1973b) pointed out, if it is necessary in a formal situation to discuss such face-threatening, "unmentionable" topics as sex, death, money, or body functions, technical terms such as *intercourse, coitus; expired; poverty, disadvantaged; defecation* will be preferred because as words belonging to a formal, technical, scientific, or bureaucratic register, they treat the threatening topics impersonally, as subjects of disinterested, objective inquiry, not as personal matters that could pertain to the speaker or addressee. In a more informal situation, speakers will offer options by using euphemisms like *sleep with, do it; gone to a better place; in difficult circumstances; go to the bathroom*; expressions that are ambiguous or, taken literally, very vague,[5] so that the addressee can choose whether or not to acknowledge that the conversation is about an "unmentionable" topic. (As with many politeness techniques, the speaker may really only be going through the motions of offering options or showing respect for the addressee's feelings. The offer may be a facade, the options non-viable, and the respect a sham. It is the fact that an effort was made to go through the motions at all that makes the act an act of politeness. In the case of euphemisms, the addressee has no difficulty recognizing what the speaker is referring to when a vague euphemism is chosen, but the fact that the reference is vague allows the addressee the option of declining to acknowledge the nature of the topic and choosing for himself what terminology is to be used in continuing the discussion, or even of changing the topic, without implying that his interlocutor was gauche to bring it up.)

---

[4]That is, we will not touch here on the ways in which choice or change of conversational topic may exemplify a politeness strategy, though this is obviously an important component. For example, a speaker may be uncooperative in maintaining conversation on the addressee's topic of conversation if the speaker feels more threatened by that than by offending the addressee by changing the topic or remaining silent.

[5]A few euphemisms (e.g., *hard up*) are not ambiguous; although their meaning is still not transparent, their only conventional interpretation is the one the speaker uses them to avoid bluntly indicating. And the literally ambiguous ones may be in fact conversationally unambiguous in context. Nonetheless, they function as euphemisms precisely because they do not refer clearly and unambiguously; as Lakoff (1973c) and no doubt others have pointed out, if a euphemism begins to refer clearly and unambiguously to its unmentionable referent (like *toilet*), it ceases to be a euphemism, and a new euphemism must be found for that referent.

In a situation where discussion of such topics is not perceived as threatening, plain English is appropriate: *die; poor; pee*.[6] Among some groups (especially groups of young males), using "rough" language particularly offensive to "polite society" for these topics[7] counts as positive politeness in that it implies that speaker and addressee are so close that they don't have to worry about offending each other with mere words.

To take another example, Brown and Levinson (1987, p. 267) cite a number of cultures where phonetic properties of speech are apparently used as politeness tactics, for example, palatalization of consonants in intimate, low face-threat situations among the Basques (Corum, 1975) and the Japanese (Sansom, 1928, p. 205; O'Neill, 1966, p. 134), falsetto in high face-threat/Don't Impose situations among speakers of Tzeltal and Tamil. Brown and Levinson suggest that the use of falsetto in highly face-threatening situations is not arbitrary, but is natural in light of the fact that falsetto approximates the acoustic properties of the speech of a child, suggesting that the speaker has little power and is in no position to impose his will upon the addressee.

As is well-known, many languages have special deferential forms, ranging from the special pronouns used for the addressee in such European languages as German and Spanish,[8] and for the speaker in Japanese, to deferential affixes on nouns and verbs typical of Japanese, to the wholesale substitution of vocabulary items among the Dyirbal (Dixon, 1971; 1972, pp. 32–34, 292–293) in the face-threatening encounters when a taboo relative is within earshot.

By convention, the use of deferential forms indicates the speaker's respect for the addressee, referent, or bystander; it is customary to use them when addressing a person to whom one is expected to show deference, for example, teachers, parents, grandparents. Using addressee honorifics minimizes face threat by implying that since the addressee is superior in status and authority to the speaker, the speaker is not in a position to demand or force any action or reaction from the addressee. All kinds of honorifics offer the speaker a means to display shared values. For example, in Japanese and Korean, special affixes are attached to verbs to indicate the speaker's respect for or humility towards a referent, and to nouns to indicate (a) the speaker's respect for the addressee or an individual identified as responsible for the noun's referent (e.g., the individual himself, a child's father, a book's author or owner), or (b) the speaker's unworthiness or low status and power if the speaker is responsible for the referent. All of this is

---

[6]It is no doubt a measure of how taboo a topic sex is in English-speaking cultures that the only expression that strikes me as approaching plain English (*make love*) is patently a euphemism.

[7]E.g., *fuck, ball, screw, lay; bought it, croaked; piss, shit.* Apparently, poverty is not quite so taboo a topic as the others; the street slang terms *broke, busted, cleaned out* are not generally considered any more offensive or disrespectful to the addressee than other slang terms like *nuts* 'crazy' or *blotto* 'drunk'.

[8]The special use of the second person singular pronoun forms in French is a slightly different case, as they are used to indicate intimacy and/or inferiority of the addressee, not deference to the addressee. The second person plural is not so much a respect form as it is a neutral form.

illustrated in the examples in (5). (The glosses NOM, GEN, ACC, DAT relate to case markers; HON and HUM to respect and humility particles or meanings; REL refers to the relative clause marker.)

5a. cə-ʉy   atʉl-i   tangsin-ʉy halabə-nim-kkesə   ssʉ-si-n
    I(HUM)-GEN son-NOM you -GEN   grandfather-title-NOM(HON) write-HON-REL

    chaek-ʉl   phyΘncipa-eke ponae-ryΘko   hamnita
    book-ACC editor-DAT   send-in order to do(FORMAL)

    'My son sent the editor the book that your grandfather wrote.'

5b. watashi-no gusoku-ga   anata-sama-ni   shachoo-no   go-shisoku-ni
    I-GEN   son(HUM)-NOM   you-HON-DAT president-GEN HON-son-DAT

    o-kome-o   o-okuri-shite-itadaki-tai   to
    HON-rice-ACC HUM-send-HUM-have(HUM)-want that

    mooshite   ori-mas-u
    say(HUM) PROGRESSIVE(HUM)-FORMAL-present

    'My son (says he) wants you to send some rice to the president's son.'

In (5a), choosing the form *hamnita* indicates the speaker's respect for the addressee, while the title *nim* and the special nominative case marker *kkesə* indicates the speaker's respect for the addressee's grandfather, and the humble form *cə* of the first person singular pronoun indicates respect for the addressee by belittling the worth or power of the speaker. In (5b), the prefix *go* on *shisoku* 'son' indicates respect for the referent of *shachoo*, the father of that son, while the *o* prefixed to 'rice,' and the formal verb suffix *mas* show respect for the addressee. The speaker also indicates respect for the addressee, as referent of *anata*, with the honorific suffix *sama*. In addition, the humiliative forms *mooshite, orimasu*, and the *o-...- shite* surrounding 'send' indicate respect for the addressee by indicating the relative unworthiness of the speaker, as do the special lexical items for 'son' (*gusoku*) and 'have' (*itadaki*).

Naturally, speakers of Korean and Japanese exploit this rich system in sarcasm and in switching levels of honorification to indicate a belief that the relationship between the speaker and the addressee has changed, or a desire that it change to the relation implied by the honorific morphemes. Similarly, in English-speaking cultures, strangers who want to have the privileges of an intimate relationship (e.g., insurance and real-estate salesmen, telephone solicitors) often use positive politeness tactics to imply that that relation already exists, asking personal questions about the addressee's family and state of mind (*Good evening. How are you tonight? And how is Mr. Eks?*). Often telephone solicitors do not identify themselves at the beginning of the interaction, speaking as if you should know who they are and reciprocate with intimate, positive politeness behavior.

Among the Dyirbal, speakers must use a special language, Dyalŋuy (the "mother-in-law tongue"), in the presence of taboo relatives. Dyalŋuy has only about one quarter as many words as the regular Dyirbal language (Dixon, 1972, pp. 292–293), so, for example, while the regular Dyirbal language has five different words for distinct kinds of grubs, and no generic term for 'grub,' Dyalŋuy has only a single word meaning 'grub'; the regular language has distinct words *nudin* 'cut deeply, cut off' and *gunban* 'cut (into)', but Dyalŋuy has only a single word dʸ alŋgan for 'cut'. Because the Dyalŋuy lexicon is so much smaller than the lexicon of the everyday language, expression in Dyalŋuy is necessarily more general and vague. This exemplifies, even ensures, a Don't Impose strategy for highly face-threatening situations.

In languages which, like English, lack special honorific affixes, existent forms are frequently pressed into service to indicate the speaker's deference to the addressee, as R. Lakoff (1972) pointed out. The politeness contrasts described above in the use of *may, should,* and *must* to offer food to a guest are an example of this. Thus, because *should* conventionally indicates that the referent of its subject ought to perform the action described by the verb phrase, the utterer of (1b) (repeated below for reference) asserts that the addressee has an obligation to have some cake, and by asserting that, implies that the addressee did not realize this, and that the speaker has the superior knowledge and position which authorize her to presume to give advice.

1a. You must have some of this fruitcake.
1b. You should have some of this fruitcake.
1c. You may have some of this fruitcake.

Speaking this way may be OK in an intimate situation, where such an act poses little or no face threat; elsewhere it is implicitly a boast, and therefore threatens the face (self-image) of the addressee. Similarly, to utter (1c) not only implies that the speaker is so far above the addressee in the social hierarchy that she has the authority to grant permission, but also threatens the addressee's face in implicitly referring to the addressee's wanting something which the speaker has, imputing less-than-praiseworthy ambitions to her. But when *must* refers to the requirement that an agent perform an action, as it does here, uttering (1a) implicates that the agent might not perform the action without prompting, and so implies that accepting some of the offered food is not something the addressee would be inclined to do, presumably because it is not appetizing.[9] Thus, in this context, the use of *must* functions like the humiliative affixes described above. Notice that (1a) is polite if the host or hostess utters it, since that person is responsible for the food offered. However, a waitress hired to serve the food

---

[9]If the addressee is known to be self-conscious about overeating, (1a) will not be so polite, because the implied reluctance will not be so unambiguously attributable to the quality of the food offered.

would commit a gross breach of etiquette in offering it with (1a), since it would imply falsely either that she was the source of the offer, or that she was in a position to give orders; such a person is expected to use a negative politeness/ Offer Options strategy, and say something like (6).

6.   Would you care for some fruitcake?[10]

Note that to the extent that (1a) involves a conventionalized politeness formula, the implicature will not necessarily be consciously intended or sincere, and the explanation will be historical, rather than an explication of actual inference in context. This is often the case with politeness forms (cf. Brown & Levinson, 1987, p. 23), including honorifics and particles like *please.*

2. TAKING TURNS

Perhaps the aspect of interactive conversation that most distinguishes it from other kinds of discourse production is the choreographing of the switch in roles from addressee to speaker and vice versa. How does an addressee A get to take the floor and become a speaker? Does he just break in at the end of a sentence, hoping that the one speaking (X) is finished? If X is not finished, how do they know who gets the floor? Is it a matter of status and deference, or persistence and brute force? If there is more than one addressee, how do A, B, and C know which of them gets to speak next? Since we are not usually conscious of having to resolve these problems while we are carrying on a conversation (whether small talk, or executive boardroom discussions), the question arises: How come? Why does conversation seem to flow so smoothly? Only a very small portion of one participant's conversation overlaps any other's, and gaps between different speakers' turns are generally measured in fractions of a second.

How participants manage this delicate task has been investigated by a group of sociologists known as ethnomethodologists. In work pioneering the microanalysis of turn-taking. Sacks, Schegloff, and Jefferson (1974) noted recurrent features of conversants' speech at points where the floor is yielded to another participant (Transition Relevance Places or TRPs). The rules they inferred are very simple, and apply recursively at all TRPs, in order:

I.   If the current speaker (S) selects the next speaker (N) in the current turn, S is expected to stop speaking, and N is expected to speak next.

---

[10]The choice of *care for* as opposed to *like* is significant. A positive answer to (i) commits the speaker (i.e., the addressee of (i)) to a stronger desire than a positive answer to (6).

   i. Would you like some fruitcake?

Thus (i) poses more of a threat to the addressee's autonomy than (6), and is therefore less polite.

II.   If S's utterance or behavior does not select the next speaker, then any other participant may self-select. Whoever speaks first gets the floor.[11]

III.   If no speaker self-selects, S may continue.

Sacks, Schegloff, and Jefferson claimed that these rules predict that speakers are able to distinguish among (a) the brief GAPS that occur when the right to speak is transferred according to the first or second rule, (b) the longer gaps that occur when the third rule is invoked, (c) PAUSES that occur in a party's speech which are not at a TRP, and (d) attributable SILENCES that occur when a selected party fails to speak. Such a party might have nothing to say, or might be too embarrassed to speak, or might intend his silence to convey (implicate) an attitude such as disapproval, displeasure, or disassociation, or perhaps something much more specific (cf. Morgan & Green, 1987).

Thus, we would expect from the content of the conversations below that the gap between the (a) and (b) contributions in conversation (7) will be shorter than in conversation (8).[12] (The notation "(n.n)" indicates time in seconds between stretches of discourse flanking it.)

7a.   Ann: Didn't you go to Haverford, Dan? (0.1)
7b.   Dan: Yeah.

8a.   Jo: Well, *I* think we should spend it all on the camping trip. (0.7)
8b.   Jo: I mean, if we're gonna do something, we should do it right.

Furthermore, we interpret the period of silence in (8) as Jo waiting for another participant to comment, while in (9) we know that she is not done speaking.

9.   Jo: That class is really (0.5) *boring*.

Finally, we would tend to invest the pause between stretches of discourse by the same speaker in (10) with more significance than either that in (8) or that in (9).

10a.   Jo: I want you to come straight home from school this afternoon and clean your room. (1.5)
10b.   Jo: You got that?

Of course, speakers distinguish all of these periods of no speech from those that occur when the conversation has simply lapsed, as in (11).

---

[11]Sacks, Schegloff and Jefferson do not mention that this speaker may defer to another whose speech overlaps his, and abandon his turn before he has a chance to contribute anything significant to the conversation. By the definition in their rule (b), he is still, of course, the next speaker.

[12]Ethnomethodologists would not approve of my using adapted and fabricated conversation here. I have chosen to do so to enable the reader to concentrate on the relevant properties of the conversations.

11a. Mo: We'll go see *Blazing Saddles* then. (16.0)
11b. Mo: Did I tell you someone stole my bike last week?

Ethnomethodologists have extended the structural, context-independent, inductive techniques used in their analysis of turn-taking to more substantive aspects of conversation as well, identifying such ADJACENCY PAIRS as question–answer, greeting–greeting, offer–acceptance, summons–answer (e.g., Schegloff, 1979) and their PRE-SEQUENCES (e.g., Merritt, 1976), and discovering preferred and dispreferred second parts of such pairs. Often the results are consistent with analyses based on the inference of speakers' plans and intentions as described here in chapters 2–6. However, the two systems of analysis are incompatible since the ethnomethodologists reject as unverifiable and premature theorizing, all reference to participants' plans and intentions, as well as reference to inferences, and all of these have been central to the investigation of pragmatics in these chapters. A close reading of ethnomethodological analyses indicates, however, that it is equally based on hypotheses (i.e., theories) about behavior, although the constructs and assumptions underlying the hypotheses are often not explicitly acknowledged.

It seems likely that further investigation will show that not only the ability to correctly interpret periods of no speech, but even the smooth and apparently effortless turn-taking that characterizes ordinary conversation involves inferring speakers' plans for the conversation, and their intent in producing utterances interpretable as selecting a next speaker.[13] For example, in a two-party conversation, a question will usually indicate that a TRP is at hand, and by default, the other party is selected to speak next, although, by definition, rhetorical questions so understood will not do this. When there are more than two participants, probably the most nearly fool-proof tactic for selecting the next speaker is to name the selected party by directly addressing him, as in (7a). Even this may fail, though; if potential (but not actual) addressee B thinks S's turn is over before S utters A's name, B may self-select according to the second rule. To forestall this, S would have to order the vocative first, as in (12).

12. Dan, didn't you go to Haverford?

Not surprisingly, (12) sounds like the speech of a schoolteacher or business executive who keeps fairly strict control over her domain. Part of the art of successfully maintaining smooth conversation must be in appearing not to manage it.

Accompanying a question or a pause at a TRP with a shift of eye gaze to the selected next speaker is an effective technique for speaker selection in face-to-face

---

[13]Ethnomethodologists would probably object vigorously to this claim, and to my assumption that inference of plans and interests is relevant or even possible.

situations. Its utility and its ubiquity are demonstrated by the difficulty speakers have conversing the first time they participate in a multi-party conference call where no one can see anyone else's face. Needless to say, the reason why eye-gaze and direct address are effective in selecting the next speaker is that conversants assume that when a speaker addresses or focuses his gaze on a participant at the end of an utterance, it is because the speaker wants and/or expects that participant to make the next contribution to the conversation.

Speakers who have self-selected regularly select the previous speaker as the next speaker (accounting for the A-B-A-B-A . . . character of conversation, even in groups larger than two participants). They use brief questions like *Where?* or *Who did?* to do this, and repetitions intended to get the previous speaker to elaborate on his contribution to the conversation (Sacks et al., 1974, p. 717). By the same token, speakers who are not ready to give up the floor, but who sense that a pause will be interpreted as indicating a TRP, may indicate that they are not done speaking by prefacing the pause with a conjunction (e.g., *And, But, Or, Yet*), which indicates that a sentence is in the process of being uttered, so that taking the floor will be have to be construed as an interruption. Or, the speaker may vocalize the pause (with *Uhhhhhhh*) while he collects his thoughts; as long as one is vocalizing, he has the floor, even if he is not saying anything.

3. FUNCTIONS OF QUESTIONS IN CONVERSATION

In chapter 4 we noted that, interpreted directly, the utterance of a question is a request for information. In chapter 5, it became evident that one could exploit this fact in a number of ways to implicate attitudes relating that information to the addressee's previous utterances or other behavior. In section 1 of this chapter, it was pointed out that the subject matter of a question, the way it is asked, even the decision to ask a question at all, will be understood as reflecting the speaker's evaluation of the social relationship between himself and the addressee. In section 2, it was seen that the basic speech act properties of questions are also exploited to manage the orderly transfer of speaking rights in conversation. In this section, we examine some of the other functions of questions in discourse, as a way of illustrating the one-to-many nature of the form–function relation that is pervasive in language use.

In chapter 4, we discussed SINCERE questions which indicate that the speaker S wants some information which S believes the addressee A has, namely, the information that provides a true answer to the question. Questions like those in (13) are likely to be sincere questions.

13a.   When was Sandy Smith's application for admission received?
13b.   Is my brown suit at the cleaners?

RHETORICAL questions, as discussed in chapter 5, include questions like those in (14), where S assumes not only that A knows the answer, but also that A knows that everyone relevant knows the answer, including the speaker.

14a. Who understands Piaget?
14b. Is the Pope Catholic?

There are also rhetorical questions such as those in (15), where the speaker assumes not only that the addressee does not know the answer, but that in fact no one does.

15a. What makes people do a thing like that?
15b. Why is the sky blue?

As discussed in chapter 5, section 2, both types function in conversation not to request information, but to implicate assertions (e.g., No one understands Piaget; The answer to that implied question is obviously "Yes"; What makes people do that is a mystery; The question your utterance asks or implies cannot be answered directly). Consequently, the speaker does not expect an answer, and often will not bother to make even a pro forma pause for one. The addressee who provides an answer risks being evaluated as foolish or hostile.

In between there are types of questions where the speaker's knowledge and her estimate of the addressee's knowledge of the answer is a matter of degree rather than an absolute. Asking a CLARIFICATION question indicates that the speaker knows that he has been spoken to, but isn't sure exactly what was said or meant (cf. Ochs, 1984). Examples range from very general questions like (16a) and (16b) to more specific ECHO questions like (16c) and (16d), and meta-conversational questions like (16e) and (16f).

16a. Huh?
16b. What?
16c. He did what?
16d. Eks said *whose* job would be on the line?
16e. A hundred fans to move air, or a hundred admirers?
16f. Did you mean that literally or as a figure of speech?

The speaker's utterance of a CONFIRMATORY question indicates that S has a hunch or assumption about what the correct answer is, but isn't sure, and believes that the addressee does know for sure. In asking the question, the speaker is seeking confirmation of the expected answer. Confirmatory questions range from tagged assertions like (17a) and (17b), to general requests for confirmation of a previous utterance by the addressee, as in (17c).

17a. University Avenue is south of Church St., right?

17b. You did put the mayonnaise back, didn't you?
17c. Really?

Sometimes a speaker S will ask a nonrhetorical question to which he knows the answer, and knows that the addressee A knows that S knows the answer, as in (18).

18a. Boy, we really beat them good, didn't we?
18b. Remember when we played baseball on the Midway without a ball or bat?

In contrast to the rhetorical questions in (14–15), where the purpose was to implicate an assertion about the discourse or its topic, with these questions the normal use is as a friendly or positive politeness technique: to display, or evoke in the addressee a feeling of agreement and solidarity. Sometimes the purpose of questions like (18) is to allocate the right to speak, and so facilitate the smooth flow of conversation. In the same vein, sometimes people use questions like those in (19) to encourage the addressee to keep talking and say more about the subject of the conversation.

19a. Is that so?
19b. Yeah?
19c. He did?

Sometimes this is a positive politeness tactic, indicating interest in the addressee. Other times, the speaker has ulterior motives as well—trying to keep the addressee talking in hopes he will let slip some piece of information that the speaker cannot, for some reason, ask for directly—or maybe just because the speaker does not want to get seriously involved in the conversation.

In general, however, there is not any one-to-one correspondence between particular question types and politeness, nor, as should be clear, between question forms and question functions. Depending on the topic, the presuppositions, and the relationship between the speaker and the addressee, asking a sincere question could be an act of positive politeness, or an act conforming to the Offer Options strategy of negative politeness, or it could be a gross violation of the injunction against imposing on the addressee. Similarly, some rhetorical questions (e.g., (14b)) will be rude if it would be rude to assert what the rhetorical question implicates, while with others (e.g., (15b)), the fact that they broach the topic indirectly allows their use as a Don't Impose or Off Record politeness technique. Clarification questions are polite to the extent that they indicate the speaker's interest in the addressee's topic, but not so polite to the extent that they indicate that the speaker has not been paying close attention. As noted, confirmatory questions may be used as a positive politeness or solidarity device, but they can also be used to pressure the addressee into admitting or agreeing to a proposition the speaker is putting forth, by speakers with little thought of genuine politeness, as in (20).

20a. And then you told Officer Bradley you'd never seen the .45 with your fingerprints on it, didn't you?

20b. And the verb has to agree with the subject, doesn't it?

20c. Don't you think that's a naive attitude?

Depending on where the speaker stands in a power relationship with the addressee, questions can be used to effect suggestions, requests, or even demands for action, as in (21a), (21b), and (21c–d) respectively.

21a. Do you want to put some salt in there?

21b. Do you think you could hand me that wrench?

21c. Why are your crayons still all over the floor?

21d. Don't you think you had better pick them up?

Readers wishing to explore these relationships in more detail are referred to Goody (1978), where many insightful observations on the uses of questions and their relation to status and deference are discussed. In any case, it should be clear that the illocutionary and perlocutionary uses of question forms, and by extrapolation, of other syntactic types, are probably limited only by speakers' imagination and ingenuity in exploiting the fact that questions demand answers (and the fact that particular kinds of questions demand particular kinds of answers) in order to further their private agendas.

CHAPTER 7 STUDY QUESTIONS

1. What are the categories of Lakoff's analysis of politeness behavior, and what kinds of linguistic usages exemplify them?

2. What are the categories of Brown and Levinson's analysis of politeness behavior, and what kinds of linguistic usages exemplify them?

3. What are the rules which, according to Sacks, Schegloff, and Jefferson, govern turn-taking in conversation?

4. What is the relation of the Sacks-Schegloff-Jefferson analysis of conversational interaction to an analysis framed in terms of participants' intentions?

8 Perspective

This book is about the factors that influence a speaker's choice to say something the way she does, and a hearer's interpretation of what has been said and what was meant by it. In chapter 2, it was shown that speakers must depend on estimates of their addressee's beliefs in order to make rational choices involving even aspects of linguistic structure assumed to be simple and straightforward, such as which pronoun or pronominal adverbial or tense to use.

In chapter 3 (and later in chap. 5), we examined the matter of what is involved in using descriptions and predicating expressions to say what we mean. We saw that choice of descriptive or predicative expression to indicate a referent depends not only on what the speaker believes, or believes the addressee believes, but also on what the speaker believes the addressee believes (the speaker believes) others believe.

Chapter 4 described the phenomena of illocutionary force and presupposition, many aspects of which, it was suggested in chapter 5, may be ultimately reducible to matters of implicature: by the act of saying something, a speaker conveys or implies something else in addition or instead, which she intends to be recognized as being intended to be recognized. Much of the value of implicature in conversation lies in its indirectness, in the fact that it allows the speaker to avoid saying exactly what she means to convey, and so (as elaborated in chap. 7) to temper any social repercussions that may arise from going "on record" with beliefs or desires that may be contrary to the addressee's.

In chapter 6, we looked at syntactic structures which reflect the speaker's plans for the discourse, interpretation of the discourse, or evaluation of language processing requirements. Chapter 7 treated the interaction of linguistic devices and mechanisms with the social goals of participants in conversation: maintaining, improving, and exploiting social relationships.

The recurring theme of these chapters has been the extent to which language interpretation and production depends on language users' reflexive assumptions and inferences about each other, varying particular aspects of the world, and even about the language they share. Elucidation of the relevant assumptions and the logic of the inferences is the domain of pragmatics, which relates to undertakings in all of the disciplines that contribute to cognitive science. Much of the impetus for the exploration of the domain of pragmatics came from issues raised in philosophical arenas, logic in particular (e.g., the distinction between sense and reference, the nature of reference, presupposition, illocutionary force, implicature, and so forth). Natural language research in these areas continues to be relevant to the resolution of these issues. It goes without saying that insofar as work in artificial intelligence purports to simulate human language processing, natural language understanding systems will need to reflect the extent to which speakers' (reflexive) models of each other's belief systems affect what is said, how it is said, and how it is interpreted. The cultural (and subcultural) assumptions that are so essential in making correct inferences (and thus essential in the inference of reference, illocutionary force, politeness moves, and implicature of all sorts) are elucidated through anthropological studies. Studies in experimental cognitive psychology both inform and are informed by studies in linguistic pragmatics of the sorts that have been discussed in these chapters. This includes the interpretation of utterances and discourses or texts, and thus encompasses, among other things, presupposition, illocutionary force, implicature, reference, metaphor, and the management of interpersonal relations.

To conclude this brief review of the significant issues in the study of pragmatics as outlined in these chapters, a metaphor that summarizes the negotiation of interpretations and roles that characterizes pragmatics: It takes two to tango.

References

Aissen, Judith. (1975). Presentational *there*-insertion; A cyclic root transformation. In Robin Grossman, J. San, and T. J. Vance (Eds.), *Papers from the 11th Regional Meeting of the Chicago Linguistic Society* (pp. 1–14). Chicago: Chicago Linguistic Society.

Allen, James F. (1983). Recognizing intentions from natural language utterances. In Michael Brady and Robert C. Berwick (Eds.), *Computational models of discourse* (pp. 107–166). Cambridge, MA: MIT Press.

Allen, James F., & Perrault, C. Raymond. (1980). Analyzing intention in dialogue. *Artifical Intelligence, 15*, 143–178.

Allwood, Jens, Anderson, L. G., & Dahl, Östen. (1977). *Logic in language*. Cambridge, England: Cambridge University Press.

Anderson, Stephen. (1971). *On the linguistic status of the performative/constative distinction*. Bloomington, IN: Indiana University Linguistics Club.

Appelt, D. (1985). *Planning English sentences*. Cambridge, England: Cambridge University Press.

Åqvist, L. (1965). *A new approach to the logical theory of imperatives*. Uppsala: University of Sweden.

Åqvist, L. (1971). Revised foundations for imperative-epistemic and interrogative logic. *Theoria, 37*, 33–73.

Austin, John L. (1962). *How to do things with words*. Cambridge, MA: Harvard University Press.

Bach, Emmon, & Partee, Barbara. (1980). Anaphora and semantic structure. In Judy Kreiman & Almerindo Ojeda (Eds.), *Papers from the parasession on pronouns and anaphors* (pp. 1–28). Chicago: Chicago Linguistic Society.

Bach, Kent, & Harnish, Robert M. (1979). *Linguistic communication and speech acts*. Cambridge, MA: MIT Press.

Baker, Carl L. (1970). Double negatives. *Linguistic Inquiry, 1*, 169–186.

Bar-Hillel, Yehoshua. (1954). Indexical expressions. *Mind, 63*, 359–379.

Bechtel, William. (1988). *The philosophy of mind*. Hillsdale, NJ: Lawrence Erlbaum Associates.

Birner, Betty M. (1992). *The discourse function of inversion in English*. Unpublished doctoral dissertation. Northwestern University, Evanston, IL.

Birner, Betty M. (1994). Information status and word order: an analysis of English inversion. *Language, 70*, 233–259.

REFERENCES

lka, S., & Olshtain, E. (1986). Too many words: Length of utterance and pragmatic failure. *Studies in Second Language Acquisition, 8,* 165–180.

Boer, Steven, & Lycan, William. (1976). *The myth of semantic presupposition.* Bloomington, IN: Indiana University Linguistics Club.

Bolinger, Dwight. (1972). *That's that.* The Hague: Mouton.

Borkin, Ann. (1972). Coreference and beheaded NPs. *Papers in Linguistics, 5,* 28–45.

Borkin, Ann. (1974). *Raising to object position.* Unpublished doctoral dissertation, University of Michigan, Ann Arbor.

Bransford, John, & Johnson, M. K. (1973). Consideration of some problems in comprehension. In W. G. Chase (Ed.), *Visual information processing.* New York: Academic Press.

Brown, G., & Yule, G. (1983). *Discourse analysis.* Cambridge, England: Cambridge University Press.

Brown, Penny, & Levinson, Stephen. (1978). Universals in language usage: Politeness phenomena. In Esther Goody (Ed.), *Questions and politeness: strategies in social interaction* (pp. 56–311). Cambridge, England: Cambridge University Press.

Brown, Penny, & Levinson, Stephen. (1987). *Politeness.* Cambridge, England: Cambridge University Press.

Bruce, Bertram C. (1980). Plans and social actions. In Rand Spiro, B. C. Bruce, & W. Brewer, *Theoretical issues in reading comprehension* (pp. 367–384). Hillsdale, NJ: Lawrence Erlbaum Associates.

Burt, Susan M. (1990). External and internal conflict: conversational codeswitching and the theory of politeness. *Sociolinguistics, 19,* 21–35.

Carlson, Gregory N. (1978). *Reference to kinds in English.* Unpublished doctoral dissertation, University of Massachusetts. Reproduced by Indiana University Linguistics Club.

Carnap, Rudolf. (1947). *Meaning and necessity.* Chicago: University of Chicago Press.

Chomsky, Noam. (1965). *Aspects of the theory of syntax.* Cambridge, MA: MIT Press.

Chomsky, Noam. (1968). *Language and mind.* New York: Pantheon.

Chomsky, Noam. (1980). *Rules and representations.* New York: Columbia University Press.

Clark, Billy. (1993). Relevance and "pseudo-imperatives". *Linguistics and Philosophy, 16,* 79–121.

Clark, Eve, & Clark, Herbert H. (1979). When nouns surface as verbs. *Language, 55,* 767–811.

Clark, Herbert H. (1979). Responding to indirect speech acts. *Cognitive Psychology, 11,* 430–477.

Clark, Herbert H., & Carlson, T. B. (1982). Hearers and speech acts. *Language, 58,* 332–373.

Clark, Herbert H., & Haviland, S. E. (1977). Comprehension and the given-new contract. In Roy O. Freedle, *Discourse production and comprehension* (pp. 1–40). Norwood, NJ: Ablex.

Cohen, Philip, & Levesque, Hector. (1980) Speech acts and the recognition of shared plans. *Proceedings of the Third Biennial Conference.* Victoria, B.C.: Canadian Society for Computational Studies of Intelligence.

Cohen, Philip, & Levesque, Hector. (1985). Speech acts and rationality. *Proceedings of the 23rd Annual Meeting.* Chicago, IL: Association for Computational Linguistics.

Cohen, Philip, & Levesque, Hector. (1990). Rational interaction as the basis for communication. In Philip R. Cohen, Jerry Morgan, & Martha E. Pollack, *Intentions in communication* (pp. 221–256). Cambridge, MA: MIT Press.

Cohen, Philip, Morgan, Jerry, & Pollack, Martha E. (1990). *Intentions in communication.* Cambridge, MA: MIT Press.

Cohen, Philip, & Perrault, C. R. (1979). Elements of a plan-based theory of speech acts. *Cognitive Science, 3,* 177–212. Reprinted in B. Webber & N. Nilsson (Eds.), (1981). *Readings in artificial intelligence.* Los Altos, CA: Morgan Kaufmann. Also in (1986) B. G. Grosz, K. Sparck-Jones, & B. Webber (Eds.), *Readings in natural language processing.* Los Altos, CA: Morgan Kaufmann.

Cole, Peter. (Ed.). (1978a). *Syntax and semantics, Vol. 9: Pragmatics.* New York: Academic Press.

Cole, Peter. (1978b). On the origins of referential opacity. In Peter Cole (Ed.), *Syntax and semantics, Vol. 9: Pragmatics* (pp. 1–22). New York: Academic Press.

Collins, Alan M., & Quillian, M. R. (1972). How to make a language user. In E. Tulving & W. Donaldson (Eds.), *Organization of memory.* New York: Academic Press.

Collins, Alan M., & Loftus, Elizabeth. (1975). A spreading-activation theory of semantic processing. *Psychological Review, 82*, 407–428.

Conklin, Harold. (1972). *Folk classification: a topically arranged bibliography of contemporary and background references through 1971.* New Haven: Yale University Press.

Copi, I., & Gould, J. (1967). *Contemporary readings in logical theory.* New York: Macmillan.

Corum, Claudia. (1975). Basques, particles, and babytalk: a case for pragmatics. In Cathy Cogen, H. Thompson, G. Thurgood, K. Whistler (Eds.), *Proceedings of the 1st annual meeting of the Berkeley Linguistics Society* (pp. 90–99). Berkeley, CA: Berkeley Linguistics Society.

Crain, Stephen, & Steedman, Mark. (1985). On not being led up the garden path: the use of context by the psychological syntax processor. In David R. Dowty, Lauri M. Karttunen, & Arnold Zwicky (Eds.), *Natural language parsing* (pp. 320–358). Cambridge, England: Cambridge University Press.

Cutler, Anne. (1974). On saying what you mean without meaning what you say. In Michael LaGaly, R. A. Fox, & A. Bruck (Eds.), *Papers from the Tenth Regional Meeting of the Chicago Linguistic Society* (pp. 117–127). Chicago: Chicago Linguistic Society.

Cutler, Anne. (1977). The context dependence of "intonational meanings." In Woodford Beach, S. Fox, & S. Philosoph (Eds.), *Papers from the 13th Regional Meeting of the Chicago Linguistic Society* (pp. 104–115). Chicago: Chicago Linguistic Society.

Davison, Alice. (1970). Causal adverbs and performative verbs. In *Papers from the Sixth Regional Meeting of the Chicago Linguistic Society* (pp. 190–201). Chicago: Chicago Linguistic Society.

Davison, Alice. (1980). Peculiar passives. *Language, 56*, 42–66.

Dinsmore, J. (1981). *The inheritance of presupposition.* Amsterdam: John Benjamins.

Dixon, Robert M. W. (1971). A method of semantic description. In Danny D. Steinberg & Leon A. Jakobovits (Eds.), *Semantics, an interdisciplinary reader* (pp. 436–471). Cambridge, England: Cambridge University Press.

Dixon, Robert M. W. (1972). *The Dyirbal of North Queensland.* Cambridge, England: Cambridge University Press.

Donnellan, Keith. (1966). Reference and definite descriptions. *Philosophical Review, 75*, 281–304. Reprinted in Jay F. Rosenberg and Charles Travis (Eds.), *Readings in the Philosophy of Language* (pp. 195–211). Englewood Cliffs, NJ: Prentice-Hall.

Donnellan, Keith. (1978). Speaker references, descriptions, and anaphora. In P. Cole (Ed.), *Syntax and Semantics 9: Pragmatics* (pp. 47–68). New York: Academic Press.

Downing, Pamela. (1977). On the creation and use of English compound nouns. *Language, 53*, 810–842.

Dowty, David. (1979). *Word meaning and Montague grammar.* Dordrecht: Reidel.

Dowty, David, Wall, Robert, & Peters, Stanley. (1981). *Introduction to Montague semantics.* Dordrecht: Reidel.

Fauconnier, Giles. (1985). *Mental spaces.* Cambridge, MA: MIT Press.

Fillmore, Charles. (1971a). Verbs of judging: an exercise in semantic description. In Charles J. Fillmore & D. T. Langendoen (Eds.), *Studies in linguistic semantics* (pp. 272–289). New York: Holt, Rinehart & Winston.

Fillmore, Charles. (1971b). Types of lexical information. In Danny D. Steinberg & Leon A. Jakobovits (Eds.), *Semantics: An interdisciplinary reader* (pp. 370–392). Cambridge, England: Cambridge University Press.

Firbas, Jan. (1964). On defining the theme in functional sentence perspective. *Travaux linguistiques de Prague, 1*, 267–280.

Fraser, Bruce. (1971). *An examination of the performative analysis.* Bloomington, IN: Indiana University Linguistics Club.

Fraser, Bruce. (1973). A partial analysis of vernacular performative verbs. In Roger Shuy and Charles-James N. Bailey (Eds.), *Towards tomorrow's linguistics.* Washington, DC: Georgetown University Press.

Fraser, Bruce. (1974). An examination of the performative analysis. [A revised and expanded version of Fraser 1971] *Papers in linguistics, 7*, 1–40.

Frege, Gottlob. (1952). On sense and reference. In P. T. Geach & M. Black (Eds.), *Translations from the philosophical writings of Gottlob Frege* (pp. 56–78). Oxford: Basil Blackwell.

Fukada, Atsushi. (1986). *Pragmatics and grammatical description*. Unpublished doctoral dissertation, University of Illinois, Urbana.

Gallagher, Mary. (1970). Does meaning grow on trees? In Anthony Vanek & Jerrold Sadock (Eds.), *Studies presented to Robert B. Lees by his students* (pp. 79–93). Edmonton, Alberta: Linguistic Research Inc.

Gazdar, Gerald. (1979). *Pragmatics, implicature, presupposition, and logical form*. New York: Academic Press.

Gazdar, Gerald. (1980). Pragmatics and logical form. *Journal of Pragmatics, 4*, 1–13.

Goodwin, C. (1981). *Conversational organization: Interaction between speakers and hearers*. New York: Academic Press.

Goody, Esther N. (1978). Towards a theory of questions. In Esther N. Goody (Ed.), *Questions and politeness: Strategies in social interaction* (pp. 17–43). Cambridge, England: Cambridge University Press.

Gordon, David, & Lakoff, George. (1975). Conversational postulates. In P. Cole & J. Morgan (Eds.), *Syntax and semantics, Vol. 3: Speech acts* (pp. 83–106). New York: Academic Press. [Originally published in D. Adams et al. (1971), *Papers from the Seventh Regional Meeting of the Chicago Linguistic Society* (pp. 63–84). Chicago: Department of Linguistics, University of Chicago.]

Green, Georgia M. (1973). The lexical expression of emphatic conjunction. *Foundations of Language, 10*, 197–248.

Green, Georgia M. (1974). *Semantics and syntactic regularity*. Bloomington, IN: Indiana University Press.

Green, Georgia M. (1975a). How to get people to do things with words: the whimperative question. In P. Cole & J. Morgan (Eds.), *Syntax and semantics, Vol. 3: Speech acts* (pp. 107–142). New York: Academic Press.

Green, Georgia M. (1975b). Nonsense and reference; or, the conversational use of proverbs. In T. J. San, L. J. Vance, & R. E. Grossman (Eds.), *Papers from the 11th Regional Meeting of the Chicago Linguistic Society* (pp. 226–239). Chicago: Chicago Linguistic Society.

Green, Georgia M. (1980). Some wherefores of English inversion. *Language, 56*, 582–601.

Green, Georgia M. (1981). Pragmatics and syntactic description. In *Studies in the Linguistic Sciences 11*, 1, 27–38. Urbana, IL: Department of Linguistics, University of Illinois.

Green, Georgia M. (1982a). Linguistics and the pragmatics of language use. *Poetics, 11*, 45–76.

Green, Georgia M. (1982b). Colloquial and literary uses of inversions. In Deborah Tannen (Ed.), *Spoken and written language* (pp. 119–153). Norwood, NJ: Ablex.

Green, Georgia M. (1983). Review of Linguistic communication and speech acts, by K. Bach & R. Harnish. *Language, 59*, 627–635.

Green, Georgia M. (1984). *Some remarks on how words mean*. Bloomington, IN: Indiana University Linguistics Club.

Green, Georgia M. (1985a). Subcategorization and the account of inversions. *Proceedings of the First Eastern States Conference on Linguistics* (pp. 214–221). Columbus, Ohio: Ohio State University.

Green, Georgia M. (1985b). The description of inversions in generalized phrase structure grammar. In Mary Niepokuj, M. VanClay, V. Nikiforidou, & D. Feder (Eds.), *Proceedings of the 11th Annual Meeting of the Berkeley Linguistics Society* (pp. 117–145). Berkeley, CA: Berkeley Linguistics Society.

Green, Georgia M. (1993). Nondescriptional accounts of word meaning and reference. *Cognitive Science Technical Report, UIUC-BI-CS-93-12*. Beckman Institute. Urbana, IL: University of Illinois.

Green, Georgia M. (1995). Ambiguity resolution and discourse interpretation. In Kees van Deemter & Stanley Peters (Eds.), *Ambiguity and underspecification* (pp. 1–26). Stanford, CA: Center for the Study of Language and Information.

Green, Georgia M., & Morgan, Jerry L. (1976). Notes toward an understanding of rule government. *Studies in the Linguistic Sciences, 6*, 1, 228–248. Urbana, IL: Department of Linguistics, University of Illinois.

Green, Georgia M., & Morgan, Jerry L. (1980). Pragmatics and reading comprehension. In Rand Spiro, B. C. Bruce, & W. Brewer (Eds.), *Theoretical issues in reading comprehension* (pp. 113–140). Hillsdale, NJ: Lawrence Erlbaum Associates.

Green, Georgia M., & Morgan, Jerry L. (in preparation). *Reference guide to syntactic description.* Manuscript.

Grice, H. Paul. (1957). Meaning. *Philosophical Review, 66*, 377–388.

Grice, H. Paul. (1975). Logic and conversation. In P. Cole & J. Morgan (Eds.), *Syntax and semantics, Vol. 3: Speech Acts* (pp. 41–58). New York: Academic Press.

Grice, H. Paul. (1978). Further notes on logic and conversation. In P. Cole (Ed.), *Syntax and semantics, Vol. 9: Pragmatics* (pp. 113–127). New York: Academic Press.

Grice, H. Paul. (1989). *Studies in the way of words.* Cambridge, MA: Harvard University Press.

Gumperz, John. (1976). Code switching in conversation. *Pragmatics microfiche* 1.4, A2-D4.

Gundel, Jean. (1985). Shared knowledge and topicality. *Journal of Pragmatics, 9*, 83–107.

Halliday, Michael A. K. (1967). Transitivity and theme, part 2. *Journal of Linguistics, 3*, 199–244.

Halliday, M. A. K., & Hasan, Ruqaiya. (1976). *Cohesion in English.* London: Longman.

Hankamer, Jorge. (1977). Multiple analyses. In Charles Li (Ed.), *Mechanisms of syntactic change* (pp. 583–607). Austin, TX: University of Texas Press.

Hankamer, Jorge, & Sag, Ivan. (1976). Deep and surface anaphora. *Linguistic Inquiry, 7*, 391–426.

Harada, S. I. (1976). Honorifics. In M. Shibatani (Ed.), *Syntax and semantics, Vol. 5: Japanese generative grammar* (pp. 499–561). New York: Academic Press.

Harrah, D. (1961). A logic of questions and answers. *Philosophy of Science, 28*, 40–46.

Hawkins, J. (1976). On explaining some ungrammatical sequences of Article+Modifier in English. In Salikoko Mufwene, C. Walker, & S. Steever (Eds.), *Papers from the 12th Regional Meeting of the Chicago Linguistic Society* (pp. 287–301). Chicago: Chicago Linguistic Society.

Heim, Irene R. (1982). *The semantics of definite and indefinite noun phrases.* Amherst: University of Massachusetts Graduate Linguistics Student Association.

Heringer, James, (1972). Some grammatical correlations of felicity conditions and presuppositions. In *Working Papers in Linguistics, 11*, iv–110. Columbus, OH: Department of Linguistics.

Hinrichs, Erhard. (1986). Temporal anaphora in discourses of English. *Linguistics and Philosophy, 9*, 63–82.

Hintikka, Jaako. (1974). Questions about questions. In M. Munitz and P. Unger (Eds.), *Semantics and philosophy* (pp. 103–159). New York: New York University Press.

Hirschberg, Julia. (1985). A theory of scalar implicature. Unpublished doctoral dissertation, University of Pennsylvania, Philadelphia.

Horn, Laurence. (1971). Negative transportation: unsafe at any speed? In *Papers from the Seventh Regional Meeting of the Chicago Linguistic Society* (pp. 120–133). Chicago: Chicago Linguistic Society.

Horn, Laurence. (1972). *On the semantic properties of logical operators in English.* Ph.D. dissertation UCLA, Los Angeles, CA.

Horn, Laurence. (1973). Greek Grice. In Claudia Corum, T. C. Smith-Stark, & A. Weiser (Eds.), *Papers from the Ninth Regional Meeting of the Chicago Linguistic Society* (pp. 205–214). Chicago: Chicago Linguistic Society.

Horn, Laurence. (1978). Lexical incorporation, implicature and the least effort hypothesis. In D. Farkas, W. Jacobsen, & K. Todrys (Eds.), *Chicago Linguistic Society Parasession on the lexicon* (pp. 196–209). Chicago: Chicago Linguistic Society.

Horn, Laurence. (1979). Remarks on neg-raising. In Peter Cole (Ed.), *Syntax and semantics, Vol. 9: Pragmatics* (pp. 129–220). New York: Academic Press.

Horn, Laurence. (1984a). Toward a new taxonomy for pragmatic inference: Q-based and R-based implicature. In Deborah Schiffrin (Ed.), *Georgetown University Round Table on Languages and*

Linguistics 1984; Meaning, form, and use in context: linguistic applications (11–42). Washington, DC: Georgetown University Press.

Horn, Laurence. (1984b). Ambiguity, negation, and the London School of Parsimony. In C. Jones & P. Sells (Eds.), *Proceedings of the 14th Annual Meeting of the Northeast Linguistics Society* (pp. 108–131). Amherst, MA: Graduate Linguistics Association.

Horn, Laurence. (1985). Metalinguistic negation and pragmatic ambiguity. *Language, 61,* 121–174.

Horn, Laurence. (1986). Presupposition, theme and variations. In Anne M. Farley, Peter Farley, & Karl-Erik McCullough (Eds.), *Parasession on pragmatics and grammatical theory, 22nd Regional Meeting of the Chicago Linguistic Society* (pp. 168–192). Chicago: Chicago Linguistic Society.

Horn, Laurence. (1989). *A natural history of negation.* Chicago: University of Chicago Press.

Horn, Laurence, & Bayer, S. (1984). Short-circuited implicature: a negative contribution. *Linguistics and Philosophy, 7,* 397–414.

James, Deborah. (1972). Some aspects of the syntax and semantics of interjections. In Paul M. Peranteau, J. N. Levi, & G. C. Phares (Eds.), *Papers from the Eighth Regional Meeting of the Chicago Linguistic Society* (pp. 162–172). Chicago: Chicago Linguistic Society.

James, Deborah. (1973). Some aspects of the syntax and semantics of interjections in English. Unpublished doctoral dissertation, University of Michigan, Ann Arbor.

Kamp, Hans. (1981). A theory of truth and semantic representation. In J. A. G. Groenendijk, T. M. V. Janssen, & M. B. J. Stokhof (Eds.), *Formal methods in the study of language.* Amsterdam: Mathematisch Centrum.

Kantor, Robert N. (1977). *The management and comprehension of discourse connection by pronouns in English.* Unpublished doctoral dissertation, Ohio State University.

Kantor, Robert N., Bruce, B. C., Green, G. M., Morgan, J. L., Stein, N. L., & Webber, B. L. (1982). Many problems and some techniques of text analysis. *Poetics, 11,* 237–264.

Kaplan, David. (1977). Demonstratives "Draft #2." Unpublished manuscript, UCLA, Los Angeles, CA.

Kaplan, David. (1978). DTHAT. In Peter Cole (Ed.), *Syntax and semantics, Vol. 9: Pragmatics* (pp. 221–243). New York: Academic Press.

Karttunen, Lauri. (1971). Implicative verbs. *Language, 47,* 340–358.

Karttunen, Lauri. (1973). Presuppositions of compound sentences. *Linguistic Inquiry, 4,* 169–193.

Karttunen, Lauri. (1977). The syntax and semantics of questions. *Linguistics and Philosophy, 1,* 3–44.

Karttunen, Lauri, & Peters, Stanley. (1979). Conventional implicature. In C. K. Oh & D. A. Dinneen (Eds.), *Syntax and semantics, Vol. 11, Presupposition* (pp. 1–56). New York: Academic Press.

Katz, Jerrold J., & Langendoen, D. Terence. (1976). Pragmatics and presupposition. *Language, 52,* 1–17.

Keenan, Edward. (1971). Two kinds of presupposition in natural language. In Charles Fillmore & D. T. Langendoen (Eds.), *Studies in linguistic semantics* (pp. 45–52). New York: Holt, Rinehart & Winston.

Keenan, Edward. (1972). On a semantically-based grammar. *Linguistic Inquiry, 3,* 413–462.

Keenan, Elinor Ochs. (1976). The universality of conversational implicature. *Language in Society, 5,* 67–80.

Kempson, Ruth. (1975). *Presupposition and the delimitation of semantics.* Cambridge, England: Cambridge University Press.

Kendall, Sue Ann. (1985). Japanese sentence-final particles as commitment markers. In Mary Niepokuj, Mary VanClay, Vassiliki Nikiforidou, Deborah Feder, with Claudia Brugman, Monica Macaulay, Natasha Berry, Michele Emanatian (Eds.), *Proceedings of the 11th annual meeting of the Berkeley Linguistics Society* (pp. 164–174). Berkeley, CA: Berkeley Linguistics Society, University of California.

Kiparsky, Paul. (1968). Tense and mood in indo-European syntax. *Foundations of Language, 4,* 30–57.

Kiparsky, Paul, & Kiparsky, Carol. (1971). Fact. In Danny Steinberg & Leon Jakobovits (Eds.), *Semantics, an interdisciplinary reader* (pp. 345–369). Cambridge, England: Cambridge University Press.

Kreiman, Jody, & Ojeda, Almerindo (Eds.). (1980). *Papers from the Parasession on pronouns and anaphora.* Chicago: Chicago Linguistic Society.

Kripke, Saul. (1959). A completeness theorem in modal logic. *Journal of Symbolic Logic, 24,* 1–14.

Kripke, Saul. (1972). Naming and necessity. In Donald Davidson & Gilbert Harman (Eds.), *Semantics of natural language* (pp. 253–355). Dordrecht: Reidel.

Kuno, Susumu. (1972). Functional sentence perspective; a case study from Japanese and English. *Linguistic Inquiry, 3,* 269–320.

Kuno, Susumu. (1973). *The structure of the Japanese language.* Cambridge, MA: Harvard University Press.

Kuno, Susumu. (1975). Three perspectives in the functional approach to syntax. In R. Grossman, L. J. San, & T. J. Vance (Eds.), *Papers from the parasession on functionalism* (pp. 276–336). Chicago: Chicago Linguistic Society

Lakoff, George. (1968). *Counterparts, or, the problem of reference in transformational grammar.* Paper presented at the July 1968 Linguistic Society of America meeting, Urbana, IL.

Lakoff, George. (1971). Presuppositions and relative well-formedness. In Danny Steinberg & L. Jakobovits (Eds.), *Semantics, an interdisciplinary reader* (pp. 329–340). Cambridge, England: Cambridge University Press.

Lakoff, George. (1972). Hedges: a study in meaning criteria and the logic of fuzzy concepts. In P. M. Peranteau, J. L. Levi, & G. C. Phares (Eds.), *Papers from the Eighth Regional Meeting of the Chicago Linguistic Society* (pp. 183–228). Chicago: Chicago Linguistic Society.

Lakoff, George. (1976). Pronouns and reference. In James D. McCawley (Ed.), *Syntax and semantics, v, 7: Notes from the linguistic underground* (pp. 275–336). New York: Academic Press.

Lakoff, George, & Johnson, Mark. (1980). *Metaphors we live by.* Chicago: University of Chicago Press.

Lakoff, Robin. (1968). *Abstract syntax and Latin complementation.* Cambridge, MA: MIT Press.

Lakoff, Robin. (1969a). A syntactic argument for negative transportation. In R. Binnick, A. L. Davison, G. M Green, J. L. Morgan (Eds.), *Papers from the Fifth Regional Meeting of the Chicago Linguistic Society* (pp. 140–147). Chicago: Department of Linguistics, University of Chicago.

Lakoff, Robin. (1969b). Some reasons why there can't be any *some-any* rule. *Language, 45,* 608–615.

Lakoff, Robin. (1971). Passive resistance. In *Papers from the Seventh Regional Meeting of the Chicago Linguistic Society* (pp. 141–162). Chicago: Chicago Linguistic Society.

Lakoff, Robin. (1972). Language in context. *Language, 48,* 907–927.

Lakoff, Robin. (1973a). Questionable answers and answerable questions. In Braj B. Kachru, R. B. Lees, Y. Malkiel, A. Pietrangeli, S. Soporta (Eds.), *Issues in linguistics: Papers in honor of Henry and Renee Kahane* (pp. 453–467). Urbana: University of Illinois Press.

Lakoff, Robin. (1973b). The logic of politeness: or Minding your P's and Q's. In Claudia Corum, T. C. Smith-Stark, & A. Weiser (Eds.), *Papers from the Ninth Regional Meeting of the Chicago Linguistic Society* (pp. 292–305). Chicago: Chicago Linguistic Society.

Lakoff, Robin. (1973c). Language and women's place. *Language in Society, 2,* 45–80.

Lakoff, Robin. (1974). Remarks on *this* and *that.* In Michael Lagaly, R. Fox, & A. Bruck (Eds.), *Papers from the 10th Regional Meeting of the Chicago Linguistic Society* (pp. 345–356). Chicago: Chicago Linguistic Society.

Langacker, Ronald. (1966). Pronominalization and the chain of command. In D. Reibel & Sanford Schane (Eds.), *Modern studies in English* (pp. 160–186). Englewood Cliffs, NJ: Prentice-Hall.

Larkin, Don, & O'Malley, Michael H. (1973). Declarative sentences and the rule-of-conversation hypothesis. In C. Corum, T. C. Smith-Stark, & A. Weiser (Eds.), *Papers from the Ninth Regional Meeting of the Chicago Linguistic Society* (pp. 306–319). Chicago: Chicago Linguistic Society.

Lemmon, E. (1965). Deontic logic and the logic of imperatives. *Logique et analyse, 29.*

Levi, Judith N. (1978). *The syntax and semantics of complex nominals.* New York: Academic Press.

Levinson, Stephen. (1979). Pragmatics and social deixis. In *Proceedings of the 5th annual meeting of the Berkeley Linguistic Society* (pp. 206–223). Berkeley, CA: Berkeley Linguistic Society.

Levinson, Stephen. (1983). *Pragmatics*. Cambridge, England: Cambridge University Press.

Lewis, David. (1968). Counterpart theory and quantified modal logic. *Journal of Philosophy, 65*, 113–126.

Lieber, Francis. (1880). *Legal and political hermeneutics*, 3rd ed. St. Louis: F. H. Thomas.

Linsky, Leonard. (1966). Reference and referents. In Charles Caton (Ed.), *Philosophy of ordinary language* (pp. 74–89). Urbana: University of Illinois Press.

Longuet-Higgins, C. (1976). . . . And out walked the cat. *Pragmatics microfiche* 1.7:G10–G14.

Lycan, William G. (1984). *Logical form in natural language*. Cambridge, MA: MIT Press.

Mathesius, Vilem. (1928). On linguistic characterology with illustrations from modern English. (Reprinted 1967 in *A Prague school reader in linguistics*, compiled by Josef Vachek, pp. 59–67). Bloomington, IN: Indiana University Press.

Matthews, G. H. (1965). *Hidatsa syntax*. The Hague: Mouton.

McCawley, James D. (1968). The role of semantics in grammar. In Emmon Bach, & Robert Harms (Eds.), *Universals in linguistic theory* (pp. 124–169). New York: Holt, Rinehart & Winston.

McCawley, James D. (1971a). Tense and time reference in English. In Charles J. Fillmore, & D. T. Langendoen (Eds.), *Studies in linguistic semantics* (pp. 97–113). New York: Holt, Rinehart & Winston.

McCawley, James D. (1971b). Where do noun phrases come from? In Danny A. Steinberg, & Leon Jakobovits (Eds.), *Semantics, an interdisciplinary reader* (pp. 217–231). Cambridge, England: Cambridge University Press.

McCawley, James D. (1975a). Review of N. Chomsky: Studies on semantics in generative grammar. *Studies in English Linguistics, 3*, 209–311.

McCawley, James D. (1975b). Verbs of bitching. In D. Hockney (Ed.), *Contemporary research in philosophical logic and linguistic semantics* (pp. 313–332). Dordrecht: D. Reidel. Also in McCawley, (1979). *Adverbs, vowels, and other objects of wonder* (pp. 135–150). Chicago: University of Chicago Press.

McCawley, James D. (1977). Remarks on the lexicography of performative verbs. In Andrew Rogers, Robert Wall, & J. Murphy (Eds.), *Proceedings of the Texas Conference on Performatives, Implicature, and Presupposition* (pp. 13–25). Washington, DC: Center for Applied Linguistics.

McCawley, James D. (1978a). Conversational implicature and the lexicon. In P. Cole (Ed.), *Syntax and semantics 9: Pragmatics* (pp. 245–259). New York: Academic Press.

McCawley, James D. (1978b). Notes on Japanese clothing verbs. In John Hinds, & Irwin Howard (Eds.), *Problems in Japanese syntax and semantics* (pp. 68–78). Tokyo: Kaitakusha.

McCawley, James D. (1978c). World-creating predicates. VS 19/20. Bompiani.

McCawley, James D. (1979). Presupposition and discourse structure. In C. K. Oh & D. Dineen (Eds.), *Syntax and semantics, vol. 11: Presupposition* (pp. 225–234). New York: Academic Press.

McCawley, James D. (1993). *Everything that linguists have always wanted to know about logic* *but were ashamed to ask*, 2nd edition. Chicago: University of Chicago Press.

Merritt, Marilyn. (1976). On questions following questions (in service encounters). *Language in Society, 5*, 315–357.

Meyer, D. E. (1970). On the representation and retrieval of stored semantic information. *Cognitive Psychology, 1*, 242–300.

Mill, John Stuart. (1843). *A system of logic*. London: Longmans.

Miller, George A. (1979). Images and models, similes and metaphors. In Andrew Ortony (Ed.), *Metaphor and thought* (pp. 202–250). Cambridge, England: Cambridge University Press.

Milsark, Gary. (1977). Toward an explanation of certain peculiarities of the existential construction. *Language Analysis, 3*, 1–30.

Montague, Richard. (1970). Universal grammar. *Theoria, 36*, 373–398. Reprinted in Montague, 1974.

Montague, Richard. (1973). The proper theory of quantification. In J. Hintikka, J. Moravcsik, & P. Suppes (Eds.), *Approaches to natural language*. Dordrecht: Reidel.

Montague, Richard. (1974). *Formal philosophy: selected papers of Richard Montague*. New Haven: Yale University Press.

Morgan, Jerry L. (1969). On the treatment of presupposition in transformational grammar. In Robert I. Binnick, A. L. Davison, G. M. Green, J. L. Morgan (Eds.), *Papers from the Fifth Regional Meeting of the Chicago Linguistic Society* (pp. 167–178). Chicago: Chicago Linguistic Society.

Morgan, Jerry L. (1970). On the criterion of identity for noun phrase deletion. *Papers from the Sixth Regional Meeting of the Chicago Linguistic Society*. Chicago: Chicago Linguistic Society.

Morgan, Jerry L. (1972a). Verb agreement as a rule of English. In Paul M. Peranteau, J. N. Levi, & G. C. Phares (Eds.), *Papers from the Eighth Regional Meeting of the Chicago Linguistic Society* (pp. 278–286). Chicago: Chicago Linguistic Society.

Morgan, Jerry L. (1972b). Some problems of verb agreement. *Studies in the linguistic sciences, 2*, 1:84–90. Urbana: Department of Linguistics, University of Illinois.

Morgan, Jerry L. (1973a). How can you be in two places at once when you're not anywhere at all? In Claudia Corum, J. C. Smith-Stark, A. Weiser (Eds.), *Papers from the Ninth Regional Meeting of the Chicago Linguistic Society* (pp. 410–417). Chicago: Chicago Linguistic Society.

Morgan, Jerry L. (1973b). *Presupposition and the representation of meaning: Prolegomena*. Unpublished doctoral dissertation, University of Chicago, Chicago, IL.

Morgan, Jerry L. (1973c). Sentence fragments and the notion 'sentence'. Issues in linguistics. In Braj B. Kachru, R. B. Lees, Y. Malkiel, A. Pietrangeli, & S. Saporta (Eds.), *Papers in honor of Henry and Renee Kahane* (pp. 719–751). Urbana: University of Illinois Press.

Morgan, Jerry L. (1975a). On the nature of sentences. In Robin Grossman, L. J. San, & T. J. Vance (Eds.), *Papers from the parasession on functionalism* (pp. 433–449). Chicago: Chicago Linguistic Society.

Morgan, Jerry L. (1975b). Some interactions of syntax and pragmatics. In P. Cole & J. Morgan (Eds.), *Syntax and semantics, vol. 3: Speech acts* (pp. 289–304). New York: Academic Press.

Morgan, Jerry L. (1976). Pragmatics, common sense, and the performative analysis. Paper presented at the 12th Regional Meeting of the Chicago Linguistic Society, Chicago, April 1976.

Morgan, Jerry L. (1977). Conversational postulates revisited. *Language, 53*, 277–284.

Morgan, Jerry L. (1978). Two types of convention in indirect speech acts. In P. Cole (Ed.), *Syntax and semantics 9: Pragmatics* (pp. 261–280). New York: Academic Press.

Morgan, Jerry L. (1979). Observations on the pragmatics of metaphor. In Andrew Ortony (Ed.), *Metaphor and thought* (pp. 136–147). Cambridge, England: Cambridge University Press.

Morgan, Jerry L. (1981). Discourse theory and the independence of sentence grammar. In Deborah Tannen (Ed.), *Georgetown University Roundtable on Languages and Linguistics 1981: Analyzing discourse: text and talk* (pp. 196–204). Washington, DC: Georgetown University Press.

Morgan, Jerry L., & Green, Georgia M. (1987). On the search for relevance. *Behavioral and brain sciences, 10*(4), 726–727.

Morgan, Jerry L., & Sellner, Manfred. (1980). Discourse and linguistic theory. In Rand Spiro, B. C. Bruce, & W. Brewer (Eds.), *Theoretical issues in reading comprehension* (pp. 165–200). Hillsdale, NJ: Lawrence Erlbaum Associates.

Myers, Frank. (1984). *The language of political elites*. Paper presented at the Linguistic Society of America/American Association of Applied Linguistics, December, 1984.

Napoli, Donna Jo, & Rando, Emily. (1978). Definites in *there*-sentences. *Language, 54*, 300–313.

Nunberg, Geoffrey. (1978a). *The pragmatics of reference*. Bloomington, IN: Indiana University Linguistics Club.

Nunberg, Geoffrey. (1978b). Poetic and prosaic metaphor. In Association for Computing Machinery (Ed.), *Theoretical issues in natural language processing, 3* (pp. 177–180). Las Cruces, NM: New Mexico State University.

Nunberg, Geoffrey. (1993). Indexicality and deixis. *Linguistics and Philosophy, 16*, 1–44.

Nunberg, Geoffrey. (1995). Transfers of meaning. To appear: *Journal of Semantics*.

Nunberg, Geoffrey & Pan, Chiahua. (1975). Inferring quantification in generic sentences. In Robin Grossman, L. J. San, & T. J. Vance (Eds.), *Papers from the 11th Regional Meeting of the Chicago Linguistic Society* (pp. 412–422). Chicago: Chicago Linguistic Society.

Ochs, Elinor. (1984). Clarification and culture. In Deborah Schiffrin (Ed.), *Georgetown University Round Table on Languages and Linguistics 1984: Meaning, form, and use in context* (pp. 325–341). Washington, DC: Georgetown University Press.

Olsen, Margaret. (1986). *Some problematic issues in the study of intonation and sentence stress.* Unpublished doctoral dissertation, University of Illinois, Urbana.

O'Neill, P. G. (1966). A programmed guide to respect language in modern Japanese. London.

Over, D. E. (1985). Constructivity and the referential/attributive distinction. *Linguistics and Philosophy, 8,* 415–430.

Partee, Barbara. (1973). Some structural analogues between tenses and pronouns in English. *Journal of Philosophy, 70,* 601–609.

Peterson, Thomas. (1969). A case for the declarative performative verb; dependent and independent conjunction in Moore and English. In R. Binnick, A. L. Davison, G. M. Green, J. L. Morgan (Eds.), *Papers from the 5th Regional Meeting of the Chicago Linguistic Society* (pp. 421–428). Chicago: Department of Linguistics, University of Chicago.

Perrault, C. Raymond. (1990). An application of default logic to speech act theory. In P. Cohen, J. Morgan, & M. Pollack (Eds.), *Intentions in communication* (pp. 161–186). Cambridge, MA: MIT Press.

Perrault, C. Raymond, & Allen, J. F. (1980). A plan-based analysis of indirect speech acts. *American Journal of Computational Linguistics, 6,* 167–182.

Pollack, Martha E. (1986). Inferring domain plans in question answering. Unpublished doctoral dissertation, University of Pennsylvania, Philadelphia. (Reproduced as Tech. Report 403, SRI International).

Postal, Paul M. (1970). On coreferential complement subject deletion. *Linguistic Inquiry, 1,* 439–500.

Postal, Paul M. (1974). *On Raising.* Cambridge, MA: MIT Press.

Pratt, Mary L. (1981). The ideology of speech-act theory. *Centrum (N.S.), 1*(1), 5–18.

Prince, Ellen. (1978a). On the function of existential presupposition in discourse. In Donka Farkas, W. Jacobsen, & K. Todrys (Eds.), *Papers from the 14th Regional Meeting of the Chicago Linguistic Society* (pp. 362–376). Chicago: Chicago Linguistic Society.

Prince, Ellen. (1978b). A comparison of WH-clefts and it-clefts in discourse. *Language, 54,* 883–906.

Prince, Ellen. (1981a). On the inferencing of indefinite *this* NPs. In A. K. Joshi, B. L. Webber, & I. A. Sag (Eds.), *Elements of discourse understanding* (pp. 231–250). Cambridge, England: Cambridge University Press.

Prince, Ellen. (1981b). Toward a taxonomy of given-new information. In Peter Cole (Ed.), *Radical pragmatics* (pp. 223–256). New York: Academic Press.

Prince, Ellen. (1981c). Topicalization, focus-movement, and Yiddish-movement: a pragmatic differentiation. In D. Alford et al. (Eds.), *Proceedings of the 7th Annual Meeting of the Berkeley Linguistics Society* (pp. 249–264). Berkeley, CA: Berkeley Linguistics Society.

Prince, Ellen. (1982). Grice and universality: a reappraisal. Unpublished manuscript.

Prince, Ellen. (1984). Topicalization and left-dislocation: a functional analysis. In S. J. White & V. Teller (Eds.), *Discourses in reading and linguistics. Annals of the New York Academy of Sciences, 433* (pp. 213–225). New York: New York Academy of Sciences.

Prince, Gerald. (1973). *A grammar of stories.* The Hague: Mouton.

Putnam, Hilary. (1962). The analytic and the synthetic. In *Mind, language and reality: Philosophical papers* (Vol. 2, pp. 33–69). Cambridge, England: Cambridge University Press.

Putnam, Hilary. (1965). How not to talk about meaning. In *Mind, language and reality: Philosophical papers* (Vol. 2, pp. 117–131). Cambridge, England: Cambridge University Press.

Putnam, Hilary. (1970). Is semantics possible? In *Mind, language and reality: Philosophical papers* (Vol. 2, pp. 139–152). Cambridge, England: Cambridge University Press.

Putnam, Hilary. (1973). Explanation and reference. In *Mind, language and reality: Philosophical papers* (Vol. 2, pp. 196–214). Cambridge, England: Cambridge University Press.

Putnam, Hilary. (1975a). The meaning of 'meaning'. In *Mind, language and reality: Philosophical papers* (Vol. 2, pp. 215–271). Cambridge, England: Cambridge University Press.

Putnam, Hilary. (1975b). Language and reality. In *Mind, language and reality: Philosophical papers* (Vol. 2, pp. 272–290). Cambridge, England: Cambridge University Press.

Quine, Willard van Orman. (1953). *Reference and modality. From a logical point of view.* New York: Harper & Row.

Quine, Willard van Orman. (1956). Quantifiers and propositional attitudes. *Journal of Philosophy, 53,* 177–187.

Quine, Willard van Orman. (1960). *Word and object.* Cambridge, MA: MIT Press.

Reddy, Michael J. (1969). A semantic approach to metaphor. In R. I. Binnick, A. L. Davison, G. M. Green, J. L. Morgan (Eds.), *Papers from the Fifth Regional Meeting of the Chicago Linguistic Society* (pp. 240–241). Chicago: Department of Linguistics, University of Chicago.

Reddy, Michael J. (1979). The conduit metaphor—a case of frame conflict in our language about language. In Andrew Ortony (Ed.), *Metaphor and thought* (pp. 284–324). Cambridge, England: Cambridge University Press.

Reinhart, Tanya. (1983). *Anaphora and semantic interpretation.* Chicago: University of Chicago Press.

Rescher, Nicholas. (1966). *The logic of commands.* New York: Dover.

Rescher, Nicholas (Ed.). (1967). *The logic of decision and action.* Pittsburgh, PA: Pittsburgh University Press.

Riddle, Elizabeth. (1975). Some pragmatic conditions on complementizer choice. In Robin Grossman, L. J. San, & T. J. Vance (Eds.), *Papers from the 11th Regional Meeting of the Chicago Linguistic Society* (pp. 467–474). Chicago: Chicago Linguistic Society.

Riddle, Elizabeth. (1978). Sequence of tenses in English. Unpublished doctoral dissertation. University of Illinois, Urbana.

Rosch, Elinor, & Mervis, Carolyn. (1975). Family resemblances: studies in the internal structure of categories. *Cognitive Psychology, 7,* 573–605.

Ross, John Robert. (1967). *Constraints on variables in syntax.* MIT dissertation. (Published 1983 as Infinite syntax, Norwood, NJ: Ablex).

Ross, John Robert. (1969). The cyclic nature of English pronominalization. In David Reibel & Sanford Schane (Eds.), *Modern studies in English* (pp. 187–200). Englewood Cliffs, NJ: Prentice-Hall.

Ross, John Robert. (1970). On declarative sentences. In Roderick Jacobs & P. S. Rosenbaum (Eds.), *Readings in English transformational grammar* (pp. 222–272). Waltham, MA: Ginn.

Ross, John Robert. (1975). Where to do things with words. In Peter Cole & J. Morgan (Eds.), *Syntax and semantics, vol. 3: Speech acts* (pp. 233–256). New York: Academic Press.

Ruhl, Charles. (1989). *On monosemy.* Albany: SUNY Press.

Rumelhart, David. (1975). Notes on a schema for stories. In D. Bobrow & A. Collins (Eds.), *Representation and understanding* (pp. 211–236). New York: Academic Press.

Rumelhart, David. (1979). Some problems with the notion of literal meanings. In Andrew Ortony (Ed.), *Metaphor and thought* (pp. 78–90). Cambridge, England: Cambridge University Press.

Russell, Bertrand. (1905). On denoting. *Mind, 14,* 479–493.

Sacks, Harvey, Schegloff, Emanuel A., & Jefferson, Gail. (1974). A simplest systematics for the organization of turn-taking in conversation. *Language, 50,* 676–735. Variant version published 1978 in J. Schenkein (Ed.), *Studies in the organization of conversational interaction* (pp. 7–55). New York: Academic Press.

Sadock, Jerrold M. (1970). Whimperatives. In J. Sadock & A. Vanek (Eds.), *Studies presented to Robert B. Lees by his students* (pp. 223–238). Edmonton, Alberta: Linguistic Research, Inc.

Sadock, Jerrold M. (1972). Speech act idioms. In Paul M. Peranteau, J. N. Levi, & G. C. Phares (Eds.), *Papers from the Eighth Regional Meeting of the Chicago Linguistic Society* (pp. 329–339). Chicago: Chicago Linguistic Society.

Sadock, Jerrold M. (1974). *Toward a linguistic theory of speech acts.* New York: Academic Press.

Sadock, Jerrold M. (1978). On testing for conversational implicature. In P. Cole (Ed.), *Syntax and semantics, vol. 9: Pragmatics* (pp. 281–298). New York: Academic Press.

Sadock, Jerrold M. (1979). Figurative speech and linguistics. In Andrew Ortony (Ed.), *Metaphor and thought* (pp. 46–63). Cambridge, England: Cambridge University Press.

Sadock, Jerrold M. (1983). The necessary overlapping of grammatical components. In John F. Richardson, M. Marks, & A. Chukerman (Eds.), *Papers from the parasession on the interplay of phonology, morphology, and syntax* (pp. 198–221). Chicago: Chicago Linguistic Society.

Sadock, Jerrold M. (1990). Commends on Vanderveken and on Cohen and Levesque. In Philip R. Cohen, Jerry Morgan, & Martha E. Pollack (Eds.), *Intentions in communication* (pp. 257–270). Cambridge, MA: MIT Press.

Sansom, G. B. (1928). *An historical grammar of Japanese.* Oxford, England: Oxford University Press.

Schauber, Ellen, & Spolsky, Ellen. (1986). *The bounds of interpretation.* Stanford: Stanford University Press.

Schegloff, Emanuel A. (1979). Identification and recognition in telephone conversation openings. In G. Psathas (Ed.), *Everyday language: Studies in ethnomethodology* (pp. 23–78). New York: Irvington.

Schiffer, Stephen. (1972). *Meaning.* Oxford, England: Clarendon Press.

Schmerling, Susan F. (1971). A note on negative polarity. *Papers in linguistics, 4*(1), 200–206.

Schmerling, Susan F. (1976). *Aspects of English sentence stress.* Austin: University of Texas Press.

Schmerling, Susan F. (1978). Synonymy judgments as syntactic evidence. In Peter Cole (Ed.), *Syntax and semantics, vol. 9: Pragmatics* (pp. 299–314). New York: Academic Press.

Schourup, Lawrence. (1982). Common discourse particles in English conversation. Unpublished doctoral dissertation, Ohio State University.

Scott, Dana. (1970). Advice on modal logic. In K. Lambert (Ed.), *Philosophical problems in logic* (pp. 143–174). Dordrecht: Reidel.

Searle, John. (1969). *Speech acts.* Cambridge, England: Cambridge University Press.

Searle, John. (1975a). A taxonomy of speech acts. In Keith Gunderson (Ed.), *Language, mind, and knowledge* (pp. 344–369). Minnesota Studies in the philosophy of science, 7. Minneapolis: University of Minnesota Press.

Searle, John. (1975b). Indirect speech acts. In P. Cole & J. Morgan (Eds.), *Syntax and semantics, vol. 3: Speech acts* (pp. 59–82). New York: Academic Press.

Searle, John. (1976a). A classification of illocutionary acts. *Language in Society, 5,* 1–23.

Searle, John. (1976b). Review of Toward a linguistic theory of speech acts, by Jerrold Sadock. *Language, 52,* 966–971.

Searle, John, Kiefer, Ferenc, & Bierwisch, Manfred. (1980). *Speech act theory and pragmatics.* Dordrecht: Reidel.

Sheintuch, Gloria, & Wise, Kathleen. (1976). On the pragmatic unity of the rules of Neg-raising and Neg-attraction. In Salikoko Mufwene, C. Walker, & S. Steever (Eds.), *Papers from the 12th Regional Meeting of the Chicago Linguistic Society* (pp. 548–557). Chicago: Chicago Linguistic Society.

Smith, Edward, & Medin, Douglas. (1981). *Categories and concepts.* Cambridge, MA: Harvard University Press.

Smith, Edward, Shoben, E. J., & Rips, Lance. (1974). Structure and process in semantic memory: A featural model for semantic decisions. *Psychological Review, 81,* 214–241.

Sorensen, Roy A. (1990). Process vagueness. *Linguistics and Philosophy, 13,* 589–618.

Sperber, Dan, & Wilson, Deirdre. (1981). Irony and the use-mention distinction. In Peter Cole (Ed.), *Radical pragmatics* (pp. 295–318). New York: Academic Press.

Sperber, Dan, & Wilson, Deirdre. (1982). Mutual knowledge and relevance in the theory of comprehension. In N. V. Smith (Ed.), *Mutual knowledge* (pp. 61–131). London: Academic Press.

Sperber, Dan, & Wilson, Deirdre. (1986). *Relevance: communication and cognition.* Cambridge, MA: Harvard University Press.

Stalnaker, Robert. (1974). Pragmatic presuppositions. In M. K. Munitz & P. K. Unger (Eds.), *Semantics and philosophy* (pp. 197–214). New York: New York University Press. (Reprinted in Andrew Rogers, Robert Wall, & J. P. Murphy (Eds.), *Proceedings of the Texas conference on performatives, presuppositions, and implicatures* (pp. 135–147). Washington, DC: Center for Applied Linguistics.

Stalnaker, Robert. (1978). Assertion. In Peter Cole (Ed.), *Syntax and semantics, vol. 9: Pragmatics* (pp. 315–332). New York: Academic Press.

Stampe, Dennis. (1975). Meaning and truth in the theory of speech acts. In Peter Cole & Jerry L. Morgan (Eds.), *Syntax and semantics, vol. 3: Speech acts* (pp. 1–40). New York: Academic Press.

Steever, Sanford. (1977). Raising, meaning, and conversational implicature. In Salikoko Mufwene, C. Walker, & S. Steever (Eds.), *Papers from the 12th regional meeting of the Chicago Linguistic Society* (pp. 590–602). Chicago: Chicago Linguistic Society.

Strawson, Peter F. (1950). On referring. *Mind, 59*, 320–344.

Strunk, William, Jr., & White, E. B. (1979). *The elements of style* (3rd ed.) New York: Macmillan.

Tannen, Deborah. (1979). *Processes and consequences of conversational style*. Unpublished doctoral dissertation, University of California, Berkeley.

Tulving, E. (1972). Episodic and semantic memory. In E. Tulving & W. Donaldson (Eds.), *Organization of memory*. New York: Academic Press.

van Dijk, Teun. (1972). *Some aspects of text grammars*. The Hague: Mouton.

van Dijk, Teun. (1977). *Text and context: Explorations in the semantics and pragmatics of discourse*. London: Longmans.

Van Oosten, Jean. (1986). *The nature of subjects, topics, and agents*. Bloomington: Indiana University Linguistic Club.

Verschueren, Jef. (1976). *Speech act theory: a provisional bibliography with a terminological guide*. Bloomington, IN: Indiana University Linguistics Club.

Von Wright, G. (1963). *Norm and action: A logical inquiry*. London: Routledge & Kegan Paul.

Ward, Gregory. (1985). *The semantics and pragmatics of preposing*, Unpublished doctoral dissertation, University of Pennsylvania.

Ward, Gregory, & Hirschberg, Julia. (1985). Implicating uncertainty; the pragmatics of fall-rise intonation. *Language, 61*, 747–776.

Weiser, Ann. (1974). Deliberate ambiguity. In Michael LaGaly, R. Fox, & A. Bruck (Eds.), *Papers from the 10th Regional Meeting of the Chicago Linguistic Society* (pp. 732–741). Chicago: Chicago Linguistic Society.

Whorf, Benjamin L. (1950). An American Indian model of the universe. *International Journal of American Linguistics, 16*. Reprinted in J. B. Carroll (Ed.), *Language, thought, and reality: Selected writings of Benjamin Lee Whorf* (pp. 57–64), New York: Wiley.

Wierzbicka, Anna. (1986). The semantics of 'internal dative' in English. *Quaderni di semantica, 7* 121–135.

Williams, Timothy. (1995). *A pragmatic account of control*. Unpublished doctoral dissertation, University of Illinois at Urbana-Champaign.

Wilson, Deirdre. (1975). *Presupposition and non-truth-conditional semantics*. New York: Academic Press.

Wilson, Deirdre, & Sperber, Dan. (1979). Ordered entailments: an alternative to presuppositional theories. In C. K. Oh, & D. Dinneen (Eds.), *Syntax and semantics, vol. 11: Presupposition* (pp. 299–323). New York: Academic Press.

Yanofsky, Nancy. (1978). NP utterances. In Donka Farkas, W. Jacobsen, & K. Todrys (Eds.), *Papers from the 14th Regional Meeting of the Chicago Linguistic Society* (pp. 491–502). Chicago: Chicago Linguistic Society.

Yanofsky, Nancy. (1980). *The semantics of NP utterances*. Unpublished doctoral dissertation, Georgetown University, Washington, DC.

Zaenen, Annie. (1982). *Subjects and other subjects*. Bloomington, IN: Indiana University Linguistics Club.

Ziv, Yael. (1976). *On the communicative effect of relative clause extraposition in English.* Unpublished doctoral dissertation, University of Illinois, Urbana.

Zwicky, Arnold, & Sadock, Jerrold M. (1975). Ambiguity tests and how to fail them. In John Kimball (Ed.), *Syntax and semantics, vol. 4* (pp. 1–36). New York: Academic Press.

Author Index

Subject Index

Acts 4-5
Addressee 1n
Adjacency pairs 158
Ambiguity 9, 11-12, 47, 51; *see also* Homonymy, Polysemy
   illocutionary force 69, 110*f*, 114
   mass-count 54
   type-token 49, 52, 54
Anaphora, *see* Reference, anaphoric

Backward pronominalization 27
Belief 2-4, 59
   normal *see* Normal belief
   reflexive 3, 12, 60

Cancellability 77
Causal theory of reference 38*f*
Causal chain, *see* Historical chain
Coherence 105-109
Compositional semantics 6, 54n, 122-124
Compound nouns 6n, 122*f*
Concepts
Conduit metaphor 9-10
Conjunctions 31*f*
Connectives 29*ff*
Connotation 38, 73-75, 86
Context 25, 26n, 59
   null 59
Conventions 5*ff*, 126*ff*
   of language 5, 112, 123
   of use 59*ff*, 112, 115, 126*ff*
Conventional meaning 54n
Conventionalization 59*ff*

Cooperative principle 89-101, 90, 105, 106, 109n, 114, 119*ff*, 125
   universality 100*f*
Coordinates, spatio-temporal 18, 19, 24, 42
Coreference 26
Counterfactive verbs 74
Counterfactual conditional 74
Counterparts 29

Deixis, *see* Reference, deictic
Deictic Indexicals 51
Deference
   forms 153-155
   uses 141, 155*f*
Definite descriptions 28
   attributive 39*ff*
   referential 39*f*
Demonstratives 24, 28
Denomination 38
Denotation 38, 42
Discourse structure 133, 135-138
Discourse particles 141*f*
 Ellipsis 32*ff*
Entailment 78*f*
Epithets 28
Euphemisms 152
Expositive 116
Extension 38, 42

Face 150*f*
Face-threatening act 150-153, 155
Felicity conditions 83

Goals 90-93, 97*f*, 116